Northwest Perspectives

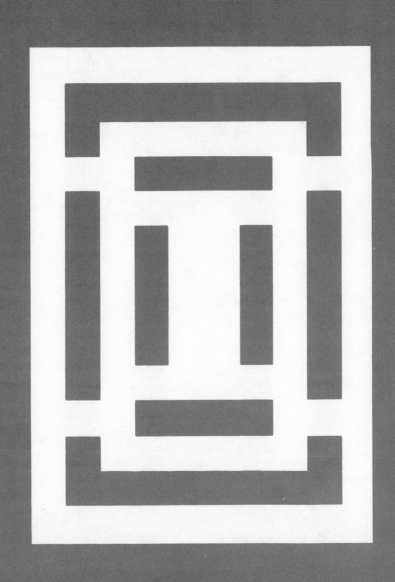

Northwest Perspectives

Essays on the Culture of the Pacific Northwest

Compiled and Edited by
Edwin R. Bingham and Glen A. Love

University of Oregon, Eugene
University of Washington Press, Seattle and London

Library of Congress Cataloging in Publication Data

Main entry under title:

Northwest perspectives.

   Presented at a symposium held at the University
of Oregon, July 6-8, 1976.
   Includes bibliographical references and index.
   1. Northwest, Pacific—Civilization—Congresses.
2. American literature—Northwest, Pacific—History
and criticism—Congresses. 3. Folk-lore—North-
west, Pacific—Congresses. I. Bingham, Edwin R., 1920-
II. Love, Glen A., 1932-
F851.N65   979.5   77-15189
ISBN 0-295-95594-5

To Harold G. Merriam,
emeritus professor of English at the
University of Montana,
founder and editor of THE FRONTIER,
early leader in helping the Northwest
find its distinctive voice

Acknowledgments

We wish to thank the National Endowment for the Humanities for its support of the 1976 Summer Institute in Northwest History and Literature, held at the University of Oregon, which provided the forum for the original presentation of these papers. We also wish to express our gratitude to the University of Oregon Development Fund, the Centennial Publications Committee, and especially Martin Schmitt for the initial grant which allowed these papers to take shape, in our thinking, as a book. The University of Oregon was then joined, in further planning and support for this volume, by the University of Washington Press in what is the first joint publication of these two great universities of the Northwest. The encouragement and helpful advice of Donald Ellegood, Director of the University of Washington Press, has been instrumental in bringing this work to completion. From the University of Oregon Publications Office, Alan Baas has ably borne major responsibility for copy editing duties, with the design assistance of the Director of Publications, George Beltran, and further helpful advice from Catherine Lauris. The index was prepared by Karen Gernant. The mutual cooperation of the two institutions in this publication suggests the hope for further joint projects in the future.

To the twenty college teachers from the Northwest who formed the 1976 Institute, Marvin Singleton, Stan Scott, Ralph Wirfs, Jane Davies, James Hitchman, Merrill Lewis, George L. Ives, Richard W. Etulain, Kerry Ahern, Gerald McCaughey, George Venn, Warren Blankenship, Donald Epstein, Pat Enders, Vernon H. Jensen, Jr., Jack W. Bennett, Hugh Nichols, Ward Tonsfeldt, Ruby Vonderheit, and Tim Tucker, we owe a special debt, both for their encouragement of such a volume as this and for, in many cases, their active participation in creating its various parts. To those other teachers and scholars who contributed to this volume and to those, like Raymond Gastil and Earl Pomeroy, who shared their insights on the Northwest with us during the Institute, we are most appreciative. This book is evidence that the teachers of a region do indeed help shape and define its culture.

Our thanks are gratefully extended to the following publishers, institutions, and individuals for permission to quote from their materials.

American Philosophical Society Library for a letter, Archie Phinney to Franz Boas, Nov. 20, 1929, from the Franz Boas Collection.

Doubleday & Company for quotations from *Straw for the Fire: From The Notebooks of Theodore Roethke, 1943-1963*, selected and arranged by David Wagoner and Beatrice Roethke, with an introduction by David Wagoner. (Copyright 1968, 1969, 1970, 1971, and 1972 by Beatrice Roethke.) Reprinted by permission of Doubleday & Company, Inc.

Also reprinted by permission of Doubleday & Company, Inc., are the following eleven materials from *The Collected Poems of Theodore Roethke* (copyright 1968): from "Four for Sir John Davies," copyright 1952 by The Atlantic Monthly Company; from "The Sententious Man," copyright 1959 by Theodore Roethke; from "What Can I Tell My Bones," copyright 1957 by Theodore Roethke; from "The Longing," copyright 1963 by Beatrice Roethke, Administratrix of the Estate of Theodore Roethke; from "Meditation at Oyster River," copyright 1960 by Beatrice Roethke, Administratrix of the Estate of Theodore Roethke; from "Journey to the Interior," copyright 1961 by Beatrice Roethke, Administratrix of the Estate of Theodore Roethke; from "The Long Waters," copyright 1962 by Beatrice Roethke, Administratrix of the Estate of Theodore Roethke; from "The Far Field," copyright 1962 by Beatrice Roethke, Administratrix of the Estate of Theodore Roethke; from "The Rose," copyright 1963 by Beatrice Roethke, Administratrix of the Estate of Theodore Roethke; from "Feud," copyright 1935 by Theodore Roethke; from "In Praise of Prairie," copyright 1937 by Theodore Roethke.

Opal Fisher for quotations from *April: A Fable of Love* (Caldwell, Idaho: The Caxton Printers, 1937).

Opal Fisher and Houghton Mifflin Company for selections from *Toilers of the Hills* (copyright 1928) and *Dark Bridwell* (copyright 1931).

The Frontier, ed. Harold G. Merriam, for "Philipsburg" by John S. Frohlicher (copyright 1931).

Harper and Row for lines quoted from Mircea Eliade's *Myth and Reality* (copyright 1963).

Mrs. Elizabeth B. Hobson and the Humanities Resources Center, University of Texas, Austin, for quotations from the H. L. Davis Manuscript Collection.

William Morrow and Company for "The Rain Crow" and "New Birds," and for lines quoted from "After Love," all in H. L. Davis's *Proud Riders and Other Poems* (copyright 1942); also William Morrow and Company for quotations from H. L. Davis's *Kettle of Fire* (copyright 1959).

W. W. Norton & Company, Inc. for Norman H. Clark's "Notes For a Tricentennial Historian" adapted from Norman H. Clark, *Washington: A Bicentennial History* (copyright 1976); published by W. W. Norton & Company, Inc. and the American Association for State and Local History, with the assistance of a grant from the National Endowment for the Humanities. Reprinted with permission of the publishers.

Reed College Library for quotations from the Papers of Simeon Gannett Reed and Thomas Lamb Eliot.

Mrs. Beatrice Roethke Lushington and McGraw-Hill Book Company for quotations from Allan Seager, *The Glass House* (copyright 1968).

Mrs. Beatrice Roethke Lushington and the University of Washington for quotations from Theodore Roethke manuscripts in the University of Washington Collection.

William Stafford for his poem, "Starting With Little Things," which appeared in *Northwest Review*, 13, No. 3 (1973), 86.

William Stafford and Harper and Row for lines quoted from "The Well Rising" and "From Eastern Oregon" in William Stafford's *The Rescued Year* (copyright 1966).

University of Washington Press for quotations from the following: Ralph J. Mills, Jr., ed., *On the Poet and His Craft: Selected Prose of Theodore Roethke* (copyright 1965); Ralph J. Mills, Jr., ed., *Selected Letters of Theodore Roethke* (copyright 1968); Arnold Stein, ed., *Theodore Roethke: Essays on the Poetry* (copyright 1965).

Acknowledgment is also due to the University of Washington Press for permission to reprint, in revised form, Jarold Ramsey's "Introduction" to *Coyote Was Going There* (copyright 1977).

E. R. Bingham
G. A. Love
Eugene, Oregon
March, 1978

Contents

Edwin R. Bingham is professor of history at the University of Oregon, where he teaches American cultural history and Pacific Northwest history. He is author of *Charles F. Lummis, Editor of the Southwest* (San Marino: Henry E. Huntington Library, 1955) and co-editor of *The American Frontier: Readings and Documents* (Boston: Little, Brown and Co., 1972). A biography of Charles Erskine Scott Wood (1851-1944), western poet, satirist, attorney, and radical, begun years ago, is still in progress. Glen A. Love is currently professor and acting head of the English Department at the University of Oregon, where he was formerly director of composition. He has published on American literature and on rhetoric and composition and is now completing a book on urban industrialism and the westerner in the American novel. His pamphlet on Northwest novelist Don Berry is soon to appear in the Boise State Western Writers series.

Introduction

Edwin R. Bingham
Glen A. Love

This collection of essays on the historical, literary, and folk culture of the Pacific Northwest is the record of a symposium held at the University of Oregon, July 6-8, 1976. The symposium was the central event of a four-week Institute on Northwest Literature and History funded by a grant from the National Endowment for the Humanities. Participating in the Institute were twenty teachers of English, history, and related subjects from Northwest colleges who came to the University of Oregon during the summer of that institution's centennial year to study Northwest culture and to vitalize its teaching in the region.

In the group's activities—pursuing individual research and seminar discussions, listening to scholars and poets, viewing films and slides, preparing bibliographies and teaching materials—as well as in the events of the three-day symposium itself, the Institute sought to explore both the image and reality of the Northwest as it appears in the works of its leading writers and historians and in the lives and lore of its people. And it sought to set these findings against the background of the larger national and international cultural setting. Is there an identifiable Northwest civilization? What are its boundaries? Its achievements? Its attributes? To what extent does it reflect the larger culture? To what extent is it unique? These were questions pursued in the four weeks of the Institute and addressed by the symposium papers presented here.

It has been thirty years since a similar group of writers and scholars gathered in the fall of 1946 at the Portland, Oregon, Library and at Reed College to examine in depth the life and culture of the Pacific Northwest. The record of that conference (*Northwest Harvest*, ed. V. L. O. Chittick, Macmillan, 1948) shows the same thrust toward cultural definition and assessment which continues to engross—and perhaps to elude—us during this year of the nation's bicentennial. In many respects, the Northwest has changed greatly since the time of the Portland conference. Certainly our attitudes toward the region have taken new perspectives. The twentieth-century westward tilt of the nation has grown more pronounced since World War II. California is now the nation's most populous state and the number of Pacific Northwesterners has grown from four million in 1946 to seven million today; if one includes that portion of the Northwest above the 49th parallel, as did our Institute, the number is nine million. Revolutionary changes in transportation and communication have given an air of quaint antiquity to those characteristic depictions of the 1930s and 1940s of the Pacific Northwest as a "far corner" or a "farthest reach." The Northwest, while still synonymous with tall timber and wood products, has undergone a rapid growth in urbanization and the concomitant homogenizing service industries, as well as in diverse forms of manufacturing and farming. The bright promise of technology which led the president of Reed College to welcome the 1946 conference by extolling "the power of a billion wild horses in the Columbia Valley" has faded with the decimation of the great salmon runs on that river. The heirs of Woody Guthrie no longer sing, as he once did, ditties praising the Grand Coulee Dam in a land where population growth and energy demands have brought much of the region's lavish natural advantages and attractions under the cloud of pollution and despoliation.

In an essential respect, however, the Northwest continues to express a coherent and unified vision of itself. If it shares a sense of environmental deterioration and disenchantment over technological progress with the rest of the nation and planet, it also holds as it did in 1946, and even in 1846, to a belief in hopeful possibilities. Students of American civilization since Henry Nash Smith have noted that the symbolic function of the American West has been to maintain the national dream after it has faded in other regions. The Northwest, in this regard, may be seen as a kind of West's West. Historically it was the ultimate goal of continental westering, a visionary land of plenty at the end of the Oregon Trail. In contemporary terms it appears as an environmental pathfinder for the nation, a region which, despite its tendency to overlook its own errors, continues to act as though the future can be shaped to avoid the failures of the national experience. It was in this perhaps naïvely optimistic spirit, coming at a time of profound and widespread loss of faith in national political processes and leaders, that the 1976 Institute was conceived. It was hoped that fuller understanding of the region would help clarify underlying patterns of conflict and commonality with the nation as a whole and help re-establish the productive balance of both. In this sense, our purpose in the Institute and in the collecting of these essays has been to foster what Josiah Royce, the California-born Harvard philosopher, called a "wholesome provincialism."

Writing early in the twentieth century, Royce was deeply disturbed by three tendencies that he felt threatened the stability and integrity of the national character. First, he feared the restlessness and mobility of his countrymen that so often left them uprooted and without a sense of community. Second, he deplored the pressures of a leveling conformity calculated to make Americans dress alike, eat alike, talk alike, and think alike. Finally, he warned against the spirit that could substitute emotion for reason and result in the most destructive kind of violence. Royce sought to combat these tendencies with his version of constructive "wholesome provincialism." He believed that individualism is best served through its expression within a group. But before man can become a citizen of the world and take his place in the world community, Royce's ultimate goal, he must first find his identity in, and give his allegiance to, a province or region and learn to function effectively at that local level. The Harvard idealist was concerned with nurturing the positive aspects of the province—its natural beauty, its cultural potential, its historical heritage, its opportunities for human contact and participation, its common and constructive interests. He was not a regional chauvinist and he warned against false and destructive sectionalism that fosters narrowness of spirit and jealousies among communities.

For Royce a province was "any one part of a national domain, which is, geographically and socially, sufficiently unified to have a true consciousness of its own unity, to feel a pride in its own ideals and customs, and to possess a sense of its distinction from other parts of the country." Doubtless Royce's idea of the province is more applicable to a subregion such as the Willamette Valley, Olympic Peninsula, or Harney Desert. Nevertheless, a sense of regional cohesion and identity is a subjective and protean matter depending on angle of vision and changing circumstance. For example, let Pacific Northwesterners learn that their thirsty neighbors to the south covet a sustained draught from the Columbia River system and overnight, citizens of Seattle and Boise are joined in a common concern—each suddenly aware that he or she resides in a sprawling, diverse, yet somehow coherent corner of the continent.

These essays, then, are for those seeking a deeper understanding of the Pacific Northwest and who would nurture a "wholesome provincialism" resting on a clear-eyed rather than a sentimental estimate of the region and its achievements. Thus far the Pacific Northwest has lacked an interpretation on the scale of Walter Prescott Webb's *The Great Plains*, or Wilbur Cash's *The Mind of the South*, or Paul Horgan's *Great River*; nor has it produced a William Faulkner or a Mark Twain. One explanation may be its relative rawness, the proximity of present to past. Or perhaps it is that the Pacific Northwest lacks the physiographic unity of the Great Plains or the psychological conditioning and congealing influence of a Lost Cause and persistent racial tensions. Still, there are materials—including, we hope, this volume—from which a reader of Northwest writing can gain some sense of identity, some consciousness of historical roots, some idea of the broad and diverse margins of existence, some promise of sustained purpose and ultimate fulfillment—all this without denying the region's physical and cultural flaws, without surrendering forbearance for those with equally ardent attachments to other parts of the planet, and perhaps without sacrificing a Roycean vision of someday reaching a kind of world community.

Artists of the Folk

This opening essay examines some of the literature of the Northwest's oldest culture, that of its Indian inhabitants. Jarold Ramsey grew up on a ranch across the Deschutes River from the Warm Springs Indian Reservation in central Oregon, where he still spends his summers with his family. Since 1965 he has taught courses in Shakespeare, modern poetry, and creative writing at the University of Rochester. He is an accomplished poet whose work has appeared in national magazines and in his book, *Love in an Earthquake,* published in 1973. To the observation of Indian literature gained from his personal background and study of anthropological records, Professor Ramsey adds the skills of the literary scholar; thus he is among the first to read and interpret American Indian stories as literature. Readers interested in pursuing further the legends of Northwest Indians should see his recent University of Washington Press anthology of Indian literature from the Oregon country, *Coyote Was Going There*, from which this essay is adapted.

The Indian Literature of Oregon

Jarold Ramsey

We should begin with the right setting. It is deep winter night along the Columbia River on the Oregon shore. Outside the lodge, the wind blows full of snow; snow covers the canoes, the fishing platforms, the drying racks, the trails east and west along the river and inland to the south. Inside, acrid smoke from the big fire drifts this way and that: and more faintly, there comes the smell of food long since safely gathered, dried, smoked, stored in corners and hung up along the ridgepole. It is winter here, and there is little for the People to do but stay indoors and try to keep warm. It is the season of *stories,* the time when Coyote and Raccoon and Tsagiglalal come back as they were in the old time. Only in winter can they come with their stories: to bring them back in summer, when the People should be out working, would be to risk a rattlesnake bite or a twisted mouth. But now it is the right time, and with the rest of the People you wait.

Pretty soon an old woman, Grandmother, comes in and hunkers down close to the fire. She spits, peers wrinkling around the lodge, and spits again. Then she asks, "If I tell the stories, what are your favors for me?"

Someone says, "Fisheyes."

Grandmother spits and says, "No-o-o."

Someone else offers, "Kinnikinnick, ready to smoke."

A negative grunt.

Someone else—your uncle—says, hopefully, "Jerky—with huckleberries?"

"Ahhh. Pretty good." Eyes fixed on the fire, voice faint above the wind, she begins. "Coyote was going there, and when he came to the mouth of the river . . . ."

Three, even two generations ago, you might have heard Oregon Indian stories told in such a setting. Now, most of the stories and much of the complex arts of reciting them and listening to them are lost like smoke through a smokehole. When the first settlers reached Oregon in the 1840s and the occupation of the land began, there were at least forty independent tribes on that land, speaking an estimated twenty-five distinct languages.[1] It was a rich matrix for the flourishing of oral literatures—made richer by Oregon's strategic location, with outland tribes bringing trade goods and (presumably) stories from California and the Great Basin to the south, from the Rocky Mountain countries to the east, and from the Walla Walla, Yakima, and Puget Sound lands to the north. There are perhaps 500 trustworthy story texts from the Oregon country in print, but the sad certainty is that this number represents only a tiny fraction of the once available total repertory. Whole tribes and their languages have vanished without leaving a trace of their mythological heritage. No wonder, then, that the dean of Northwest anthropologists, the late Melville Jacobs, could ask grimly in 1962, "Are the state's Indian literatures so shabbily represented, in such deteriorated versions, or so bleakly unaccompanied by backgrounds of the socio-cultural systems which had maintained them, that annotative commentary on their features of expressive content and style is not possible?"[2]

How we happen to possess even those 500 texts today is a story of heroic proportions itself, written largely by a few dedicated anthropologists and linguists from outside Oregon like Jacobs and before him Edward Sapir, Franz Boas, and Albert Gatschet who, recognizing the native literatures of the region were rapidly vanishing, sought with a kind of frenzy against time to learn the languages and accurately transcribe the myths before the old tellers died and their younger listeners perhaps forgot forever. What the transcribers accomplished—without the aid of tape recorders!—is prodigious. The trouble, however, is that the fruits of their labors went into academic journals and monographs and thus largely disappeared from public knowledge. The northwesterner interested in Indian arts, or to put it more crucially, the young Oregon Indian trying to repossess his cultural heritage, may very well not know that impressive remnants of what he's looking for have been preserved but are inaccessibly scattered through university libraries. With the exception of Ella Clark's very readable collection, *Indian Legends of the Pacific Northwest* (itself flawed by exclusion of all bawdry and by a narrow choice of narrative forms), he has had nothing but a variety of garbled, romanticized, usually bowdlerized texts and "popular versions" to work with. The numerous florid redactions of the "Bridge of the Gods" story are fair examples.

What I have discovered in the course of ten years or so of study of western Indian mythology is that many of the scholarly transcriptions into English have real literary merit and can serve as the basis of serious interpretation and appreciation. By *scholarly* I mean work that attempts to be faithful to the original Indian wordings in performance and is in touch with the cultures the myths represent. There is no use denying Professor Jacobs's view of even these texts as a sorry vestige in proportion to the rich regional literature we might have possessed. But what we *do* have is not "sorry," surely, when taken on its own terms, and it is high time we began the difficult work of reclaiming it as native American literature from the learned journals and monographs where it has lain in general neglect for forty, sixty, even seventy years. The attention now being given to western Indian lore by poets and writers, though often misguided, points the way.

Admittedly, there is a wide diversity in literary sophistication and readability among the scholarly texts; some are literal, "word-for-word," others are essentially paraphrases; some early texts are stilted and prudish, other more recent ones are unsqueamish and colloquial; some are simple transcriptions from English-language recitals, others, like Melville Jacobs's *Clackamas Chinook Texts* and Archie Phinney's *Nez Perce Texts,* are superb achievements in transcription and translation.[3] Yet from the standpoint of editing, interpretation, and teaching, from now on it is surely better to accept this diversity and work through it critically than to carry on the unhappy tradition of "re-telling" Indian stories so as to give them a factitious stylistic consistency—and a false conformity with Caucasian printed literature.

Now it may well be that most of the scholarly transcribers of Oregon's Indian myths never thought that their transcriptions would ever be collected in anthologies as literature, or taught in literature courses. Some might object strenuously on ethnological grounds that the stories are simply unintelligible without full annotations, or at least woefully subject to the distortions of ignorance, unless an editor stands between a lay reader and an Indian text at every sentence. Against such objections on behalf of the scholarly collectors and editors, to whom every credit is due (short of proprietorship), I can only argue from teaching and reciting the stories that they seem to make very good imaginative sense to college classes and general audiences with a modicum of footnoting, and express the hope that general readers will be allowed to discover for themselves how richly imaginative and expressive the stories are, and how deserving of their full attention, as well as that of the specialists.

How expressive, *why* deserving? Well, for anyone who cares about the mountains, lakes, rivers, forests, deserts, seashores, weathers, and climates of the Oregon country, these stories will strike a deep chord, filled as they are with a vivid sense of place. As a settled region Oregon is still too new for white men's legends to have taken very deep root. No sooner does a promising story get told about Dirty Pat McGinty's escapades in the Ochocos, say, than someone denies it all on historical grounds—"Naw, it wasn't that way at all!" One remembers Robert Frost's haunting description in "The Gift Outright" of the American land slowly taking shape in westward waves, but lacking story, art, imaginative enhancement until the white settlers fully gave themselves to it.[4] But in a special sense Frost's poem contains a profound untruth. In the traditional narratives of the Coos, the Wascos, the Paiutes, the very terrain these native people lived on *is* storied and enhanced, is lifted imaginatively into indisputable myth. The natural features that still delight and haunt us are given supernatural dimensions they otherwise lack, are given a native "local habitation and a name."

It is no exaggeration, I think, to claim that you can't really "possess" the countries of the Columbia or the Klamath, say, until you have experienced the sense of these places evoked in the Indian stories set in them. A typical Wasco story about Coyote is wholly lacking in "local color" in the self-conscious literary sense, but from first to last it eloquently implies a climate, a landscape, a set of ecological conditions that the Indians had been coming to terms of existence with since the beginning.

Geographically and ecologically, Oregon is a very diverse state, and yet within its present official geopolitical unity, and corresponding to it, there is a certain natural wholeness of parts that Indian groups who lived from the Columbia to the Klamath and from the Pacific to the Snake seem to have recognized in their sense of "home" and their awareness of each other's territorial claims. At any rate, so far as the stories in my own collection, *Coyote Was Going There*, are concerned, I have tried to regard "Oregon" not just as a limited geopolitical fact but also as a viable and I hope not merely arbitrary concept of selection and organization—as an ecological idea.[5] Thus besides strictly "domestic" materials, I have included Paiute stories that were in fact recorded across the California and Nevada borders, and Nez Perce stories that were probably as current among Idaho and Washington bands as they were among the "Oregon" Nez Perce. To refrain from thinking in terms of an "Oregon country" beyond state boundaries would surely be perverse.

Bearing in mind, then, the diverse terrains and climates that constituted "Oregon" to its first peoples as they still do for us, I have tried in *Coyote Was Going There* to select and arrange the myths by major ecological regions—the northeastern Oregon of the Nez Perce, Cayuse, and Umatillas; the Columbia River region of the Wishrams, Wascos, and Warm Springs Sahaptins; the Willamette Valley of the Clackamas Chinook, the Kalapuyas, and the Molalas; the coastal country of the Tillamook, Alsea, Coos, and other groups; the southwestern Oregon region of the Klamaths, the Modocs, and the Takelma; and the Great Basin desert land of the Northern Paiute bands. Such an organization might be applied to the Indian literature of almost any state or region; what it does, at least in the case of Oregon, is to emphasize how deeply and variously the literature of the state's native inhabitants reflects their responses to the special natural environments they knew as home, and of which we are the unlikely inheritors.

(Just how unlikely can be seen, metaphorically, by considering that the names of four of Oregon's biggest cities are "Portland," "Eugene,"

"Salem," and "Medford." Their equivalents in Washington State are *Seattle, Tacoma, Spokane,* and *Yakima.* Why did the empire builders north of the Columbia accept native place-names while those to the south ignored or avoided them? In fact, not one major city in Oregon bears an Indian name—unless one counts *Klamath* Falls or *Coos* Bay. And moving from nomenclature back to the question of native literature, it is a scandalous fact that to date just one scholarly book or monograph on the mythology of Oregon Indians has been published in the state, Elizabeth Jacobs's excellent *Nehalem Tillamook Tales* [Eugene: University of Oregon Books, 1959]. Except for university presses in California, Washington, Indiana, New York, and elsewhere, there would now simply not be a transcribed native Oregon literature to consider!)

For the modern reader—Oregonian or not—the best stories from Oregon and elsewhere in the Northwest possess an extraordinary strength and simplicity of imagination against which category-words like "primitive" seem to lose their usefulness. It is an imagination that celebrates a profound sense of harmony with the Natural Order. For the Indian who lived *on* the land, nothing could be taken for granted about man's place in that generous, unforgiving Order. To slacken even momentarily his animistic piety, his alertness to the great inexorable orbit of Nature, was to risk expulsion from that orbit—"death from natural causes," a she-bear, a rattlesnake, winter starvation. In mythic terms, in the Wasco story "The Elk, the Hunter, and the Greedy Father," the hunter, by yielding to his father's demands for bigger, more wasteful kills, offends and is abandoned by his spirit guardian, and subsequently dies.

The distinguished Oregon poet William Stafford, a keen observer of western Indian culture, often summons in his poems this mentality and the imagination that sustains it; one poem in particular, "The Well Rising," though not given an Indian setting, memorably expresses the Indian's reverential view of his world, concluding, "I place my feet with care in such a world."[6] *Feet placed with care, nothing taken for granted*: how different from our presumptions today, living off, under, above, across, but seldom truly *on* or *with* the land! Now that our presumptuousness (our fatal lack of imagination) has begun to haunt us with images of perpetual smog over the Willamette Valley and befouled rivers and eagles preserved only in aviaries, these stories of how men and women once found and kept their place in Nature seem downright indispensable. To feel this is not, I insist, to sentimentalize them.

How to understand, how to "take" them? Although most of the recorded Oregon texts have been in print for at least forty years, we are only just beginning to recognize them as *literature* at all. And the analytical and interpretive study through which any literature unfolds and in an important sense fulfills itself is to date nonexistent, except for fine pioneering efforts by Melville Jacobs, Dell Hymes, and a few others.[7] For the present (and with hopes for the future), my basic contention is that these stories are imaginatively so strong and so rooted in the Oregon earth we still know that we can begin to take them to heart without volumes of ethnographical commentary on their undeniable obscurities. This is a necessary generalization, for these stories, even to the critic and ethnographer, are like pictures that lack frames to limit and orient their meanings. Even the most enigmatic picture by Klee or story by Kafka is limited and clarified by the cultural "frame" around it—that is, the context of cultural assumptions and conventions that we share with the artist. But what assumptions and conventions circumscribe these anonymous and traditional Indian stories? They first strike the modern mind very much as the Indian pictographs and petroglyphs on our native cliffs do—vividly *there*, but unlocated, unlimited in their implications. So much seems to be implied, taken for granted, left operating beneath the surface of the narrative—as an old Papago woman, Maria Chona, once explained to her transcriber, "The song is very short because we understand so much."[8]

First of all, in their thrust of imagination these are in most cases truly *mythic* stories. Assuming a fixed present reality, they carry us back to beginnings, to a Time before time when the natural and human world we know was being irrevocably established, feature by feature, through the decisions and actions of the First Beings. Supernatural in their power to set precedents for all life to come, these beings, like their equivalents in all mythologies, are often all too human in their careless exercise of that power. In the Wasco Orpheus story, "Coyote and Eagle Visit the Island of the Dead," for example, death becomes an irreversible fixture of human life because in fetching his wife back to life, impatient Coyote does *not* "place his feet with care" in the unfinished world; he desires his wife too much, it seems, for him to be patient or careful. But even in such unhappy myths, there is felt, as Mircea Eliade has suggested, a sense of human knowledge and power in being imaginatively "in on the beginnings" of things.

In experiencing mythically *how* the local world first became what it is, one perceives *why*, and thus shares in the logic of creation, according to one's own culture. To know how Coyote first caught and prepared salmon is to know how these crucial acts are to be performed, and why they must be done "just so" as rituals—"as it was in the beginning." As Eliade explains in *Myth and Reality*, myth is always related to a creation, to how things came to be, or to

> how a pattern of behavior, an institution, a manner of working was established; this is why myths constitute the paradigm for all significant human acts . . . . By knowing the myths one knows

the "origin" of things and hence can control and manipulate them at will.

More generally, Eliade declares that

the man of the societies in which myth is a living thing lives in a World that, though "in cipher" and mysterious, is "open." The World "speaks" to man, and to understand its language he needs only to know the myths and decipher the symbols. Through the myths and symbols of the Moon man grasps the mysterious solidarity among temporality, birth, death, and resurrection, sexuality, fertility, rain, vegetation, and so on. The World is no longer an opaque mass of objects arbitrarily thrown together, it is a living Cosmos, articulated and meaningful. *In the last analysis, the World reveals itself in language*. It speaks to man through its own mode of being, through its structures and its rhythms.[9]

So, in a mythopoetic Northern Paiute text taken down by Isabel Kelly in the 1930s, an old shaman named Sam Wata tells his version of the Paiute creation and then explains how it happens that the whites have violated the mythic order of the Paiute "way": "Maybe white people don't know about the beginning of this earth."[10]

Now it is frequently difficult in reading the stories to know "what time it is," mythologically speaking. Oregon's Indians apparently did not worry very much about eras, or follow the Greeks in dividing the history of their world into Ages of Gold, Silver, Iron. But most of their narratives do seem to be set in one or another of three loosely defined and overlapping periods —the Myth Period, the Period of Transformation, and the Historical Period.[11] In the earliest of these, the Myth Age, the great primal beginnings took place; there were no human beings yet; the world was peopled with animal-spirits in more or less human form; monsters, freaks, and confusions of nature were abroad, threatening general disorder. The Myth Age flows into the Age of Transformation, when Coyote or some other transformer went about fixing up the world (not "perfecting" it—is it perfect now?), turning animal people into animals *per se* and certain beings into natural landmarks—usually with the unsettling prophecy that "The People" (i.e., the real Indians, like those listening to the story) "are almost here now."

The third age is "Historical" only in the sense that its events are not cataclysmic or precedent setting; transformations still occur but not as a matter of course; the world with its human and animal inhabitants has settled down and pretty much taken on its present reality. Narratives set in this age are really more stories or tales than myths; the realistic main events of a Wasco story in which a woman feigns death in order to leave her family and live in a nearby village with her lover will illustrate the distinction. A full collection of Indian literature would properly include some texts of a fourth, truly "historical" kind: prophecies, hero stories, personal memoirs dealing with the advent of the white men in the nineteenth century and expressive of the Indians' response to the onset of this ultimate and shattering "Age of Transformations." Historians and students of myth alike have neglected the whole field of native oral history.

Reading these stories off the printed page, we are inclined to forget that they have been utterly transformed for us—taken down from a wholly oral/traditional mode of existence in an unthought-of mode, print, and translated out of the original languages into an alien language, English. More seriously, seeing them unfold in orderly rows of type across uniform pages we may fall into the habit of reading them simply as stories in our terms, as prose narratives. To experience them in this way is to lose imaginative contact with the artistic and social conditions that govern them. When Archie Phinney, a Nez Perce trained by Franz Boas, returned to his tribe near Culdesac, Idaho, and began transcribing their myths (from his mother), he became so distressed by what he was losing in the process that he wrote to Boas, "A sad thing in recording these animal stories is the loss of spirit—the fascination furnished by the peculiar Indian vocal tradition for humor. When I read my story mechanically I find only the cold corpse."[12] What Phinney implies about Indian stories, Melville Jacobs and others have emphasized: they are essentially *dramatic* in conception, monodramas in which one highly skilled actor-narrator played all the parts before an enthralled audience who knew the stories backwards and forwards and thrilled to the vividness of the narrator's impersonations and to his skill in weaving familiar episodes into new cycles.[13] As in reading our own drama-scripts, in reading myth-texts we must make imaginative allowance for the fact that characters' emotions and motives are invariably left *tacit*; there is no authorial voice to tell us what to feel, only the dramatic situations and the dialogue.

Reconsider the probable setting with which we began. After the Grandmother had well begun her acting-out (with elaborate gestures, grimaces, vocal mimicry) of the roles of Coyote and his neighbors, she would, according to Wasco Indian sources, suddenly break off with an interrogatory grunt—"Unnhhh?"—that is, *are you following?* And the audience, so long as it wanted more, would respond emphatically, "Nunnhhh"—*yes, keep going!* This periodic deliberate breaking of the dramatic illusion may very well have served, I think, to *intensify* that illusion, bringing the audience back to itself so as to send it off again with a renewed sense of participation in the illusion of the play.

At the heart of these dramatic forms lies, I think, a rich convergence of myth and ritual. The chief religious ceremonies *per se* of the Oregon tribes were (for that matter still are) the solitary quest for a personal guardian spirit, the communal exercises of naming, and singing and dancing in winter for spirit power. Yet surely the public acting-out of the myths of the tribe must be reckoned as one of the tribe's primary rituals, too. The rituals of storytelling seem to have been less infused with sacred purpose and more concerned with moral and existential education, to be sure (literature is not liturgy). But they dramatically set forth, one by one, the mythic origins and rationales of particular tribal rites (as for mourning, "first fruits," and so on), and conveyed directly a sense of the power informing all ceremonies based on mythic beginnings. That refrain of Transformation Age myths, "The People are almost here," must have evoked in Indian listeners at once a sense of tribal identity and purpose (they *were* "the People") and a sense of wonder at a time before them, when they had no being, but were being anticipated.

To deny ritual significance to the dramatic recitation of myths, to desacralize them to the status of pedagogical entertainments, is to ignore, among other things, how intimately drama has been linked with ritual and ceremony in other cultures, including classical Greek and medieval European, and how an intensely dramatic acting-out in heightened language of inherited stories would inevitably partake of the power of the tribe's formal acting-out of private and (especially) public ceremonies. I do not deny that on one end of a scale of "ritual gravity" the stories might be told or referred to very casually. Rather, I argue that on the upper end of such a sliding scale (we have no modern counterpart to it), the same stories would in their full winter's-night recitation be ritually dramatic, intensely so, and best understood as such.[14]

At issue here is what Oregon's natives would come to "know" through their ceremonies and through their story-recitations. I submit: essentially *one* kind of knowledge about the human order, relative to the rest of the world; not two kinds of knowing, "ritual" as distinct from "mythic," and not an abstract knowledge either, but (as Eliade observes) "a knowledge that one experiences ritually, either by ceremonially recounting the myth or by performing the ritual for which it is the justification. . . . In one way or another one 'lives' the myth, in the sense that one is seized by the sacred, exalting power of the events recollected or enacted."[15]

Nowhere is this fundamental relationship between ritual and myth in the Indian storytelling more clearly revealed than in an ending formula used by Clackamas Chinook recitalists at the conclusion of extended performances, according to Melville Jacobs. At the end of the telling the various beings the teller had been impersonating would say, through him, "Now let us . . . separate and go our ways to the rivers, the mountains, or into the air."[16] The lodge had been full of the presence of these spirits from the Old Time and full of their powers, invoked by the art of the storyteller, embodied in him, and communicated by him to his audience. Now he had to release them ceremoniously to return to their mythic elements, like Shakespeare's wizard Prospero releasing his "elves of hills, brooks, standing lakes and groves" from the summons of his "so potent art."

The prominence of conventional elements and repeated motifs is striking in these myths, but hardly surprising, given their oral-dramatic basis and the storyteller's natural dependence on repeatable formulae to organize and draw out his story material. Some of these formulae are clearly *ritualistic*. It seems, for example, that everything of importance must happen a magical five times, with the fifth time being the charm. Coyote disguised as Frog in the House of the Dead in a Wasco tale must take five leaps to the moon; he accosts five sisters along the Columbia and comes to grief with the fifth (as in European stories, the youngest sibling is always the smartest or at least the most successful). Most accounts suggest that an Indian recitalist would not have been likely to abridge these sequences of five for the sake of brevity, nor would a formal audience have expected it: that would be an impatient white man's trick! Frequently, too, the action involves rituals of divination, as when Coyote, in a quandary, defecates and consults his excrementa about what to do next—a detail linking the mind and the bowels that should have caught Freud's eye. Further, every tribe seems to have had some formulaic way of ending its cycles of stories, ranging from the dramatically elaborate Chinook dismissal of spirit actors described above to the casual ending of the Coos narrators, *k'ani k'ani* ("story story").

Periodically, in the grip of strong feeling, actors in the myths break into brief *songs* which in their lyric repetitiousness seem very ritualistic. Again, a leap of the imagination is required to hear them properly as dramatic songs. In some transcriptions the music was actually taken down, or even recorded. Hundreds of Ediphone recordings by Melville Jacobs, for example, are stored away in neglect in the University of Washington Library. Did the songs represent a formal shift in the story from "prose" to "verse," or should we think of each myth-drama as essentially poetic, in terms of cadence and line-units, rising to formal lyricism in the songs?[17] Could there have been a place for *dance* in formal recitals, either by the recitalist himself or by a "chorus" as in North Coast ceremonials? Were the stories invariably recited with word-for-word fidelity to traditional versions, in keeping with the general Indian respect for the tradition and the power of words, or did the performer sometimes break into innovations, creating as well as performing? Were some stories considered more open to such innovations than others, were some tribes more likely to innovate and improvise than others?[18]

These questions about possible interactions between the Indians' performing arts are as fascinating as most of them are presently unanswerable; the same must be said about another possible interrelation: between the stories and Oregon's plentiful pictographs and petroglyphs. In only two recorded stories that I know of is there any reference to rock paintings and carvings; otherwise, the two art forms (unlike their counterparts in Australia and Africa) simply do not illustrate each other. Are the crudely vigorous human and animal figures on Central and Eastern Oregon cliffs actually portraits of Coyote, Bear, and so on; or were these rock figures either too insignificant to be mentioned in the stories, or too sacred, or too old?

Although the fact is necessarily somewhat obscured in any survey or collection of stories, certain narrative motifs and stock situations reappear from story to story and indeed from tribe to tribe, just as in any other folklore. The Ascent to the Land of the Sky People (usually by means of a chain of arrows), the Descent to and Return from the Land of the Dead, the Marriage of the Living Bride and the Dead Groom, the astonishing story of the Toothed Vagina and how this terrible predicament was resolved, the Discovery of Fire, the Rolling Head or Skull, the Eye-juggling Contest, and of course Coyote's metamorphoses and embarrassments (notably the loss and recovery of his penis)—versions of these motifs and others are found in Indian mythology all over western America and suggest, if not a common origin, then a continual process of cultural interaction among the tribes through marriage, slave-trading, bartering expeditions, and the like. Our efforts to grasp the deep mythic seriousness of many of the narratives should not keep us from recognizing that the Indians simply loved to hear a good tale well told and, when they liked an outlander's story, would add it to their own repertory.

Witness the Ptciza stories of several Willamette Valley tribes, to take an extreme example. When French-Canadian trappers of the Hudson's Bay Company retired to Valley farms in the 1830s and 1840s (many took Indian wives), they evidently spent much time entertaining their Indian neighbors with French tales, especially those dealing with the Provençal folk hero "Le Petit Jean." The Indians must have been charmed, the "Ptciza" becomes a native hero as well, in a cycle of stories at once European in content and Indian in narrative method and detail. (Other tribes— the Nez Perce, for example—also picked up "Petit Jean" stories, presumably from Hudson's Bay engagés traveling through. The Nez Perce called him "Laptissan." In an even more outlandish kind of assimilation many tribes took over Bible stories, often preserving the plots but twisting the Christian morals thereof beyond recognition—a sort of revenge, one suspects, on the missionaries.)[19]

It seems likely that the Indians of the Oregon country took an exotic figure like Le Petit Jean to heart not because he was exotic but because he embodied a kind of wily, resourceful, questing heroism that they were prepared to enjoy. And to conclude these introductory notes, we should move from mythic and literary questions about the stories to ask what was their relation to the Indian cultures that sustained them? Beyond education and exaltation through myth, what cultural purposes did they serve? Again, such ethno-cultural knowledge as we can bring to the stories is in large part derived *from* the stories, but at least a few values can be established without danger of interpretive circularity.

The mythological literature of each tribe seems to have served, along with the winter "power" ceremonies, as a chief source of the continuity of its culture. For the stories are, on one level, thoroughly *didactic*. They tell the people who know them how to be most fully "The People." They are designed to convey social and moral instruction as well as delight—indeed, the two purposes, generally at odds in our culture, strike a remarkable imaginative balance in them. Almost any myth from any of the Oregon transcriptions offers dramatic affirmations of what must have been central cultural values to its audience: unstinted hospitality, respect for elders, unceasing caution and alertness in all dealings with people and animals, the subordination (at least officially) of women to men, the superiority of one's own tribe or clan to all others, the necessity of adjusting individual personality to the identity of the tribe, the importance and dignity of work, and so on. By the same token, most of these stories dramatize the dire consequences of rejecting or neglecting these values: death to the unwary, the taker-for-granted; "social death"—exposure, shame, ostracism —to the flaunter of morés, the self-seeking, the disrespectful.

Take just one example, a story from the Warm Springs Reservation, "Raccoon and His Grandmother." In this tale a spoiled brat named Raccoon digs up all his grandmother's acorn caches, eats the contents, and refills the caches with his dung. When she finds out and whips him (the lashes give him his raccoon's stripes), he runs away, is scorned by all he meets, and goes into hiding. Grandmother at length relents and, feeling guilty, searches for him. When she finds him, he abuses her cruelly, making sport of her choking thirst, and at last she turns into a bluejay.

Now a Wasco-Warm Springs listener would have understood that "justice prevails" in this Myth Age story more or less as follows. Raccoon's Grandmother deserves some of her grandson's insolence for spoiling him unduly; he should have been gathering food like everybody else. After he steals the acorns and tries to replace them with his dung, Raccoon learns to his shame that news of one's bad deeds always travels quickly. The painful metamorphosis of the Grandmother into a scolding bluejay is a direct consequence of his cruel delays in helping her to drink. Childlike, he only obeys the "letter" of her request for water, not the "spirit," and this disrespect results in calamity for them both.

I am not suggesting that recitals of such stories were followed Aesop-like with a set of moral truisms like these. The story carried its own meaning;

its action dramatically confirmed without direct moralistic commentary the values of the audience. But it is a fact that Indian parents did frequently invoke such stories to their children, as occasion—and misbehavior!—suggested them. One of my informants, a member of the Confederated Tribes of the Warm Springs Reservation, remembers being told as a child to wait on her own grandmother with deference and dispatch—"If you're poky, she'll turn into a bluejay too!"

In the stories featuring Coyote, the cultural meanings of these myths can be seen most clearly, perhaps, and in something like their full complexity. In their way, Coyote's adventures must have served a didactic purpose, too, but in no simple fashion. If he was a sort of culture hero to tribes as diverse as the desert Paiutes and the seacoast Coos, his "heroism" was of a very ambiguous kind. His doings, taken together, seem patterned to satisfy a wide and sometimes contradictory variety of felt needs in Indian life. In his innings as Transformer, of course, he can appear to be a straightforward mythic hero—the conqueror of At'at'ahlia the Owl Woman, the Engineer of the Columbia River, the Inventor of salmon fishing and its rites. It is noteworthy, however, that he performs most of his good works as Transformer out of selfish motives and not for philanthropic reasons, or in keeping with a divine plan. And in other kinds of stories, even sometimes within the Transformer stories, he becomes "secularized." As the protagonist of these stories he is by turns Delightful Rogue and Horrible Example, and his Promethean deeds give way to self-seeking schemes and deceptions that often backfire uproariously. Assuming that Coyote *is* a single personage, how can he still be understood as a "hero?"

In this way, I think. The social fabric of the Oregon Indian tribes from which these stories come must have been in some respects quite rigid and repressive. They were "shame societies," maintaining order through a tradition of community approval and disapproval that must have been in its way tyrannical. Instead of fearing a guilty conscience, a potential wrongdoer in an Indian community feared public exposure and shame above all. A bad conscience can be eased, even put aside, but a morality based on fear of social castigation is unrelenting; its pressures cannot be ignored. Now in such a shame society, Coyote's outrageous sexual antics, his selfishness, his general irresponsibility in the stories allowed the "good citizens" of the tribe to affirm the systems of norms and punishments that Coyote is forever comically running afoul of; at the same time that they could vicariously delight and find release in his irresponsible freedom. My point is that through the "heroic" mediation of Coyote the Trickster, the people could have their morality both ways. They knew that his scheming but always reckless pursuit of women, wealth, and status would come to no good end, according to tribal values, but before that end arrived they could richly enjoy themselves, as if on holiday!

Perhaps it is not too far-fetched to recall Freud's observations about the culture-preserving functions of art: "Art offers substitutive satisfactions for the oldest and still most deeply felt cultural renunciations, and for that reason it serves as nothing else does to reconcile a man to the sacrifices he has made on behalf of civilization."[20] As the all-too-human inventor of the arts of civilization, Coyote is not one to make such sacrifices; my point is that both his self-indulgences and his embarrassments may have made his Indian audiences feel better about *their* personal renunciations on behalf of tribal order. Coyote is often, in Claude Lévi-Strauss's engaging word, a *bricoleur*, a sort of roving "handyman" in the midst of mythic creation, working with "the available material" with humanly mixed motives and with mixed success.[21] Like Loki in Scandinavian myth, like Anansi the Spider in African tradition, like Crow in other Indian literatures, Coyote keeps mediating, now creatively, now mischievously, between the received Way of the Tribe and the Way of the unrestricted "natural" Self. We have our own Tricksters, I reckon; in literature, take for example, Ted Hughes's *Crow*; in popular culture, who else but our own Merry Prankster, Ken Kesey?

Maybe a sufficient last word here on Coyote is that of a Thompson River Indian of south central British Columbia, who, in the course of comparing Coyote favorably to Jesus Christ, observed that Coyote

> taught the people how to eat, how to wear clothes, make houses, hunt, fish, etc. Coyote did a great deal of good, but he did not finish everything properly. Sometimes he made mistakes; and although he was wise and powerful, he did many foolish things. He was too fond of playing tricks for his own amusement. He was also often selfish, boastful, and vain.[22]

I have said nothing but I hope I have suggested something of the rich humor in these stories. Nothing in them is more expressive of the Indians' freedom of imagination—or more perplexing. Anthropologists have largely ignored the subject; anthologists have uniformly followed mid-Victorian standards in excluding all the vivid sexual and scatological comedy from their collections. Surely it is time, surely we are ready for that comedy, and for the recognition that the Indians may have been as bawdy-minded as we are, only much more open about it. The humor in Indian myth-narrative is generally broad, often outrageously physical, even manic; in significance, it is predominantly social and satiric, perhaps cathartic. It ought to warn us against the temptations to prettify the Indians' literature *a la Hiawatha*. The stories directly or slyly invite laughter *at* characters who are stupid, or unsophisticated, or recklessly bent on deception, like Coyote —presumably, solid citizens like Eagle or Salmon would never get into such predicaments and become public butts. Among modern Indians, this sense of humor survives, in part as a defense against white society.

Today's Northwest Indians themselves do more than survive, certainly; they begin to flourish anew in Oregon and elsewhere in the region, and the wonder of it is that they have brought so much of a viable Indianness with them through their ordeals. Inescapably, I have used the past tense here in trying to introduce their myths to general readers, but in dwelling so much on matters of tradition and pre- and mythic history I do not want to imply that the continuities of Indian life, culture, and art have been broken. Much *has* been lost or at least attenuated—the opportunity to hear formal recitals of stories in Indian languages, for example, and the deep ties to specific homelands—but more goes forward in the Indian Way than is commonly recognized by whites. Anyone who hopes to engage and cherish these stories should understand, if he is not Indian, that without taking pains to acknowledge the continuity of Indian life, its *futurity* as well as its history, he is in danger of merely sentimentalizing a rich native literature. And such sentimentality—which says in effect, "Lo! the poor Indian, exotic, pathetic, bound to a classical past, and safely in hand"—is ultimately vicious. It is a way of keeping a wise and gifted people in the place we have made for them, a way of continuing to ignore what they and their traditional literature might give us now.

What I cherish in these stories, beyond their Northwestern settings, is their wide, healthy emotional range, the openness and strength of the imaginative energy working in them, the sense of celebration of life's natural simplicities they convey. Are they not powerful accommodations to living? But re-reading them, trying to *hear* them, I am haunted by the way their art serves to call into question so many of the personal and collective sacrifices we feel we must make to maintain our evermore demonic Myth of Progress. It is the earth itself we have sacrificed, these stories seem to tell us, the mythic earth which might seize our imaginations still, as an avid intelligible World, ours because we know we belong to it, like the other creatures.

What if you and I had been named by our family and friends according to the Wishram ceremony, given the names of some long dead illustrious tribesmen and identified as human beings in the presence of all the communities of our lives on this earth, natural, supernatural, human? A ritual leader speaks to the group, and it responds in unison—

This person will be *Spédis.*

   A-xi.

This name used to belong to *Spédis,* who died a long time ago.

   A-xi.

We want the mountains, creeks, rivers, bluffs, timber to know that this
   person is now named *Spédis.*

   A-xi.

We want to let the fishes, birds, winds, snow, rain, sun, moon, stars to know that *Spédis* has the same as become alive again. His name will be heard again when this person is called.

A-xi.[23]

---

1. Melville Jacobs, "The Fate of Indian Oral Literatures in Oregon," *Northwest Review,* 3 (Summer 1962), 90.
2. Jacobs, p. 97.
3. *Clackamas Chinook Texts,* Parts One and Two (Bloomington: Indiana Univ. Press, 1958-59); *Nez Perce Texts,* Columbia Univ. Contributions to Anthropology, No. 25 (New York: Columbia Univ. Press, 1934).
4. Robert Frost, *Selected Poems of Robert Frost* (New York: Holt-Rinehart, 1963), p. 299.
5. *Coyote Was Going There* (Seattle: Univ. of Washington Press, 1977). All Oregon Indian stories referred to here can be found therein.
6. William Stafford, *The Rescued Year* (New York: Harper and Row, 1966), p. 31. See also the "Wind World" section in *Someday, Maybe* (New York: Harper and Row, 1974).
7. See Jacobs's *The People Are Coming Soon* (Seattle: Univ. of Washington Press, 1960) and *The Content and Style of an Oral Literature* (New York: Wenner-Gren Foundation for Anthropological Research, 1959), both works based on his monumental study of the Clackamas Chinook language and literature; and Hymes's model structuralist interpretations, "The 'Wife' Who 'Goes Out' Like a Man: Reinterpretation of a Clackamas Chinook Myth," in *Structural Analysis of Oral Tradition,* ed. Pierre Maranda and Elli Köngäs Maranda (Philadelphia: Univ. of Pennsylvania Press, 1971), and "Louis Simpson's 'The Deserted Boy,'" *Poetics,* 5 (1976), 119-55. See also J. Barre Toelken's essay on texture in a Navajo story, "The 'Pretty Language' of Yellowman," *Genre,* 2 (1969), 211 ff.; and my "The Wife Who Goes Out Like a Man, Comes Back as a Hero: the Art of Two Oregon Indian Narratives," *PMLA,* 92 (1977), 9-18. The best, most *useful* collection of North American Indian literature is still Stith Thompson, *Tales of the North American Indians* (1929; rpt. Bloomington: Indiana Univ. Press, 1968).
8. "The Autobiography of a Papago Indian," ed. Ruth Underhill, *Memoirs of the American Anthropological Association,* 46 (1936), 23.
9. Mircea Eliade, *Myth and Reality* (New York: Harper and Row, 1963), pp. 18-19, 141-42. A useful brief survey of schools of interpretation is Percy Cohen's "Theories of Myth," in *MAN, New Series,* 4 (1969), 337-53.
10. Isabel Kelly, "Northern Paiute Tales," *Journal of American Folklore,* 51 (1938), 436.
11. The Klikitat narrator Joe Hunt explained to Melville Jacobs that his people recognized "a former world" when all living things were persons which was followed by a "Great Change" resulting in the present world. Myths from the former world, including the events of the Transformation, are *wat'i't'ac*; stories from the latter days are *txa'nat*, "happenings" or "customs." Hunt also gave Jacobs examples of Klikitat *cu'kwat*—"knowledge, learning, teaching," often in the form of reflections on the meaning of myths and stories. In fact, most Northwest tribes had some such division according to "kind." See Melville Jacobs, "Northwest Sahaptin Texts," *University of Washington Publications in Anthropology,* 2, No. 6 (1929), 244.

12. MS letter, dated Nov. 20, 1929, in the collection of the American Philosophical Society Library in Philadelphia and printed with the permission of the Library.

13. Jacobs, *Content and Style,* p. 7, and *The People Are Coming Soon,* pp. ix-x. See also Phinney, *Nez Perce Texts,* p. viii. Probably the fullest study of the social circumstances of storytelling in a western Indian tribe is Theodore Stern's "Some Sources of Variability in Klamath Mythology," *Journal of American Folklore,* 69 (1956), 1-9, 135-46, 377-86.

14. For a different view of the relationship of myth and ritual in Northwest Indian life, see Dell Hymes's "Two Types of Linguistic Relativity," in *Sociolinguistics,* ed. William Bright (The Hague: Mouton, 1966), pp. 114-57.

15. Eliade, p. 19.

16. Jacobs, *Content and Style,* p. 73.

17. The work of Jerome Rothenberg and Dennis Tedlock (formerly co-editors of *Alcheringa: A Journal of Ethnopoetics*) points in this direction. Tedlock's brilliant translation of Zuñi narratives, *Finding the Center* (New York: Dial Press, 1972), is keyed to performance and is cast as poetry, and I believe that most of the items in the Northwest repertories would be best rendered as verse, if we could re-transcribe them from performance. But in most cases that would be impossible in the Northwest today.

18. See Dell Hymes's essay on "Breakthrough into Performance" in *Folklore: Performance and Communication,* ed. Dan Ben-Amos and Kenneth Goldstein (The Hague: Mouton, 1975), pp. 11-24; see also May Edel, "Stability in Tillamook Folklore," *Journal of American Folklore,* 57 (1944), 116-27.

19. The subject of Indian assimilation of European stories has been oddly neglected. Such study might shed light on the fundamental principles or "rules" by which native narratives were generated. See Stith Thompson's early study, *European Tales Among the North American Indians,* Colorado College Publications, Language Series No. 34 (Colorado Springs: Colorado College, 1919), and for examples see his *Tales* and the British Columbia texts of James Teit, especially those issued in the volumes of the Jesup North Pacific Expedition. I have drawn on Teit's work in "The Bible in Western Indian Mythology," *Journal of American Folklore,* 90 (1977), 442-54.

20. *The Future of an Illusion,* transl. W. D. Robson-Scott (Garden City, N.Y.: Anchor-Doubleday, 1961), p. 18.

21. See *Structural Anthropology* (Garden City, N.Y.: Doubleday, 1967), "The Structural Study of Myth," especially pp. 250 ff. For the most penetrating study of the Indian Trickster yet made, see Paul Radin, *The Trickster* (New York: Philosophical Library, 1956). I have discussed Ted Hughes's Crow as a latter-day Trickster in "Crow, or the Trickster Transformed," forthcoming in *Massachusetts Review.*

22. James Teit, "Folk-tales of Salishan Tribes," *Memoirs of the American Folklore Society,* 11 (1917), 82.

23. Adapted from Edward Sapir and Leslie Spier, "Wishram Ethnography," in *University of Washington Publications in Anthropology,* 3, No. 3 (1930), 258-59.

As the Indian literature of the Northwest has comprised one part of the region's covert culture, so the folklore of its more recent inhabitants represents another. Like Jarold Ramsey, Barre Toelken is interested in bringing an essentially oral, and thus perishable or overlooked, form of Northwest culture to the attention of a contemporary audience and to the work of scholarly inquiry. Professor Toelken teaches at the University of Oregon, where his classes in folklore attract large numbers of students and where he has won that University's Ersted Award for distinguished teaching. He was editor of the *Journal of American Folklore* from 1973 to 1977 and is now president of the American Folklore Society.

Northwest
Regional Folklore

Barre Toelken

In his introductory remarks to *Northwest Harvest*, V. L. O. Chittick expressed a reasonable certainty that the Northwest was ripe for a folklorist's services.[1] Nonetheless, he declined to print as a chapter of that book the conference contribution of Professor William L. Alderson which was, lamentably, "more of a performance than a paper" (p. xv). Nothing could more forcefully represent the gulf that has existed through the years between literary scholars and folklorists. Similarly and ironically, nothing could more clearly demonstrate the difference between folklore and other forms of expression than the very factor of *performance*, for folklore exists in the performance: not in what a dialect word looks like but how, and under what circumstances, it is said; not in the barn but in the barn raising; not in the quilt only, but in the quilting bee; not in the song text in the scholar's speech, but in the performance of the song within its traditional habitat. In fact, it will be the contention of this essay that if there is a distinctive Northwest aspect to our culture, much of it involves the ability to "perform" in locally viable genres of traditional expression. The spirit of the region is to be found primarily among the people in how they say and do things, and only secondarily in the works of literature and art that may be based on these everyday performances of local culture. It is probably safe to say that if a Northwest "Homer" had come along, as many in Professor Chittick's 1946 conference hoped, he would have been dismissed as a semi-literature entertainer, for both performance and oral tradition in our own culture have been generally denigrated or ignored by literary scholars until very recently.

Alderson himself fought a losing battle to acquaint Oregonians with the riches of real oral traditional song; at least he was tolerated as a reasonably articulate spokesman for illiterature, and was in some demand as a singer of songs at parties. His last article, published posthumously, concerned a gold-rush song, "The Days of '49," and there are still those who puzzle quietly over the Reed College English professor so interested in something "far out of his field."[2]

Less fortunate was Randall V. Mills, a professor in the English Department at the University of Oregon, who was kept at an instructor's salary for most of his career by a department head who felt his interest in folklore (including string games) proved his inability to deal with "real" literature.

The folklore archives at the University of Oregon are today named in his honor, but when he died in the 1950s, folklore had not yet become locally respectable. Robert Winslow Gordon, one of the founders of the Archive of Folksong at the Library of Congress and a person largely responsible for the development of disc recording (RCA Victor pioneered disc machinery for his field work)[3] was denied tenure in the English Department at Berkeley because his publications were all in folklore and, to the dismay of dean and department head, his most prominent writings were monthly folksong columns in *Adventure* magazine (now obligatory reading for folksong scholars). Gordon's personal collection of American folksongs, one of the largest outside the Library of Congress, is now at the University of Oregon because his alma mater, Harvard, declined it.

What accounts for this former academic devaluation of field-collected folklore generally, and what has impeded its study in a region so "ready" for the folklorist's ministrations? For one thing, there has been the curious assumption among scholars that writing affords a more reliable—hence a more valuable—way of transmitting important matters. This, coupled with the complementary belief that in oral tradition all things break down and wear away, has led to an operational premise that views oral materials as preliterate, as lying previous in time to what we should be interested in now. We study the presumably oral poetry of *Beowulf* or Homer in written text, but few have followed Albert Lord's lead and actually become interested in the oral poetry of Yugoslavia. Rather, the Yugoslav epic is seen as an illumination of such higher pieces as the *Iliad*. And we recall that Professor Child of Harvard felt the printed ballads in his British sources to be superior to anything that might still be found in oral tradition in America; hence he ignored almost completely the live oral resources which surrounded him in abundance. Most of these views are not held to by modern folklorists (though some survive among professors of literature). The devolutionary premise in folklore studies has been challenged.[4] The idea that folklore dies as literacy expands has been denied. The notion that oral tradition is backward and that interest in it is regressive has been neatly put away. Perhaps the field of folklore is ready now, in a way that Chittick's conference could not have been ready, to take a profitable look at the traditions of this region.

The job itself will be in some ways a difficult one, for strangely enough at least four groups of prominent opinion makers have helped to confuse, warp or ignore the real regional traditions that should be the basis of our speculation. The politicians and businessmen have encouraged a view of the region that focuses on state lines, marketing centers and transportation systems, not on the natural networks of tradition that hold people together and mold their expressions. The scholars have watched on the one hand for the "regional Homer" (that is, someone from here, but who in spite of that can write well) and have feared on the other hand that an overt interest in regionalism might brand them as provincial. The blatantly regional writers have used Northwest geographical imagery strongly but when it came to lore and tradition have often invented what eastern readers would accept as folksy; the creation of Paul Bunyan by professional writers like James Stevens is an example of this and will be discussed further herein. Finally, the middle- to upper-class descendants of the Northwest pioneers have tried continually to depict their grandparents as farsighted, godfearing folk who had no superstitions, sang no earthy songs, and who, if they had oral traditions, gave them up quickly as proof of their willing-ness to pull themselves up by their bootstraps. In this view, tradition is something backward, something no right-minded person would want to have pinned on him. Taking the place of tradition in the reminiscences of these families are the expurgated myths of the Founding Fathers and Pioneer Mothers; their genteel necrophilia is encouraged by some historical societies whose chief concerns are dates, names, and museums full of lace-doilies-and-violoncellos-brought-safely-across-the-plains-and-around-the-Horn-by-grandfather-at-terrible-risk-and-great-bother, and whose least interests are in the feelings, jokes, songs, dances, games, cus-toms, cultural aberrations and real-life traditions of pioneer forebears.

The result has been, in this region and in others, that we have been en-couraged to look not at the soul of the people in the area but at their epitaph, not at the live tradition but at the dead fact. And in many cases, indeed, the antiseptic facts have not expressed for us a rich sense of locality, of shared cultural experiences and expressions tied to a region, for these elements are naturally abstract and emotionally charged.

What resources are there, then, if we seek these elusive and subtle ex-pressions? Where will we find those culturally dynamic materials that may help us see this area as distinct in the minds of its inhabitants in their own expressive terms, not in scholarly descriptions? It will not be to the authors and scholars that we must turn, but to the actual informal oral and physical expressions of the people themselves, especially as they are modi-fied and developed through the continually changing, but locally conserva-tive, processes of tradition.[5] Not to do so will result not only in secondhand information, but may invite outright mishandling of the materials by anyone who would like to promote a particular view. James Stevens, a moderately successful regional writer, provides a good example of the dislocation that can occur when a literary composition is passed off as a product of the folk. Stevens's composition, "The Frozen Logger" (by rumor constructed with the help of H. L. Davis and Stewart Holbrook), while it may sound to a non-logger like something a logger might sing, is a clever monument to pre-expurgation, to the recognition that folk material common to one group may be unacceptable or even objectionable to another if phrased in terms actually used by the first group. Set to the tune of an old music hall song, "When I was Young and Foolish," Stevens's piece gives a polite story, with the central scene left out entirely, using conventional and "acceptable" words and images, including some superficially rough but carefully chosen descriptions of a logger's toughness. The song has never become part of active logger tradition but has maintained its stability as a humorous pop song. It is commonly accepted in the East as a logger folksong.

> As I sat down one evening
> In a timber town cafe,
> A six-foot-seven waitress
> To me these words did say:
>
> "I see that you are a logger,
> And not just a common bum,
> For nobody but a logger
> Stirs his coffee with his thumb.
>
> "My lover, he was a logger,
> There's none like him today.
> If you'd pour whiskey on it
> He would eat a bale of hay.
>
> "He never shaved his whiskers
> From off of his horny hide:
> He'd just drive them in with a hammer
> And bite them off inside.
>
> "My logger came to see me,
> 'Twas on a freezing day;
> He held me in a fond embrace
> That broke three vertebrae.
>
> "He kissed me when we parted,
> So hard that he broke my jaw;
> I could not speak to tell him
> He'd forgot his mackinaw.
>
> "I saw that logger leaving,
> Sauntering through the snow,
> Going bravely homeward
> At forty-eight below.
>
> "The weather it tried to freeze him,
> It tried its level best;

At a hundred degrees below zero
He buttoned up his vest.

"It froze clear through to China,
It froze to the stars above;
At a thousand degrees below zero,
It froze my logger love.

"We tried and tried to thaw him,
And if you'll believe me, sir,
We made him into ax blades
To cut the Douglas fir.

"And so I lost my lover,
And to this cafe I come,
And here I wait til someone
Stirs his coffee with his thumb."[6]

The problem for Stevens clearly lay in trying to champion the image of the old time independent logger—a prime symbol of American free enterprise until the evil unions forced the timber industry into the modern world—without using words and phrases which would alienate the public; in other words, how to present the logger image without doing it the way the loggers themselves would. This kind of pseudolore, created *for* the tastes of the buying public rather than *from* the real cultural tastes of the presumable folk it represents, has been justly termed "fakelore" by Professor Richard Dorson. The fakery lies not in the commercial aspect itself but in the disguise presumed necessary in order to sell a product. The result is most often typified by a quaint, cute, hyperliterary style that actually leads away from the powerfully rich speech, image, and character of the folk. Take another example of Stevens's, his attempt to create epic stories glorifying the lumber industry, claiming that the Paul Bunyan stories were actually told around the bunkhouse: one must imagine a logger looking out of his bunk to his mates, shifting a wad of snoose out of the way, and beginning a story,

> The blue snow fell first in the North. It fell scantily in its earlier
> hours, its sapphire flakes floating down on the waves of a mild
> winter wind, and glittering in an ashen cold light, a sober pale
> radiance which shimmered through silver mists. There was poetry
> in the spectacle of those hours.[7]

Perhaps it is unfair to pick on James Stevens over all the others guilty of the same kind of well-intended distortion. Obviously, the point here is not Stevens's writing, which can stand or fall on its own merits, but the extent to which we are exposed to or shielded from Northwest folklore in the printed works available to us, many of which were produced by people

who were, as Stevens was, "participant-observers" among the folk they
sought to describe. The problem is magnified astronomically in the Northwest by the many occupations, ethnic communities, localities and layers of
settlement that have produced partly separate, partly overlapping, folk
traditions that need to be perceived and understood before the nature of
the region's cultures can be appreciated. Clearly this cannot be done if the
view is only through mauve-colored windows. Although there is not much
Northwest folk material available in print, a look through any folklore
archives or almost any field research project in folklore will turn up a rich
store of unsterilized natural organic traditions which do not require the
artificial fertilizer of a scholarly meeting to grow and prosper and nurture
their communities. An overview of this bounty, first in terms of the folk
groups and areas, then in terms of the lore itself and its relation to Northwest culture, will demonstrate the ample supply of folklore *in* the Northwest and will show the existence of some strong local traditions *of* that
region as well.

For folkloristic purposes we may set one of the northern limits of the
Northwest at the Canadian boundary, for although there are occupational
and geographical and climatological similarities which know no border, the
general cast of western Canada is British (or attempts to be), and this sets
the cultural context of western Canada quite apart from the essentially
New England and Southeast United States settlement roots of the Northwest. It will become immediately apparent, however, that if one studies
the folklore of logging, western Canada must be included. Obviously,
then, there are some ways in which folklore will not be restricted in scope
to political bearings. Another northern part of the Northwest is Alaska,
which shares occupational, ethnic, and geographical roots with the rest of
the region more than it does with Canada. Yet, because Alaska is still
chiefly native in population, the whites being—even now—a motley group
of intruders settled mostly in small urban areas, there is the strong likeli-
hood that the character of Alaska will grow to be something other than
what developed in the Oregon Territory a hundred years ago when Indians
could be exterminated or pushed aside with a clear conscience.

For the sake of clarity and convenience, then, we may say that the
Northwest is certainly made up of central and western Washington, and
central and western Oregon, probably eastern Washington and eastern
Oregon, probably (in that case) northern Idaho, and maybe far western
Montana and a small strip of northern California. This total area has a
coherence that overrides the tremendously varied topography within its
borders: the traditional occupations throughout are heavily related to
forests, horses, mines, and boats; its geographical "feel" seems to be mountains, rivers, desert, and ocean; its center of gravity tends to be coastal
(that is, when people go to the big city, it is most likely to be Seattle or

Portland rather than Omaha, Salt Lake City, Denver). Much of its quality derives from its having been the end of the trail for so many western
pioneers; much of its character is geographical, for it clearly is not easily
confused with the Great Basin or with the Great Southwest.[8]

Within this area are a good number of well-defined, often sizeable, ethnic
and religious communities quite in addition to the generally white European Protestant immigration tide from Northeast and Southeast. Since
these groups have maintained their identity, often because of the outside
pressure of their neighbors, they function as all folk groups do, providing
a rich network of expressive culture informally exchanged through time
among members of the group. There are Dunkers in southcentral Washington; Russian Old Believers in Woodburn, Oregon; a few Amish near
Amity, Oregon; Mennonites at Albany, Oregon; Buddhists (Japanese-
Americans) at Hood River, Ontario, and Nyssa, Oregon and at Nampa,
Idaho; Basques in Idaho and both eastern and central Oregon; Slavs
(many of them fishermen) on the islands of Puget Sound; Icelanders in
Seattle and in Eugene; Mexican-Americans throughout the area (they
are the largest single "minority" in Oregon); Finns in Astoria; Chinese
in Portland and Seattle; Scots in Portland and Seattle; Blacks throughout
(though some smaller towns still claim to have "sundown laws" and
several locals of the Klan exist, it is true that towns in Washington were
founded by Blacks, and a Black family in northern Idaho still lives on land
it homesteaded in the 1800s); Germans at Aurora, Oregon (where one of
the only European medieval-style barn courtyards in America and a
three-story log cabin still stand); Scandinavians of all varieties at Junction
City, Oregon (which becomes *Forbindelsestad* every summer). Each of
these groups has maintained its own traditions and has, furthermore, en-
riched its area by initiating or enlarging local traditions in architecture,
boatmaking, games, dances, farming and ranching customs, cooking and
foodlore, and language, all in peculiar combinations not to be found in
other areas of the country.

If one adds to this collection of peoples the recollection of the original
inhabitants—who have by no means vanished—one begins to see the complexity of the cultural bearings of the Northwest. Even a brief, super-
ficial list of the Indian peoples still remaining would necessarily include
the small settlements of Neah Bay and La Push in Washington as well as
the larger reservations of the Yakima and Colville there; the Nez Perce
the Blackfoot reservations in Idaho; and the Warm Springs, Klamath, and
Umatilla areas of Oregon. These groups are important for our study, for
there was as profound an impact on white custom and tradition from the
Indians as there was an irremediable impact on the Indians from the whites.
We are daily witnesses to the latter, but the former often goes unacknowl-
edged. Not only did Indian families customarily adopt white children

whose families could not support them, but in their food and animal lore they gave the Northwest many of its distinctive dietary ingredients and considerable food preservation techniques. Forestry and fishing practices developed long ago by the Indians are only now beginning to be understood by the white culture, so there is ample proof that the impact persists. So close were the relations between white and Indian in the late 1800s that at the turn of the century Chinook Jargon was apparently spoken by more whites than Indians (perhaps an element of pride in a demonstrable pioneer heritage). There are letters to the editor written in Chinook Jargon in nearly every newspaper in the region, as well as hymns passed down through oral tradition in white families:

> Kah alta kloshe Old Man Daniel? [three times]
> [where now good]
> Si-ah saghalie kopa kloshe illahee.
> [far off heaven over there good place]
> Alki nesika klatawa nanitch,
> [by and by we travel to see (him)]
> Si-ah saghalie kopa kloshe illahee.[9]

This version of "Where oh Where is Father Abraham? (Way Over in the Promised Land)" may stand as a typical example of the vitality of a singing tradition that triumphed over ethnic enmities and sectarian meanings to become a kind of cultural badge for the Northwesterner. It is not an isolated instance.

Turning from the folk to the folklore, we must take a different approach than that used in either literary studies or history. Unlike our colleagues in literature, we do not study the unique, identifiable artists, their lives, times, ideas, and works. Quite to the contrary, we look primarily for the anonymous, non-unique, generally-shared traditions that have become, in spite of individual generation, identified with a whole group of people who share such close ties (ethnic, occupational, familial, geographical) that their expressions are typical of the group and its interests more than they are indicative of individuals' taste. Unlike our colleagues in history, we do not primarily look for or interpret the "hard" data of facts, dates, names, places, and sequences of events. Rather, we watch for expressions of all sorts that have become viable among the members of close communities over time.

Nonetheless, such expressions are susceptible to the kind of discussion normally found among literary critics, for not only are many of the expressions themselves phrased in generic categories akin to (and precedent to) written literature (ballad, tale, riddle, proverb), but there are also aspects of the expressions (symbol, metaphor) that can be fruitfully discussed through the methods normally used in literary analysis. Similarly, while historical detail is not central to the study, it must be recognized that an item of tradition can hardly be appreciated outside its historical context, and therefore the approaches and perspectives of the historian are essential to the discussion. Further, since most folklore exists in the actual performance within a particular live cultural milieu, discussion and analysis of traditions in any region require the perspectives of anthropology, particularly those developed recently by the social anthropologists. In addition, since many items produced in traditional ways are actual physical artifacts such as barns, quilts and carvings, the views of art history, design, and vernacular architecture are equally demanded. And since much of folklore is orally transmitted and performed by people who prefer to use in their close groups the manner of speaking most congenial and familiar to the group, the matter of dialect (ethnic, occupational, social, geographical, generational) enters the picture so strongly as to demand further the expertise and perspectives of the professional linguist. Much of folklore is made up of gesture, body movement, proxemic adjustments, and bodily art, thus requiring the dance ethnologist's knowledge as well. Finally (although this by no means exhausts the list of necessary special approaches), we recognize that many folk traditions are responses to, or expressions of, tension and fear, thus requiring that we not overlook the psychological aspect of the subject. All of these matters must be juggled, as it were, by someone who has training in, or a deep understanding of, demography and geography. This is why it is possible to say without derogation to Chittick and his earnest colleagues that the Northwest was not ready to mount a full study of its folklore in the 1940s or 1950s.

In any case, it is clear that this combination of interests must be applied if we are to get a sense of the groups of people who settled the Northwest and gave it its personality. We need to know their tastes, feelings, attitudes, their own sense of region, their sense of being at home, as these abstract qualities find expression in ways continually valid to those groups, in their own language.

Did the Northwest, for example, produce narratives and beliefs about characters like Paul Bunyan, Pecos Bill, Davy Crockett, and other real and presumed demigods? The answer, not surprisingly at this point in the discussion, is no. The "hero" most enshrined in actual folk tradition is the local character, the village liar whose self-proclaimed exploits are known primarily to his own small community and are locally thought to be clever tall stories or "windies" made up by the Münchausen himself. On examination, these stories most often turn out to be from a fund of European-American materials known to have been in circulation for years. The local character (for example, Reub Long of Fort Rock, Oregon; Len Henry of Lapwai, Idaho; Hathaway Jones of Rogue River, Oregon; Benjamin

Franklin "Huckleberry" Finn of Finn Rock, Oregon) spends much of his time telling lies, mixing his own compositions with international tradition, forming yarns that are cameos of local application. Often the tales are still being told locally by others in the third person long after the original Münchausen himself has passed on, indicating that both the character and the yarns retain a meaning in the locale. But what is the point of these characters, and why should they be found more solidly in oral tradition than are the political and economic superheroes like Davy Crockett and Paul Bunyan?[10] If they answer some local need, what is it?

First of all, local lies allow local people to focus on the emotional and personal factors of their environment in ways not normally countenanced or encouraged in everyday discourse. One is not supposed to complain loud and long about weather and circumstance; one is not supposed to crow unduly about his successes in farming. In the local lie, however, both the negative and positive aspects of the region are expressed in humorous hyperbole. In eastern Oregon the wind blows so hard that cattle have to stand on their hay to keep it from blowing away; a stiff breeze is indicated by links being snapped off a horizontal logging chain. In central Oregon it gets so dry, according to Reub Long, that their rain water assays out at 31% moisture; Long himself never saw rain until he was eighteen and then was knocked unconscious by a huge desert raindrop ("They had to throw six buckets of sand in my face to bring me around"). In the wet, western part of Oregon, as it is well-known, natives are identified by webbed feet, moss between the shoulder blades and soggy curls; here it is so wet and fertile that squash have to be put on sleds to prevent them from wearing out being dragged through the mud by rapidly growing vines. And it is such a healthy climate that they had to shoot a man just to start the first cemetery. The old lie of the stretching buckskin harness is told, one version attributing the phenomenon to a heavy rain, another to driving a team across a turbulent river. Such humorous lies as these may be told by many people throughout a region, but they seem to reach their zenith as folk expression when they are "taken on" by a local raconteur and made a part of his distinctive repertoire, especially if the person is himself a real character with noticeable oddities which also then become part of the performance of these items.

Such a character was Hathaway Jones, an early twentieth-century mail carrier along the Rogue River in southwest Oregon. He had a cleft palate and a "hare lip," and all his pronouncements were of course colored by this condition (accordingly, the effect is attempted by anyone retelling the stories today, to the utter puzzlement of outsiders). His yarns and remarks were almost entirely in the category of pioneer frustrations, anxieties, and mistakes: the stories abound with accounts of encounters with bears, falling rocks, stupid hunters, and wily game; with forgetfulness (a watch abandoned in the woods is found, still ticking three years later); with poor aim (an attempt to shoot a flock of geese all in a row with one shot results only in a "bucket of bills"); with the problems and triumphs of building a fireplace (his father's drew so fiercely that they had only to open the front door and the suction would pull wood right in from the pile). The list is limited only by the fact that Jones's stories were not all collected before his death. But from a close examination of the evidence available to us, it is clear that Hathaway Jones, like other local Münchausens, gave a focused, culturally acceptable expression to the themes and concerns that were of greatest moment to local people.[11]

This is why Paul Bunyan stories rarely get outside the classroom and into tradition. They represent not the local and the down home but the larger interests of the forest industry seen from an economical, national point of view. Bunyan, a French Canadian according to Stevens, jumps across the border to freedom, has dreams of the forests being felled, sees "to work" spelled out in the stars, and organizes a giant gang of timber harvesters to provide homes for all mankind. While this can be a rather clever metaphor for the lumber industry, it is not the way loggers themselves view the task. They face day-to-day danger which comes out in folk expression in the form of local jokes, lies, pranks, and the like. The spirit of local character, then, is found in the local specifics of tales and lies that actually provide a performance of those concerns most central to the people in their own context.

A corollary to this observation is that the performances are so local that they also create a distinct delineation of insider-outsider relations.[12] Very often a lie is so subtle, the terminology so specialized, that it takes an insider to know whether it is indeed a lie. Add the further dimension of Hathaway Jones's nasal speech, and the outsider may be completely fogged. The continued performance of local lies, then, gives us not only an idea of some of the deeper concerns of the local community, but it also demonstrates an awareness in that community of its own sense of locale. This is to say that "local color" is not accidental or unconscious, that very likely it is an animating force in a people's sense of who and where they are.

The same shaping force is seen in the regional pronunciation of place names. An aspect of folk speech, or dialect, place-name pronunciation can function to strengthen esoteric identity as well as to define exotic identity. Outsiders almost invariably mispronounce "Willamette," "Yachats," "Heceta," and "Coos" in Oregon, "Boise," Kooskia," "Kamiah," and "Weiser" in Idaho, "Cle Elum," "Puyallup," and "Sequim" in Washington. And the word "Oregon" itself is so commonly mispronounced outside the Northwest that one workable definition of the Northwest region might be "that part of the country where people in general know how to say 'Oregon.'" Such locally specific pronunciations may operate to keep the outsider out, of course, but they may also be used as a means of integrating the outsider into the local proprieties. A person from another area does not escape correction in the Northwest; at the first "Awragawn" or "Will-mét," he is usually interrupted in mid-sentence and told, "Orygun," "Wil-LAM-it."

Thus, we can see not only the lore being brought in and made a part of regional expression (as noted above in the case of internationally known lies now at home in the Northwest), but people who come to the Northwest are also converted, as it were, to the locally appropriate ways of speaking.[13] This dual process of regionalizing bespeaks a powerful and unapologetic sense of place, especially as it is expressed in culturally meaningfully ways.

In Northwest folksong there are the same two processes at work. The earliest song made up in the Northwest (as far as we know) uses as its basic ingredients the figures of speech, attitudes, and hyperbolic descriptions that had already become characteristic of the area, the author obviously having felt more drawn to local expressive notions than to those of his eastern place of birth. And the later songs that came into the area were maintained in oral tradition but were sharply changed to align their contents and implications with those of the region. Thus, both the people and the lore were being regionalized at an early date. The flavor of the region, the taste of what the area is like for its everyday inhabitants, can be perceived very strongly in these songs, which sharply reinterpret the pioneer experience not only in terms of geographical locale but also through the traumatic realization of what it means to be at the end of the trail: surprise, rationalization, disappointment are qualities better handled in song than in history texts, as the following examples show.

The first regional song to be composed in the Pacific Northwest, as far as we know, is "The Old Settler," more often known by its punchline, "Acres of Clams." The uncopyrighted composition of Frank Henry, pioneer of 1847, its actual date is unknown; it first appeared in print in 1927 and is even today widely sung in the Northwest.[14] It is one of the best examples of the "regionalization of the people," for Frank Henry put into the song a number of metaphors, exaggerations, and figures of speech which he undoubtedly heard in circulation among other pioneers trying to express themselves about the area. Many of these figures are still in use on the western slope of the region in daily conversation and in literature. Here, in other words, the song reflects usages being developed by early settlers. As we see in several other songs below, however, there was later the conversion of pre-existing songs from other areas to suit this growing "set" of regional differences. "The Old Settler" is difficult to label "folksong," for it lacks the wide variation in tune and words normally encountered when any item has passed through oral tradition. Moreover, the song has become so well-known on menus and other advertisements that its text has been virtually fossilized for many of its singers (except for the comparatively recent change from "niggered" to "labored" in verse 5). Nonetheless some variations have occurred and this may be thus one of the few indigenous songs in the area really to have been retained in local informal performance. It is sung to the tune of "Rosin the Bow."

1. I've wandered all over this country, prospecting and digging
     for gold;
   I've tunneled, drilled, and I've lumbered, and I have been
     frequently sold.

Chorus: And I have been frequently sold, and I have been
            frequently sold;
         I've tunneled, drilled, and I've lumbered, and I have been
            frequently sold.

2. I made some money at minin' but I saw lots of people get poor,
   So I tried my hand at wheat farmin'—the only pursuit that is
     sure.

Chorus: The only pursuit that is sure; the only pursuit that is sure;
         I tried my hand at what farmin', the only pursuit that
            is sure.

3. But one day I rolled up my blanket, and left all my wheat in the
     ground,
   And started out early one mornin' for a country they call Puget
     Sound.

Chorus: For a country, etc.

4. I got there dead broke in the winter and found it all covered
     with fog,
   And growin' all over with timber thick as hair on the back
     of a dog.

Chorus: Thick as hair, etc.

5. I staked out a claim in the forest and got myself down to
     hard toil;
   For ten years I chopped and I labored, but I never got down
     to the soil.

Chorus: But I never, etc.

6. I tried to get out of that country, but poverty forced me to stay,
   Until I became an old settler—now nothin' can drive me away.

Chorus: Now nothin' can, etc.

7. No longer the slave of ambition, I laugh at the world and
   its shams,
   And I think of my happy condition, surrounded by acres
   of clams.

Chorus: Surrounded by acres of clams, etc.

It is important to note that this is not called "The Founding Father,"
and that it celebrates not the achievements of the elite but the frustrations
of the everyday settler. The movement of the persona is westward through
the mining country (maybe up from California?), through the dryland
farm area of the eastern Northwest, then on to the coast, and finally he is
too broke to go back. No triumph here, but rather a humorous account of
hardship, digging through the humus, resignation. Reub Long of central
Oregon once interrupted someone who was singing the praises of the
pioneers of that area: "Do you think they settled here because they liked
it? Hell, they were just too broke to go home!" And although it is said
that one could live around Puget Sound with no labor except for the digging of clams ("when the tide's out, the table's set"), the price of that
monotonous fare was that a person would spout instead of belch and his
bladder would rise and fall with the tide. These of course are not the facts
of history, but they are the facts of human emotional response to environment, phrased in communally recognizable performances.

Compare such a regionally valid set of references to the following song
which was also brought into the region from elsewhere, in this case from
Scotland, although most likely the trip was not a direct one. Here there
has been a distinct change of setting, and therefore of words, from the Scottish "Barnyards of Dilgatty" to the Northwest loggers' "Too Ree Ama."
Even the nonsense chorus, which in the Scottish version has, phonetically,

linten addie, toorin addie, linten addie, toorinee;
linten lowren, lowren, lowren, the barnyards of Dilgattee,

is quite different. But in this case the modification is not primarily regional, with the one exception being the reference to cutting the redwood
tree, which at least suggests the more-or-less Northwest coast. The modification here is primarily occupational; the song is sung mainly by loggers
in those few taverns in Oregon and Idaho where singing is not considered
deviant behavior. Thus, while the song is sung in the Northwest, its
rhetorical strategies are not centrally regional.

My eyes look like dried-up raisins,
My nose is a purple red,
I wear a coat of many colors
And it smells like something dead.

Too ree ama, too ree ama
Too ree ama, too ree-ay. [Twice]

I can tame a wild hootnanny,
I can chop a redwood tree,
I dip snuss and chew tobaccy;
Will you marry me, me, me?

I went down to see my girlfriend,
When I got there she was sick;
In her gut they found a peavy,
Three pulaskis and a pick.

I can drink and not get drunken,
I can fight and not get slain,
I can kiss another man's girlie
And be welcome back again.[15]

The same observation may be made of the following verses from "Halle-lujah, I'm a Bum" (sung in the 1930s as a parody of the hymn "Halle-lujah, Thine The Glory") which emerged in Portland and Seattle along the skid road areas during the "recession" of the 1950s. These are political and social comments, although the agricultural exploitations they refer to are those that were centrally northwestern at the time. Still, the flavor and the rhetoric of the Northwest are not essentially here.

Chorus: Hallelujah, I'm a bum,
Hallelujah, bum again,
Hallelujah, give us a handout
To revive us again.

"Why don't you work like other men do?"
"How can I work when there's no work to do?"

"Why don't you pick my apples for me?"
"I done it before and you starved my family."

"Why don't you cut my wheat crop for me?"
"You don't need help, with that big subsidy."[16]

Contrasted to these songs which are in fact Northwest songs without being northwestern as such, there are some songs that came to the region in oral tradition and made themselves at home, as it were, by virtue of a congruity in subject and tone. These songs retain much of their earlier wording but change slightly here and there to accommodate the new setting. For example, the earliest American song we know of, "Springfield Mountain," celebrates the death by rattlesnake bite of Timothy Myrick of Wilbraham, Mass., in 1761, while he was mowing hay with a scythe. The song is sung in many parts of the United States and has been collected in Oregon as "Brownsville Mountain," naming that place (presumably near Brownsville, Oregon) instead of Springfield Mountain as its setting. But very likely the song was considerably aided in its survival in the Brownsville area by virtue of the fact that a lot of hay was mowed there by scythe (attested to by personal recollections of farmers and by several scythe-whetting songs still in oral circulation in the 1800s, and by the fact that rattlesnakes have always been common threats to workers in the field in that area). Moreover, since many of the settlers of early Oregon came from New England, there is the possibility that the song represents a cultural nostalgia, a retention of a song from the old environment because it still "fits in," given minor adjustments.

An even greater case of congruity is the song "Girl With The Striped Stockings," as sung by Clarissa Mae Judkins of Eugene, Oregon, daughter of pioneers. She learned the song by listening to her brothers sing it "out behind the barn." She was sure it had been brought from back east by the pioneers, perhaps as a popular song, but she was equally certain that the reason for its retention in western Oregon (in addition to its turn-of-the-century risqué topic) is the fact that "it rains in every verse." Here, then, the flavor is perceived as appropriate for adoption by Northwest singers without further modification.

> 1. One rainy day I'll never forget,
>   The prettiest girl I ever met:
>   When she raised her skirts to the wet—
>   I saw she had striped stockings on.
>
> Chorus: She was always out when the wind blew high,
>   When the weather was wet, she'd walk or die;
>   By the raisin' of her skirts as she passed by
>   I saw she had striped stockings on.
>
> 2. The color of her hose was red and yeller,
>   Says she to me "You're a mighty fine feller,"
>   So I walked her home under my umbrella,
>   The girl with the striped stockings on.
>
> Chorus: She was always, etc.
>
> 3. And when we parted in the rain
>   She says "We'll never meet again,"
>   And so she hooked my watch and chain,
>   The girl with the striped stockings on.
>
> Chorus: She was always, etc.[17]

The regionalization of a folksong, that is, the conversion of an existing traditional song into a strategy and image-set more at home in the region, is more clearly seen in the progression of folk parodies on the hymn "Beulah Land." Originally a physical description of the bounty of heaven—

> I've reached the land of corn and wine
> And all its riches now are mine;
> Here shines undimmed one blissful day,
> For all my night has passed away.
>
> Oh Beulah Land, sweet Beulah Land
> As on thy highest mount I stand:
> I look away across the sea
> Where mansions are prepared for me,
> And view the shining glory shore—
> My heaven, my home, forevermore

—it was sung by many of the later pioneers apparently as a hopeful portrait of the land they envisioned at the end of the trail. When some of them ran out of luck and money in the dry lands of the Dakotas, frustration and comic bitterness led to hellish parodies of the scene they were now forced to inhabit:

> We've reached the land of dying wheat
> Where nothing grows for man to eat,
> Where the wind it blows the fiery heat
> Across the plains so hard to beat.
>
> Dakota Land, South Dakota Land,
> As on thy burning soil I stand;
> I look away across the plains
> And wonder why it never rains
> Til Gabriel blows his trumpet sound
> And says the rain's just gone around.

And nearly every western and midwestern state developed its local phrasing of the lament. In New Mexico one hears it thus:

> This is a land of dusty roads
> Of rattlesnakes and horny toads;
> It never rains, it never snows,
> The doggone wind just blows and blows.
> New Mexico so fertile and rich
> We think you are a honey.
> [The last two lines are to the tune of the first line of
> "Oh Christmas Tree."]

In some states, where nearby settlements were far off and the chances of visiting suitors were slim for the girls, young women were advised to grab any man who came to the door, even if he were begging. Some areas became famous for "flirts":

> Oh Kansas girls, dry Kansas girls,
> With laughing eyes and sunny curls;
> They'll sing and dance and flirt and play
> Til some sodbuster comes that way;
> They'll grab him at the dugout door
> And stick by him forevermore.

By the time pioneers made it to the Oregon Territory, the Beulah Land parody custom was very likely familiar to everyone, and of course, since much of western Oregon *did* seem like Beulah Land, a kind of reverse parody arose, keeping the form of "Beulah Land," retaining some of the cliches and formulas of the parodies from other states, but now "complaining" (of all things) about the greenness and abundance of rain—a turn of strategy and phrase and humor that certainly must have seemed insane to those poor Dakotans still waiting for a small cloud to pass over. In the Oregon version of this parody we see the real inside flavor of the western slope mood:

> I've reached the land of rain and mud,
> Where flowers and trees so early bud;
> Where it rains and rains both night and day
> For in Oregon [pronounced O-ree-gun] it rains always.

> Oh Oregon, wet Oregon
> As through thy rain and mud I run;
> I stand and look out all around
> And watch the rain soak in the ground,
> Look up and see the waters pour
> And wish it wouldn't rain no more.

> Oh Oregon girls, wet Oregon girls,
> With laughing eyes and soggy curls;
> They'll sing and dance both night and day
> Til some webfooter comes their way:
> They'll meet him at the kitchen door
> Saying, "Wipe your feet or come no more."[18]

The last three lines bring open laughter to a western Oregon or Washington audience even today, but they are greeted by polite puzzlement outside the region. The humorous use of dry and wet weather in daily conversation and in common interchange extends the field of the hyperbolic Münchausen performances mentioned previously. The *Corvallis Gazette* (February 5, 1892) had a small item on the difference between eastern and western Oregon which told of an old lady getting on a passenger boat heading down the Columbia to Portland. Asked why she was making the trip, she replied, "Going to where there's water enough to wash my clothes; we don't have enough for that in eastern Oregon." A month later, the purser noticed the old woman was again a passenger headed upstream (east) and quipped, "How do you do ma'am; have you got your washing done?" "Yes," the old lady said, "and now I'm going back east of the mountains to get my clothes dry."

Another clear case of regionalizing in folksong is seen in the variations on a song that must be honestly titled, "Don't Marry the X Boys," the X to be filled in with the local area name and the verses riddled with specific references to the hazards of local marriages. In Utah one hears

> Come girls come and listen to my noise,
> Don't you marry the Mormon boys,
> For if you do your fortune it'll be
> Johnnycakes and babies is all you'll see.

> The Mormon man's delighted to see
> His Mormon family all agree:
> A prattling baby sitting on each knee
> Shouting "Daddy, I'm a Mormon!"[19]

Important to our perception of this song's function and meaning is the observation that this is sung by Mormon traditional singers. That is, rather than being a satirical portrait drawn from without, it is a kind of ironic humor from within: Mormons do customarily have large families, do customarily eat plain but wholesome fare, and *do* want their girls to marry Mormon boys. The song seems to say, then, if you marry within the group you'll get stuck with exactly what you should get stuck with. The limitations of provincialism are proclaimed thus to be advantages. The same function and flavor are found in an Oregon variant of the song, but of course the "limitations" are spelled out in distinctly regional terms, using both local place names and reference to local conventions in building, hunting, and cooking. The town of Alsea lies between Corvallis and the Oregon coast.

> Come you Alsea girls and listen to my noise,
> Don't you marry the Oregon boys,
> For if you do your fortune it'll be
> Cold johnnycakes and venison is all you'll see.

> They'll take you to a side-hewed wall
> Without any windows in it at all;
> Sandstone chimney and a button door,
> A clapboard roof and a puncheon floor.

Every night before you go to bed
They'll build up a fire as high as your head,
Rake away the ashes and in they'll throw
A great big chunk of old sourdough.

When they go a-milkin' they milk in a gourd,
Strain it in the corner and hide it with a board.
Some gets little and some gets none,
And that's how things in the Oregon run.[20]

Yet another kind of regional flavor comes from attitudes quite apart from the geographical or meteorological setting. Anxieties and tensions relating to ethnic minorities, especially Blacks, Asians, and Indians, are expressed in jokes and tales, in comic references in popular plays, and in songs such as the following. "Judge Duffy," a song of uncertain, perhaps of music hall, origin, entered folk tradition and was sung in widely separated places —Florence, Idaho; Jacksonville, Oregon; Seattle, Washington—all of which had considerable Chinese populations. It praises the wit and practicality of a local judge who passed down the most convenient judgments for his community. Several locales are named in local legends as "the very place" where the incident happened, but it is likely that the historicity of the piece lies chiefly in its sentiments, feelings which did in fact give rise to numerous outrages perpetrated on ethnic minorities. It is important to note that the song is considered lighthearted and humorous and that the "punchline" usually provokes, even among sophisticated audiences today, hearty laughter.

Old John Martin Duffy was judge of the court
In a small mining town in the West;
Although he knew nothin' 'bout rules of the law,
At judgin' he was one of the best.

One night in the winter a murder occurred,
And the blacksmith was accused of the crime;
We caught him red-handed and gave him three trials
But the verdict was "guilty" each time.

Now he was the only good blacksmith we had
And we wanted to spare him his life,
So Duffy stood up in the court like a lord
And with these words he settled the strife:

"I move we dismiss him—he's needed in town."
Then he spoke out these words, which have gained him renown:
"We have two Chinese laundrymen, everyone knows—
Let's save this poor blacksmith and hang one of those."[21]

It should be clear in the above examples from Northwest tradition that regionalism in folklore as well as in literature is not a matter of real isolaation, of festering parochialism, of dull provincialism. Rather it is a state of mind based on culturally-shared postulates which are the bases for meaningful and moving expression among people who can share the same system of references. As folklore studies have shown, people in a given area are not in any way *limited* to their regional orientation: they will also belong to other folk groups based on other familiar, informal sharing of traditions. Some will spend a good part of their waking hours participating in an occupational set of traditions (logging, farming, fishing, ranching, herding, mining); some will be, in addition, participants in ethnic folk groups (Indians, Basques, Scandinavians); others will be members of groups whose principal orientation for folk exchange will be essentially creative or artistic (quiltmakers, cooks, whittlers); others will be members of groups concerned with folk science (dowsers, midwives, herbalists, curanderos). And many other such groupings could be mentioned. The point is that none of these orientations excludes any of the others, and indeed, the most common situation is that a person is a member of several folk groups, the particular set of references determined by what traditional network the person is "performing" in at a particular time. Thus, regionalism in Northwest folklore is that quality of phrase which comes about when, to paraphrase Jones's definition, northwesterners are identifying themselves to each other (and to "outsiders") by performing folklore which is theirs by the circumstance of their residence in the Northwest and their association with other northwesterners—not, at least at that moment, because they happen to be also loggers or fishermen or Basques.[22] The people's awareness of a shared regional identity as expressed richly through their various genres of folklore provides us with the certainty that this cultural frame of mind, far from being a negative geographical fence, is a positive creative force that is no doubt the matrix of the really powerful aspects of Northwest art and literature. The humble origin of this force, its wide, general occurrence in the area's folklore, is ignored at great risk to our understanding of the region and its dynamics.

---

1. V. L. O. Chittick, ed., *Northwest Harvest: A Regional Stock-Taking* (New York: Macmillan, 1948), p. xvi.
2. William L. Alderson, " 'The Days of '49,' Reprise," *Northwest Folklore*, 1 (Summer 1965), 1-10.
3. Norm Cohen, "Robert W. Gordon and the Second Wreck of 'Old 97,' " *Journal of American Folklore*, 87 (1974), 12, 36.
4. Alan Dundes, "The Devolutionary Premise in Folklore Theory," *Journal of the Folklore Institute*, 6 (1969), 5-19.
5. See J. Barre Toelken and John Wilson Foster, "A Descriptive Nomenclature for the Study of Folklore," *Western Folklore*, 28 (1969), 91-111, for a dis-

cussion of the "Twin Laws" of Dynamism and Conservatism.

6. In a letter to the author, Stevens insisted these were his original words.
7. James Stevens, *Paul Bunyan* (New York: Garden City Publishing Co., 1925), p. 11.
8. Jan H. Brunvand, "Folklore of the Great Basin," *Northwest Folklore*, 3 (Summer 1968), 17-32.
9. From the author's private collection.
10. Richard Dorson notes this interesting contrast in *American Folklore* (Chicago: Univ. of Chicago Press, 1959), pp. 214-31.
11. See Stephen Dow Beckham, *Tall Tales From Rogue River: The Yarns of Hathaway Jones* (Bloomington: Indiana Univ. Press, 1974), for the only full treatment of Jones and his storytelling.
12. Professor William Hugh Jansen gives a valuable account of this phenomenon in "The Esoteric-Exoteric Factor in Folklore," originally published in *Fabula: Journal of Folktale Studies*, 2 (1959), 205-11, and reprinted in Alan Dundes, ed., *The Study of Folklore* (Englewood Cliffs, N.J.: Prentice-Hall, 1965), pp. 44-51.
13. The most cogent discussion of this phenomenon (and the only one with some direct reference to the folklore of the Northwest) is Suzi Jones, "Regionalization: A Rhetorical Strategy," *Journal of the Folklore Institute*, 13 (1976), 105-20. The present essay is considerably indebted to Ms. Jones's clarity of vision.
14. In *Transactions of the Fifty-fifth Annual Reunion, Oregon Pioneer Association*, June 23, 1927 (Portland, Ore.: F. W. Baltes), p. 27.
15. Sung by Verne Strain, Salmon, Idaho; from the author's collection.
16. Sung by anonymous itinerant laborers, Portland, Oregon, and Seattle, Washington, summer 1958.
17. For a fuller account of Mrs. Judkins's repertoire, see Russell M. Harrison, "Folk Songs from Oregon," *Western Folklore*, 11 (1952), 174-84.
18. Regional variants of the "Beulah Land" parody are from the author's field collections. Actually fragments of longer renditions, they are presented here for purposes of discussion only.
19. As sung by Fabian Giroux in 1957 at Ogden, Utah.
20. Collected by Walter Bolton; sung by Orlo Flock near Bend, Oregon (Flock lived in the Willamette Valley). The reference to Oregon as "the Oregon" is encountered elsewhere; probably it is a vernacular truncation of "the Oregon country," or "the Oregon Territory." The singer used it in conversation as well as in the song text.
21. Collected by Marion Cupp and F. C. Michel, summer 1959; sung by Henry Tams, retired logger, at Moscow, Idaho.
22. Jones, p. 107.

Founders and Settlers

For many years Norman Clark taught American history and history of the Pacific Northwest at Everett Community College with an occasional stint at the University of Washington where he obtained his doctorate. Among his books are *Mill Town,* a highly respected social history of Everett, Washington; *Deliver Us From Evil: An Interpretation of American Prohibition*; and the recent volume on the state of Washington in the Norton bicentennial state histories series, from which the following essay is adapted. Since 1975 Norman Clark has been president of Everett Community College. In this overview of Pacific Northwest history Clark measures regional claims to distinction against broader, universal standards, and warns against tendencies to see the Pacific Northwest's past in complacent or simplistic terms.

Notes
For a Tricentennial Historian

Norman Clark

In the history of American democracy we now stand at year 200, and it
is surely appropriate to raise questions that may help us to identify or to
define the spirit of the American nation. My purpose, however, is at once
more limited and more difficult, because I intend to consider a narrowly
regional dimension of the American spirit—that of the Pacific Northwest.

One might begin with a very personal inventory of regional achievements, an inventory from which might be drawn a proud and confident
sense of national identity, an inventory that would include achievements
that are industrial as well as artistic, political as well as intellectual. I am
thinking of an abundance of hydro-electricity, of the preservation of
wilderness areas, of initiative and referendum, of a remarkable architecture.
But on second thought, it seems to me that while these achievements do in
part illuminate the spirit of the republic, they should not so simply be
regarded as distinctly regional achievements. Virginia, after all, has no
special claim to the American Declaration of Independence. Nor has Pennsylvania any special or exclusive role in shaping the American Constitution. In our own region, it seems hardly fair to regard the Olympic
National Park or the Oregon System of William S. U'Ren, or the work
of Mark Toby or of Pietro Belluschi as uniquely regional distinctions.

In fact, it seems to me as we consider the Bicentennial, that most of us
will not look for the unique distinctions of any state or region. Most of us,
I believe, will not suppose that the purpose of the state of Washington or
of Oregon is to produce singularly meritorious achievements. Yet many
of us will hope that the people of each state, in their public and private
lives, might enrich the traditions that since 1776 have defined the transcendent purposes of our nation. From the long view of two centuries, how
well, we may ask, have the citizens of any state or region secured the rights
of life, liberty, and the pursuit of happiness? To ask that question is to
invoke the Jeffersonian legacy, and at the level of regional history, it is
perhaps the ultimate Bicentennial question. From this perspective we can
begin our strictly regional considerations.

During the first hundred years after the American Declaration of Independence, American consciousness of the Pacific Northwest evolved from
hazy myths of a fabled river through lively dreams of Oriental commerce
to urgent desires for continental supremacy. This consciousness guided

the westward course of empire, but even in 1876 the Pacific Northwest was too remote to have attracted more than a few thousand people, including explorers, fur traders, missionaries, industrialists, tradesmen, and statesmen. It was the reach of transcontinental railroads after 1876 that dramatically refreshed the visions of life, liberty, and happiness for hundreds of thousands of men and women. As they came to make new homes, they were often keenly aware that their first social and political experiences would shape the character of their new states for years to come, and they often approached these experiences with an exhilarating confidence and optimism. As they formed new governments, they quite deliberately extended the functions of democratic institutions. As they shaped a sense of community, they offered refuge to many who needed refuge. As they developed the economy, they presented an expansive range of opportunities to those who could make the most of them. In the same spirit, they were eager to fashion a way of life clearly hospitable to the values of self-reliance, self-esteem, and self-discipline. Now we know that life, liberty, and the pursuit of happiness often unfold in the dimensions of refuge, of economic opportunity, and of chances to develop self-reliance and self-discipline. Such experiences and conditions make the history of the Pacific Northwest in many ways consistent with the most noble of American traditions.

But it is also a history haunted by melancholy images. Suppose today that we had stood together on the gray green heights of Cape Flattery, looking out beyond the great waves that wash white against the walls of Tatoosh Island. We could there have contemplated the fate of Makah Indians, of maritime fur traders, of Spanish and English explorers—and this would have been to contemplate the dark depths of culture, the mystique of adventure, the energies and the aspirations of the new American nation. Or suppose today that we had been together near the Rogue River, on that high mesa called Table Rock, where in 1853 white people fashioned what they called a treaty—a sorry abstraction—into language and then law which would accelerate the destruction of the proud but bewildered Rogue River Indians. Our thoughts then would have been of lost cultures and of the harsh violence implicit in ethnocentrism. And suppose we could drift tomorrow with the Columbia River as it sweeps broadly around the great White Bluffs toward the Yakima confluence. It is for a moment there a passage of free-flowing water, graced on its western shore with the artifacts of lost cultures: walls of an abandoned ranch house made of white river rock, spokes of a broken wagon wheel bleached by a hundred years of rain and scorching sun, mounds that mark the forlorn graves of forgotten Indians. The majesty, however, is brief, and our passage would soon edge a bleakly lunar landscape insulated by armed guards who protect our latest nuclear installations.

Between the broken wagon wheel and the latest nuclear installations lie the years of regional history of most significance to our Bicentennial celebration, and they are the years that have been of most concern to me during my career as a historian. My study of these years has helped me develop certain prejudices which I care neither to conceal nor to defend. I can accordingly state them clearly. They are, first of all, that serious history should not serve a society's need for flattery or justification—that serious history cannot evoke a vision of nobility, past or present, for a people whose lives do not in fact support such a vision. In such matters, the historian must make his judgments. In my own system of moral accounting for the Pacific Northwest, I list certain vivid debits: a mindless violence against a delicate ecology, episodes of racial warfare, a history of racial discrimination. Others might add to this list with equal vividness: attempts to repress those who criticized social inequities; governments that have refused to provide the education, the care for the aged, the relief for the unemployed, which in any society are necessary for a Jeffersonian sense of dignity and freedom.

There are of course many credits, and some shall be mentioned, but what follows is not so much a deliberately balanced account of regional history as it is a personal view that I will try to keep focused on the Bicentennial question—what have the people of the Pacific Northwest done to secure life, liberty, and the pursuit of happiness for themselves and for their children and their children's children? Now there are of course many ways to define life, liberty, and happiness. But one of the strengths of American society may be that the definitions of life, liberty, and the pursuit of happiness are revised with the experiences of each generation. Very likely when Jefferson wrote that phrase he was thinking of opportunity, the opportunity to enhance what we call today the quality of life, the opportunity to be creative in an atmosphere of intellectual and spiritual and economic freedom. But the generation that opened the Pacific Northwest had lost at least a part of the Jeffersonian vision and the generation that came with the railroads made its definition of life, liberty, and the pursuit of happiness too crassly and too brashly in terms of economic opportunity, in terms of straightforward materialism. Life, liberty, and the pursuit of happiness meant then the unalienable right to industrialize the frontier. It meant that economic growth and development were to be pursued passionately, to be given precedence over any other consideration. This seems at best a mixed legacy. The economic growth and development of that railroad period was usually good for investors, creditors, salesmen, industrialists, and builders —so good, in fact, that however honorable these people may have been, they were quite naturally reluctant to consider the social impact of their windfalls and exploitations. If there is a central theme for this history, it would be that growth and development have always been at the unconscionable expense of life and liberty for those least able to defend themselves against growth and development. And rapid growth has usually meant a kind of social pestilence of political corruption, of rural-urban conflicts, and of environmental pollutions.

This may sound like a severe application of moral hindsight—which it is—and I grant for a moment the hazard that moral hindsight makes an amateur moralist out of a professional historian. This risk demands that I reveal what I would hope to see in regional history, and I will say simply that a healthy society might reasonably expect the kind of slow and cautious growth that encourages a creative exploration of opportunity. A healthy society might want the kind of restrained growth that rewards wisdom more than it does competition, disorder, and exploitation. If in our region such a society has no past, we may surely hope that it has a future. Our Bicentennial legacy, as I see it, is the challenge to see opportunities for life, liberty, and the pursuit of happiness in a renewed and refreshed definition. And this is why we need to think for a while about the years between the broken wagon wheel and the latest nuclear installation. Let's now go back a century to find a focus for our historical perceptions.

In the centennial year of 1876 the Pacific Northwest was to most Americans a broad expanse of hope and mystery, the land of open promises—few of them even articulated, few of them in any way fulfilled. It was, in the broadest imagination, a few scattered settlements laced together by water routes—the unmeasured Empire of the Columbia.

The upper Columbia River in 1876 still flashed through deep and crooked canyons, its flow so clear and violent that men stood away from it breathlessly, startled by its brilliance and surging speed. Where the Wenatchee entered, sun washed and crystal pure from the Cascade Mountains, the river was for a while a perfect avenue, smooth and broad and deep. There was a cabin there on the southwest shore in 1876, a shack where for years restless traders had found precarious opportunity in selling whiskey to the Indians. Beyond the cabin a wide line of water defined the edges of the Great Columbia Plain from which a trader might look west to the snows of the Cascades, south to the Blue Mountains, northeast to the Coeur d'Alenes. But then the white-water passages began again: Long Rapids, Rock Island Rapids, Priest Rapids, on toward the flat water where a ferry boat served the few settlers who had entered the Yakima Valley after the Indian wars of the 1850s. To the east and south the Palouse hills rolled in high crests, covered with grass, the richest and the sweetest on earth. Wheat farmers, coming then from depression-ridden towns and villages, were planting belts of wheat and series of settlements from Lewiston to the Blue Mountains, discovering to their amazement that the Palouse country was arable without irrigation.

Below the Walla Walla, the portages of Lewis and Clark were marked by rail lines in 1876 and Portland, on the south shore, was a prosperous and stable community given even to the sophistication that came with new money, railroads, steamboats, fish, wheat, and lumber. To the south, the Willamette Valley had of course been settled and reasonably prosperous for a generation.

North of Cape Disappointment, however, except for the casual excursions of a few reckless whites, the wilderness in 1876 stood as dense and as pervasive as the Indians had known it in the age of stone and bone. At Willapa and at Grays' Harbor, the shallow and treacherous river bars restrained all but the most determined Americans. Point Grenville, surrounded by its shoals of black rock, rose abruptly through the fog like a dark fortress. The Quinault River flowed quietly through rich and unviolated forests. To the north—from the Quinault to the Quillayute—no whites knew the forests or the rivers or the beaches except as they had seen them from ships passing beyond Destruction Island. No white man of record had ever crossed the Olympic Mountains or knew what might lie at the interior of this vast peninsula. The Quinault Indians were regarded by whites as practically inaccessible, the Hoh Indians as absolutely inaccessible. At Cape Alava, there was no sound or signal to warn the seaman. There were in fact no navigational aids between Willapa and the Strait of Juan de Fuca, where from Tatoosh a feeble light swept over the jagged teeth of Skagway Rocks and north toward Vancouver Island.

Around Puget Sound, there were cheerful signs of relief from the stagnation and gloom that in the Pacific Northwest had followed the Indian Wars and the Panic of 1873. In the summer of 1876 there were as many as 5,000 people in Seattle. They were people eager for a saltwater cargo trade—railroad ties to Latin America, raw lumber to Hawaii, fish to California—and they crowded day and night across soggy streets to make their purchases and to talk at length with friends and newcomers on the muddy boardwalks. During the week of the Centennial Fourth of July, columns of the Seattle *Intelligencer* recorded the delivery of a Centennial sermon, the theme of which was that "We must stand by our Constitution and religious principle." A Centennial editorial began with these words: "The ship of state has swept with dizzy speed forward over this hundred years of its course in the career of empire. . . . The shoals of treason have yawned around her, and the lee-shore of corruption threatened her with destruction," and a Centennial oration: "We have experienced here much of the same kind of discouragements and dangers that were the lot of the first colonies upon the Atlantic Coast." The days in Seattle progressed in lively talk about coming railroads and increasing land values, and, with appropriate frivolity, a regatta, a military procession, public fireworks, a Centennial Ball.

These activities were conspicuously more spirited than those at the southern tip of Puget Sound, where the town of Olympia in 1876 numbered perhaps 2,000. The early settlers there had come to preempt the falls of the Deschutes River and had later captured the territorial seat of government. For two decades their growing village had been the center of American activity north of Oregon City. In time, however, it was clear that steam-powered machines would take from them whatever advantage the settlers had in a small waterfall and that the railroad, running fifteen miles to the east, would leave them in isolation. Their most prominent landmark in 1876 was the capitol, a sagging, oblong building of two stories topped by a bell tower and fronted with a narrow portico—a sort of midwestern barn with windows. It was not, clearly, in good repair. The Secretary of Washington Territory had recently informed the United States Secretary of the Interior that the building was approaching "a state of utter decay and wretched worthlessness." The wooden-block foundation, he wrote, was rotted, causing the building to tilt precariously at one end. For more than a decade there had been no paint applied to the exterior, which was "a sad picture of melancholy dinginess." Inside, the "faded, soiled, and ragged" carpets could not lend even the appearance of "shabby gentility." The several stoves in the legislative chambers were a hazard to those who needed heat. Situated on the edge of town and bordering the forest, the building was enveloped by undergrowth, and legislators were demanding a meeting place which would not be, as they complained, "a standing reproach" to their dignity.

Under these rather seedy circumstances members of the Legislative Assembly appointed a joint committee "to wait upon the Hon. Elwood Evans" and request that he favor them with a reading of the address he had delivered during the Centennial Exposition in Philadelphia, where as Centennial Commissioner he had represented Washington Territory before the nation. Evans had come west early, in 1851, when he was twenty-five years old. He had married in Olympia and had supplemented a law practice with service as deputy collector of customs and as the governor's secretary. He had made influential friends in the Whig Party, but he had been ardently anti-slave and he had led local Whigs into the Republican ranks in 1856. He was himself acting governor during the Civil War and then Speaker of the House in the 1870s. Among the most literate of the territorial barristers, his experiences left him with an intense interest in the drama of those early years. His appointment as Centennial Commissioner was in grateful recognition of his writing and speaking about historical matters upon which most citizens regarded him as their leading authority.

When he appeared before the Assembly, Evans was a stout and vigorous man of fifty-one, wearing a full mustache and beard much in the fashion of General U. S. Grant. His address was, for the time and circumstances, fashionably elegant and adequately windy, an extended description of both the historical and the physical features of the Pacific Northwest (over fifty pages in the printed version), the reading of which must have consumed a full afternoon in Philadelphia as well as in Olympia. Paying his respects to the early explorers, he of course reviewed the story of the Greek mariner, Apostolos Valerianos, whose alleged discoveries had evolved into the myth of Juan de Fuca. He gave oratorical tribute to the aspirations of the Spanish during the eighteenth century, then to the "illustrious but ill-fated Captain James Cook" and his futile search for a northwest passage. He saluted the maritime fur traders, John Meares and Robert Gray, and the more scientific explorers, George Vancouver and Lewis and Clark. He recounted briefly the disastrous adventures of the Astorian expeditions by sea and by land. Then he approached his own personal involvement by reviewing the "Oregon Controversy" of the 1840s between the United States and Great Britain.

From his earlier orations, his Olympia audience already knew that Evans was an Anglophobe of the old order, always ready with a belligerent outburst of patriotic sentiment against England, its monarchs, and its Hudson's Bay Company. In his youth he had in fact been an emotional proponent of the "54-40 or fight" slogan, eager even then to drive the British from all of North America. He had again solemnly urged war with England during the petty dispute over international boundary lines through the San Juan Islands.

It was, however, in his recital of what he called "the irrepressible conflict between the settler and the Indian race" that Evans became even more emotional, and he reminded his audience of the "difficulties and dangers" to Americans who had come, as he himself had done, to claim their share of the Oregon Country, to take land, to build a new home. At this point his address became the determined cry of the apologist:

Our pioneers, he said, "were subjected to the usual difficulties and dangers consequent upon the presence of aborigines, dangerous in their native disposition. . . . On the 29th November, 1847, within our present territorial limits . . . Dr. Marcus Whitman and his excellent wife were murdered in cold blood, together with nine others. . . . Every white American within reach fell victim to the merciless perfidy of the treacherous Cayuse Indians. A rude mound, overgrown with weeds, enclosed only by a plain fence, marks the last resting place of these victims of Indian jealousy, superstition and hate." During this time, "treaties were negotiated by Governor Stevens with the various Indian tribes, by which the so-called Indian title to the lands was extinguished upon the most liberal concessions to the Indians, and with scrupulous regard for their welfare."

"In 1855," Evans continued, "gold was discovered in paying quantities . . . near the 49th parallel. Miners journeying to the new gold fields necessarily traversed country hitherto unfrequented by the white man. . . .

Unarmed miners alone or in small parties, were frequently murdered. . . . The Indian war know as the 'Oregon-Washington Indian War' was the necessary result of these repeated outrages." He said, "in its inception, its causes, its progress," the people of Washington and Oregon had no cause for reproach or shame. "In no respect were they aggressors—no act of theirs provoked its commencement—they were innocent of every justifying incentive for its being forced upon them, save their lawful presence in the country. That war was prosecuted solely with a view to secure peace within our borders."

Evans had little to say about the Civil War years, which were perhaps yet too delicate for evaluation. He skipped quickly to 1872, a year of happy memory because it was marked "by the commencement . . . of that grand enterprise [the transcontinental railroad], which will utilize and benefit not only our own people, but add great wealth to the nation." Forty miles of the track of the Northern Pacific, he announced, "were in running operation." In this beginning Elwood Evans saw a promise of golden opportunity and he told his listeners that the Northern Pacific Railroad, like a miracle ordained for their special destinies, would soon unlock inestimable treasures. It was the will of God, he thought, that the treasures should be opened for his generation. When Evans finally alluded to Divine Providence, it was with a short prayer to the "Father of light, liberty and law" that Heaven might protect the glorious future of the United States and the Pacific Northwest, where to the "western verge of the broad continent have been carried the spirit and teachings of 1776."

The editorial response to Evans's remarks was a call for their public printing and distribution. The state legislature complied by ordering 5,000 copies. Of the centennial sentiments then floating around the Pacific Northwest, Evans's were certainly the most popular and the most eloquent. He had described the past as his contemporaries wanted it described. He had served their need for a flattering historical identity. He had defined for them a satisfying role in a heroic and divinely ordained mission to "subdue," as he had said, the wilderness of the Oregon Country and to "dedicate it to American civilization."

These were sentiments which Elwood Evans later elaborated in several volumes of regional history—volumes which have inspired later generations of revisionist historians. For example, Evans's view of native Americans was, as we see it now, rooted in prejudgments and most of us today would probably say that Marcus Whitman and the murdered miners were in large measure responsible for their own destruction. And most of us would note that following the diseases that whites inflicted on the native populations, the treaties written by Governor Stevens were, in large measure, responsible for the destruction of most of the remaining Indians. It would be difficult today to see the "Spirit of 1776" in the Indian wars. It would be even more difficult to find historians believing that God ordained Americans to eject the British, to build railroads, to destroy the wilderness. It would be difficult today not to notice how Evans's passion for economic development and for American expansion distorted almost all of his conclusions. You would today have to turn over almost every rock in the region to find an Evans-model manifest-destiny historian.

But this is the cutting edge of a revisionism to which revisionists themselves shall be ultimately subjected, and we should not flatter ourselves that in it there is any ultimate wisdom. In regional history, as in personal history, there are certain periods of acceleration and of dislocation. In regional history, as in personal history, there are certain points of departure so abrupt or of beginnings so new that the established expectations of a way of life are never again the same. Evans was looking into one of these periods, and his vision was a remarkably clear one. Within a decade following the Centennial there were thousands of people in places where Elwood Evans had known only a few dozen. And as they quickly industrialized the frontier, people came then by the hundreds of thousands.

Even from their railroad car windows, those who came in the 1880s could look out over marvelous fields of opportunity. For the poor farmer, there was a cheap rail ticket and cheap land, credit easy to come by, friendships easy to make, and bankers, merchants, and neighbors eager to help him "get established." For example, in 1889—the year of Washington statehood—a farmer from Nebraska bought 100 acres of railroad land near Colfax and planted his wheat. With the harvest of one season (and his experience was not uncommon) he paid for his land, his fencing, his sowing and hauling—he paid for everything, and he still had $98 to put in the bank. For the urban worker, there were new mills and factories opening every day, new construction projects, work almost anywhere he wanted it. A man might earn wages for a year, then own his own shingle mill or logging outfit. For the European immigrant, there were urban neighborhoods of predominantly Scandinavian or German or Italian antecedents. The native-language church, the fraternal organizations, and the national social clubs embraced the newcomer and carried him into a rich fabric of new associations. For most people, the Pacific Northwest was not opened by a few mountain men trapping furs or by missionaries preaching Christianity, or even by pioneers shooting Indians; it was opened by the railroads, by the Northern Pacific and the Great Northern, by the corporations which made it easy for a farmer or a farm hand to get to Spokane or a wage earner to reach Seattle or Everett or Tacoma or Portland. There had been nothing like it in the history of American economic opportunity since the opening of the Louisiana Territory—golden years when no personal ambition, however grandiose, seemed at all unreasonable, when it seemed that every venture might prosper and every family might share in the nobility of wealth because of the democracy of profit.

When the journalist Ray Stannard Baker visited the region in 1903, he was amazed to note that everything "seems to have happened within the last ten years," and he was himself swept up in the excitement of change and growth. He found everyone full of hope and pride and even friendship, welcoming newcomers not as rivals but as developers who would contribute to—and share in—a common destiny. As the crops of wheat and hops and the yields of lumber and fish attained national prominence, thoughtful entrepreneurs looked toward the opportunities that would be opened by the Panama Canal—easier access to world markets, a view of the future that kindled even the most cautious imagination. Thus people worked together without feeling threatened, and they expressed their confidence in the parades, street fairs, and community projects which amazed Ray Stannard Baker—amazed him because he knew of eastern towns and cities where there had been no examples of such public activity for generations.

He delighted in the bustle and hustle of a Chamber-of-Commerce society. Most people he met belonged to several interlocking organizations—Eagles, Elks, Masons—and they were intensely involved with the boasts, predictions, and friendly rivalries of boosterism. Was Seattle better than Portland? For investment, for residence, culture, education, for wages? Was Spokane the greatest railroad city in the West? Should the mountain be called Rainier or Tahoma? Was the future brighter in Sprague than in Colfax? Was the high school football team at Wenatchee the best in the nation? These were considered serious questions.

The goal of a Chamber-of-Commerce society, Baker understood, was to develop, to capture, whenever possible, the many pearls of economic and industrial expansion. Thus a town acquired a new railroad or a new real estate company, or a new mill, all amid general rejoicing and speeches about community achievement. In 1909, for example, the brightest pearl was the Alaska-Yukon-Pacific Exposition and the federal monies poured into it. An editor of *Harper's Weekly* commented that this was not an exposition to commemorate anything at all because there was nothing to commemorate. It was rather an exposition to celebrate the fact "that in the story of civilization there is probably no record of more astonishing growth" than that which had recently occurred in the Pacific Northwest.

Another writer for the same magazine, inclined to ridicule places like Yakima, stopped there one day to discover that barren hills and sagebrush had indeed become the base of a prosperous and even beautiful community. Where cattle had starved to death a decade before, farmers were tilling topsoil twenty to a hundred feet deep. Diverting water from the Yakima River, they had opened opportunities that were positively lyrical: twenty dollars would clear an acre of sagebrush and provide it with ditches, and for the man who would cultivate it diligently, it could in two months yield a cash crop of vegetables or alfalfa; in a season, a bounty of hops, wheat, or grapes; in two years, peaches of real distinction; in three years, apples and pears that could make his orchard world-famous. The writer found a city of shaded lawns, handsome homes and new stores. Every house, he wrote, stood proudly by itself "embowered by fruit trees, in yards green with grass or gay with a riotous growth of roses." Each quiet street had its irrigation ditch for home gardens, and in space, pride, and abundance the city indeed presented a face of harmony amid plenty. One could see Yakima as the goal of much American experience. It was new and optimistic, firmly structured to shelter the values of ambition and self-discipline, and to offer opportunities—all because of the railroads—which were perhaps without parallel in the history of the nation.

Thus the widowed mother of William O. Douglas moved there in 1905 and built a comfortable home for $600. She was often nearly penniless, but she could keep a garden and a cow and could stay in her home to raise a distinguished family. While the boys worked for the money the family needed—tending yards, delivering newspapers, picking fruit and berries—the mother patched their coats and trousers, scrubbed them for church and school, and with pride and dignity faced her community. The boys yet had the kind of leisure and liberty that allowed them a wholesome progress toward manhood. At the age of eleven, Douglas could go off into the mountains for days at a time without adult supervision—go off to learn from an Indian how to find berries and roots, how to catch a fish, how to find a sense of confidence and maturity. At Yakima High School, even though he was working for wages during most of his out-of-school hours, Douglas received a superior education. When he was graduated in 1916, he was sensitive to literature, fluent in Latin, knowledgeable in biology—a young man admirably literate and articulate, the classical poor-boy valedictorian.

The achievements of the Douglas family—and there were surely hundreds, maybe thousands, of families like them—illuminate a history of hope and motive, a history, as it were, of aspirations, which, of all histories, is perhaps the most mercurial. But it does raise again the ultimate Bicentennial question. In shaping their lives, were these people actually advancing the rights to life, liberty, and the pursuit of happiness? At this point our answer must be that indeed they were—that their pursuit of growth and development did indeed expand opportunities that would have pleased Thomas Jefferson.

But we know now that many of their expectations were both fragile and tentative. As early as 1910 the limits of an easy optimism were almost distressingly apparent. The pace and the process of frontier industrialization were stripping away the very resources upon which progress depended.

The timber cuts, everyone knew, had already left grotesque scars across hundreds of square miles, creating debauched and abandoned wasteland. The plowing of grasslands, which always promised a splendid yield of wheat, nevertheless removed the rich grasses. On parts of the Columbia Plateau where the annual rainfall was inadequate for sustained dry farming, the ploughed soil blew with the winds, and this land too became wasted. Along the Columbia, huge fish wheels could scoop 50,000 salmon a day from the river. On Puget Sound, a single set of a purse seine could net a thousand fish. The depletion of resources was as conspicuous as it was unremedied.

Furthermore, the period of rapid development had fastened on most people of the region some inordinately optimistic assumptions about industrialism and about the inevitability of growth—assumptions which were locked into the almost sacred slogans of the Chamber-of-Commerce society and almost impossible to revise or abandon. The conviction seemed ubiquitous that the measure of social health was growth and growth alone—rather than, say, stability, or harmony, or a quality of life expressed in some other, perhaps non-material achievements. After 1912, however, the people stopped coming, and it was soon clear that rapid growth would not again open opportunities for that generation.

The realization that growth, and all that it had gloriously implied, had practically ceased would not come easily to a culture rooted in a strident boosterism. This was particularly so east of the mountains, where the areas that could sustain wheat were fairly well identified and where the good land was, quite simply, already taken. Some land on the margins of semi-aridity had been purchased but never cultivated; some cultivated lands had been abandoned. By 1912 people in dozens of towns were brimming with confidence in anticipation of a growth that they would never see. To the confusion and bitterness of their founding fathers, some small towns became skeleton villages, and even established cities knew a loss of pride and energy. Walla Walla, for example, a city of 20,000 in 1910, despite its supply outlets and storage facilities, its manufacturing of farm machinery and flour, its tree-lined streets, lost twenty percent of its population in the next decade. Spokane, which had grown so spectacularly to over 100,000 by 1912, gained only thirty-five people between that year and 1920.

In the highly specialized economy west of the mountains in Oregon and in Washington there was by 1912 a deep unrest. There was a sickness not always obvious to those who suffered from it. The timber products industry employed two-thirds of the wage earners. Yet except for a few small manufacturers of finished items like residential porch posts—for local use, mostly —the industry was still the raw lumber industry of very little healthy diversity. In fact, because it added so little value to the timber, the industry of logging and milling lumber could hardly be regarded as manufacturing at all. The refinement of raw lumber, and the value added to it, occurred usually in Chicago, St. Paul, or New York. The region's timber economy was thus an extractive and export economy which—unless American cities were to burn with some regularity—had no reliable future.

The terrible fires of San Francisco had been the great bonanza, luring thousands of marginal operators into the industry after 1906. But inevitably the market slowed, the smaller mills cut prices, the larger mills dismissed their crews, and the commerce for a while collapsed. It was alarmingly apparent then that twentieth century American builders were turning away from timber products and constructing more and more with brick, cement, steel, glass, and composition roofing. Storage lots everywhere were saturated with lumber and shingles. Within two decades after the railroads opened the Pacific Northwest, the productive capacity of its primary industry was far in excess of the nation's—or even the world's—capacity to absorb its products. In that fact we see a poignantly ironic development.

By 1914 then, it was contraction, stagnation, and failure that seemed to be the legacy of men and women whose fathers had lived with the legacy of Elwood Evans. William O. Douglas, for example, broadened his experiences to include the migrants and the hoboes who formed their own society north of the city. They gathered by the river, under the railroad bridge, and they included restless, hungry, and sometimes desperate men. In that image of desperate men gathering under a railroad bridge we see a deeply ironic symbol.

Many people in the Pacific Northwest came rather quickly to know what Earl Pomeroy has called the "Limits of Western Opportunity." "Every Western Frontier," Pomeroy wrote in *The Pacific Slope*, "yielded both fulfillment and disappointment, but none attracted, rewarded, and punished those who came to it so much as the farthest . . . frontier of all, that frontier west of the Rocky Mountains." Pomeroy, in that chapter, goes on to write of disappointment, bankruptcy, hardship, and of a social and political discontent.

This punishment, and this discontent, are topics that have commanded the attention of almost every serious social historian of the region—and for good reason. The punishment and the discontent ignited some of the nation's most vigorous and enduring achievements in political reform and in environmental conservation. The pervasive character of these concerns with reform was clear evidence that the right to life, liberty, and the pursuit of happiness was being given yet another definition.

As Raymond Gastil explains in a new and brilliant book called *Cultural Regions of the United States*, it was not an easy revision. Obsessive dreams of growth and development can impose a brash materialism upon the dreamers. In writing about the Pacific Northwest, Gastil says that "the dream of an ever-expanding future made it difficult for man to accept the challenges of sin and failure, of struggle and loss."

But the revision was occurring. In the 1920s Mark Toby could find artistic substance in the quality of life in Seattle. The poet Vachel Lindsay settled in Spokane, feeling that truly creative individuals might live there and fulfill lives of sensitivity and purpose. H. L. Davis was then beginning to look deeply into the quality of life in Oregon. That none of these efforts endured as we might have wished them to endure is perhaps not relevant: they marked a refreshing beginning.

In the year of the Bicentennial, we may be close to a refined revision. It seems to observers like Earl Pomeroy and Ray Gastil and Thomas Griffith (whose analysis appears in the April 1976 issue of *The Atlantic*) that the definition of life, liberty, and the pursuit of happiness in the Pacific Northwest is now articulated in a new dimension. Economic opportunity is a necessity, of course, but we find now an enduring hostility to growth, to development, and to what used to be called "progress." The kind of opportunity that today seems to command our attention is the opportunity to create an individualistic lifestyle—a lifestyle fashioned from the aggregate of opportunities that include clean air and water, superior educational facilities, a vigorous urban culture, and reserves of pure wilderness.

It would be a pleasure to recite the happiest expressions of this lifestyle, to inventory our recent achievements. These achievements would fill the credit side of my moral bookkeeping—achievements that are evidence of racial harmony, of political democracy, and of environmental reverence.

But my purpose has *not* been to recite achievements but to ask questions —and the ultimate question for the Bicentennial *is* a *moral* one: how well have people of the region secured for themselves and for their posterity the traditions that since 1776 have defined the transcendent purposes of our nation? To look back a hundred years is to see an ambiguous and complex answer—it is to see the tradition of opportunity glorified, then distorted, then soured, then redefined with a refreshed vision. If this view implies the arrogance of hindsight, I hope it will also sustain the humility of introspection. After all, the circumstances of our own lives in 1976 seldom reflect our ideals, and we may suppose that in time our flaws, like those of our forefathers, may perhaps obscure our motives, even our achievements. However exalted these achievements may now seem, they may by the year 2076 appear as perversions. I hope then, that my view of our past is a generous one, for I wonder what generosity there may be for *us* in pages to be written by a Tricentennial historian. What difference, he may ask, would it have made to the civilizations of the world and to the ability of humans to live harmoniously with each other—what difference would it have made if there had never existed the states of Washington, Idaho, or Oregon? It is a stunning question.

Barnett Singer has a Ph.D. in
modern European history from the
University of Washington and has
developed a second field in American
cultural history with a regional accent.
His study of the "Village Schoolmaster as
a Notable in Brittany, 1880-1914" led
him to investigate Simeon G. Reed and
Thomas Lamb Eliot as examples of
Oregon notables in the nineteenth century.
Singer takes these two Oregonians of
distinction and sketches their impact as
shapers, builders, and refiners in a young
and relatively raw society. At the same
time, he raises the question as to whether
they consciously regarded themselves as
regionalists. Professor Singer has been a
lecturer at St. Anne's College in Nova
Scotia and at the University of Washington. From 1974 to 1975 he worked in
Pacific Northwest history and fiction and
in American intellectual history as a
research assistant at the Battelle Institute
in Seattle. At present Professor Singer is
visiting lecturer at the University of
Alberta.

Oregon's Nineteenth-Century Notables: Simeon Gannett Reed and Thomas Lamb Eliot

Barnett Singer

The study of Pacific Northwest history through its elites has been recently initiated with biographies of Eugene Semple, Judge Thomas Burke, and other important figures of the nineteenth and early twentieth century Northwest.[1] The present paper discusses two kinds of Northwest notables —Simeon Reed, business notable, and Thomas Lamb Eliot, moral notable. In part my meaning of the word "notable" is derived from studies of nineteenth-century French elites, particularly André Tudesq's groundbreaking *Les Grands Notables en France (1840-1849)*, and from my own work on local French notables of a lower order than Tudesq's but also important as providers of values and of guidance at the grassroots.[2] The Pacific Northwest, of course, had its own specific conditions in the nineteenth century, being a new and frontier society, and the opportunities for mobility within growing institutions of civilization in the area were legion. The case of George Law Curry is typical: born in 1820 in Philadelphia, an apprentice printer in Boston at eleven, an immigrant on the Oregon Trail (after reading adventure tales) in 1846, Curry rapidly became editor of the *Spectator* and, after forced resignation, publisher of the rival *Free Press* in Oregon. By 1854 he was a territorial governor—an Oregon notable. Eugene Semple, from a more affluent family in Illinois, came West in 1863 and became, among other things, lawyer, journalist, amateur engineer, farmer, and land speculator, as well as territorial governor of Washington in the late 1880s.[3]

As for Simeon Gannett Reed and Thomas Lamb Eliot, they fared better than most at the game of ascent. By the end of the century their names could already be counted among the most important in Oregon history. Yet their successes, as will be shown, both symbolized the close of an era and helped doom their type to extinction. Today commentators like Daniel Bell wonder even whether the capitalist system that men like Reed embodied will survive in the near future, and as for moral norms such as Reverend Eliot discussed in his sermons, these have been increasingly uncertain in our century. Both men were extremely hardworking and found gratification in their work; today the work ethic is of low priority and America finds itself in the throes of what Edward Shils calls "progressive populistic hedonism." Both expended their energy in part for their family; the family is now threatened as a sacred American institution. Both seized new opportunities and, like earlier Northwest explorers, outdid their fathers; today the emphasis on academic degrees prolongs adolescence, and opportunities for mobility in a regimented and overloaded world are more restricted. But the main issue is the concept of a directing minority. Today the notions of deference and of calibration of statuses are under intense attack, and Tocqueville's predictions are beginning to appear prophetic. Yet, we have a Peter Schrag, who had already said "good riddance" to the reign of the Wasp, now wondering in a recent *Harper's* whether indeed America does not need some new elite. And one thinks back to Ortega y Gasset's warnings in the 1930s that no civilization can remain effective without some directing minority, whether ascriptive or meritocratic. And there is the adage that when everybody is somebody, nobody is anybody. So there is some utilitarian justification for a portrait of such nineteenth century notables and of the bases of their distinctiveness.

Simeon Gannett Reed was born in East Albington (now Rockland), Massachusetts, April 23, 1830.[4] His schooling lasted until age fifteen, and he subsequently acquired experience in dry goods, shoe cutting, and the grain and flour trade. A wealthy marriage helped improve his condition—a marriage that would be without children—and in 1852 Simeon went out as a merchant to California and thence to Oregon where he would reside almost permanently after 1853. At first Reed dealt in lumber and flour, which he shipped at great profit to San Francisco, and then he opened a general merchandise store at Rainier on the Cowlitz River, dealing in sundry items, mainly liquor. In 1855 he hired on with the Portland investment concern of W. S. Ladd and Company as a clerk; by 1859 he had become in Algeresque fashion a partner with the Ladd Brothers in banking. Their main focus of investment was the burgeoning Columbia River steamer trade, and Reed rapidly attained vice-presidency of the company that would control that trade and which included the Ladds on its board, the Oregon Steam and Navigation Company. From there he branched off into other transportation concerns, especially railways and "electric railways," and became president of both the Oregon Central Railroad Company and the Electric Railways of the United States. He also purchased mines and invested in stocks and Portland real estate, at the same time divesting himself of some of the concerns listed above when they turned sour. He bought up large farms—one in the Willamette Valley on which he raised imported sheep and cattle of the highest quality extended for over 3,000 acres. He spent the latter part of his life on activities like racehorse breeding, took his wife on a grand tour of Europe, and began to enjoy the various accoutrements of his station. Having moved to Pasadena in 1892, he died there of a stroke in 1895.

The era during which Reed and other Northwest entrepreneurs like Henry Pittock or Arthur Denny came into prominence was one of great transformation in America. It is tempting, of course, to describe every era as a kind of watershed, but the post-Civil War industrial thrust seems indisputably crucial in American history. The railway boom that linked up far-flung towns of the continent and brought homogenization came in a rapid burst of activity; in the eight years following the Civil War 35,000 miles of new track were laid, and soon the nation's railway map looked like a Jackson Pollock painting. The communications revolution also included telegraph, telephones (widespread by the 1880s), linotype, better ocean steamers, refrigerator railway cars, dependable and cheap postal service, and of course electricity.[5] A new race of men came to prominence in these enterprises, men who were Reed's contemporaries and in some cases model providers—Leland Stanford, Jay Cooke, Mark Hopkins, Commodore Vanderbilt.

But of course Reed did not start on steel, he started on water. And he did not start out in a metropolis, he began in the Portland area—the city itself containing no more than 1,000 people at the outset of the 1850s. And he represented a vigorous capitalist minority in Oregon, of New England stock and differentiated from the larger run of farmers that was frequently midwestern or southern in origin.[6] We might indeed call this a rural capitalism, one that benefited from the need for supplies in the new gold-struck areas of eastern Washington, Oregon, and the Fraser River Valley, a kind of capitalism that stimulated other, complementary rural industries such as woodcutting (for steamers) and boatbuilding. Atypical in its independence from eastern financing, the Oregon Steam and Navigation Company until sold in 1879 was all-western owned, apart from a brief period in the early 1870s under Jay Cooke's partial control. Still, the way the company came to monopolize the Columbia trade places it within the Gilded Age. If the brilliant inheritor of "Drake's folly" charged "all that the traffic would bear," so the small-time Reeds emulated the Rockefellers —molasses that cost 70 cents a gallon in Portland traveled the Columbia by steamer (and then by portage) and retailed for $6.00 a gallon in Boise. Oregon Steam men bought up individual steamers as rapaciously as Rockefeller did oil drillers, and despite great expenses (the *Shoshone* steamboat alone cost $100,000 to build), large profits were made, especially when the completion of mechanical locks at Oregon City assured continuous Willamette Valley transportation to Portland.[7] These monopoly profits aroused the ire of the press and of groups like the Grangers in the Willamette Valley. Meanwhile, as early as 1866 Reed was lobbying for the company back in Washington, D.C., which in turn introduced him to railway interests and to wider possibilities for making money. Reed greatly admired these railway men—on the officers of the Union Pacific he wrote J. C. Ainsworth: "The fact is this Company . . . [is] a live institution and such men as Oakes Ames, T. C. Durant, Glidden and Williams . . . are getting *big* rich out of it."[8] For Reed the name of his work—and of the era itself—was expansion.

It would be distortion, however, to skip to the profit and omit the work. Reed's meticulous business letters and accounts and his private notebooks filled with figures, excerpts from technical journals, information on pipes, mines, compressed air processes, Henderson grass seed, average consumption of charcoal per ton, the cost of making pig iron, the record-breaking production of the Ashland blast furnaces, new elevators, machine grease, the hiring of stone masons, the quality of farm animals, show the man behind the wealth. Today we often seek the man in his private moaning—not the *Economic Consequences of the Peace*, but Keynes's homosexuality; not Mackenzie King's record as prime minister but his whore fixation—and yet with Reed I think we can safely linger over the large amount of evidence available on his working life. It is clear that efficient money-making was the focus of his existence. Efficiency and precision characterize almost every page of the voluminous business correspondence. In 1884 he bought a passenger coach in excellent repair from Northern Pacific; he noted that it cost 2,400 dollars, is 48 feet, eight inches long, seats 48 people.[9] In a letter of the next year he desired a bull of the following description: "Horns not heavy, short legs and heavy body. Good behind the shoulders. Good back and loins and *excell* in hind quarters. For a Bull answering this description I am willing to pay a fair price, but not a fancy price."[10]

A kind of industrial enlightenment figure, Reed was always on the lookout for new equipment and techniques, providing the cost factor was not prohibitive. In 1872, having read a book called *The Handy Book of Husbandry*, he learned of steam plows and wondered whether they could be adapted to his farm. Immediately, he dispatched a letter to an English manufacturer asking the cost, weight, fuel requirements, and capabilities of the machine: how many men were needed to handle it, how much land could it plow in twelve hours? An article in *Scientific American* of 1890 led him to the new Stevenson's Shaft Lighter, which he hoped could be installed in the elevator shaft of a five-story building he owned. And when he hired a new man Reed was just as careful, always trying to get the very best for the best price. ("There is an Italian here named 'Canuto' a stone Mason and one of the best men *I ever saw* to handle men but he has one or two jobs on hand and could not leave just now.")[11] Reed's balance sheets are neat, his notations to the point, and there are no frills in this day-to-day record, no sense of self-irony or play.

Ordering for private consumption Reed also seeks out "the best." This applies to spring carriages (make sure they are well boxed), to horses' harnesses, to his cigars, which he gets from P. Pohalski, New York, and to his business suits. One of his letters to V. P. Despierres, New York, on the matter of suits somewhat reminds one of a capitalist calling a bookstore for "a load of books" to fill his new library: Reed wants a suit "of fashionable cut and material suitable for Fall and Winter wear"—period.[12] Pohalski sends Reed 2,000 "assorted" cigars as ordered, and adds another 3,000, making "the *prices* as low as they are sold to the largest jobbers, hoping through you to introduce them in your section without trouble and expense."[13]

The contradiction is obvious. Where Reed could make huge transportation concerns run so well and raise prize race horses and sheep, his private life and tastes invite irony. Certainly his taste in art was classic nouveau riche. In his big house big statues abounded—Carrera marble figures, for example—and mediocre pictures of subjects like racehorses dwarfed the occasional small painting of worth he owned (such as a Titian). When Simeon and wife Amanda toured Europe they had a "courrier" guide them around in the required fashion, though Amanda did get to visit Paris *couturières*. And Simeon, not a spontaneous type, jotted down ribald jokes in his notebooks so he could shine for the boys; he also noted titles of songs, for he fancied himself, and probably was, a rather good singer. He would sing both at church and at parties.[14] Reed's other extracurricular activities included hunting, for which he procured the finest of guns and dogs, and of course his horses. He also loved children, having none of his own, and with Amanda would give parties and stereopticon slide shows for the tikes.[15] His wife's nephew, Martin Winch, who became the chief manager of his interests by the 1880s and who figures prominently in the business correspondence, was a surrogate son. So was his nephew Arthur, whom Reed supplied with money and advised along the lines of a Lord Chesterfield or a Polonius. In a letter of 1883 Reed told Arthur not to bother his own father for money; Reed himself would pay for schooling, board, and clothes, and offer an allowance as well, provided Arthur remained sensible and worked at self-improvement. Demanding a detailed statement of Arthur's expenses, he concluded as follows: "I *do* hope Arthur you will try and improve your present opportunity, and above *all* choose suitable companions."[16] Reed implicitly offers himself here as a model of behavior, as do most self-made successes; and in fact in all his private notebooks there is little that really shows him with his guard down. One final and curious detail that *may* do so should be mentioned in passing—a half-page entry he made on a *Cure for Alcoholism*, obviously copied verbatim from some publication. It tells how to prepare a certain quinine mixture and gives the exact dosage for it as well. Was someone in the family an alcoholic? There is no other evidence to go on, and this notation may have been just for Reed's general edification.

His private notebooks, as I have noted, are mainly filled with "hard" data; there is, however, an entry entitled "Data of early times in Oregon" that does show real feeling for his section, as well as for his own part in its fortunes. Also, when a railroad was being discussed for the Willamette Valley in the late 1860s, Reed demonstrated a regional affiliation (though, as will be pointed out, this should not be overemphasized). He thought "a Road from Portland, up the Willamette Valley would greatly benefit Portland [and] at the same time benefit the State." He hoped that "Portland and the State will reap the benefits and *not* the State of California and her Rail Road Capitalists."[17]

So one can find in Reed a kind of business idealism, and details of a certain human interest. But for all that, Reed's life was mainly concerned with profits, and in the open manner one would expect of his age. To E. C. Darley in 1890 on Portland real estate he wrote, "It is hardly necessary for me to tell you that there is *big* money in this property if properly handled. . . . There are three (3) propositions in connection with this property, either one of which is *first class* in itself, viz—a Real Estate proposition—a Water Power proposition—and third an Iron proposition."[18] To the railway mogul Henry Villard in the same year, on more financial possibilities in an urbanizing Portland:

> The time is coming when they have got to do away with horses, and adopt either the cable system or the electric system, as it strikes me. The former is too expensive, and if the latter is adopted in this city, then it seems to me that the water power of the Oregon Iron and Steel Co., at Oswego is almost a key to the situation. If you could send some one out here upon whose judgement you could rely, to act quietly in these matters, without being known, I think you could bring matters about that would be satisfactory, and afford you a large margin of profit for future operations.[19]

Along with the naked profit motive one notes here the economic influence on politics that so aroused Northwest progressive theorists like J. Allen Smith and Vernon Parrington as well as the political reformers of the La Follette stamp. Reed went from steamer monopolist to railway monopolist when he joined the board of the Northern Pacific in the early, scandal-ridden 1870s. He had joined a concern that would become a monster controller of timberlands and of mines, and W. S. King, in a letter to Reed, also stressed the political possibilities: "the almost supreme control of the great Enterprise . . . properly Manipulated will Enable you to dictate the politics of your North West."[20] A year later Reed's brother Edward made a veiled criticism of Reed's activities, saying that when he read of the Credit Mobilier scandal he was glad *he* didn't belong to the

Republican party.[21] Reed, as has been said, met important politicians on trips back East, among them the pro-railway expansion Congressman Thaddeus Stevens, and on one such trip ate lunch with President Grant. To promote a certain candidate for an Idaho judgeship, Reed said (in a letter of 1891) that he had talked to several senators.[22] There were many other letters to government officials about land and river privileges and appropriations. He was involved in failing companies, mining baths, political squabbles with stockholders (one of whom tried to blackmail him), in the granting of monopolies (as to Villard in Portland), in stringent rent collection (though his nephew called him one of Portland's fairest landlords), and the like.[23] Reed thus formed part of that plutocratic contingent that furnished grist for the mills of the Age of Reform, itself just beginning to boom when he died in 1895.

His very will typifies the age. Leaving an unspecified portion of his estate, which came to some one-and-a-half million dollars in cash, for the enhancement of Portland, Reed, like Rockefeller and like Carnegie, if on a smaller scale, was using his money in an acceptable way; scholars call this stewardship. Reed's object was "the cultivation, illustration or development of the fine arts in the city of Portland, or to some other suitable purpose, which shall be of permanent value and contribute to the beauty of the city and to the intelligence, prosperity and happiness of the inhabitants."[24] He had already been persuaded by the minister of the church where he prayed to give money to an Old Ladies' Home and to a Boys' and Girls' Aid Society. That minister then prevailed on Amanda Reed to leave Reed's money for what would become a Northwest educational arena for intelligent offspring of the middle class, Reed College. After Amanda's death in 1904, Martin Winch, a trustee of her will, toured technological and trade institutions of the country for possible models and then called in a distinguished educator, Wallace Buttrick, as a consultant. Buttrick's opinion was that what Portland and the Northwest needed was a small liberal arts college, and that was the college that opened its doors September 18, 1911. Its guiding intelligence and president of the trustees was the minister who had procured the Reed money—a man whom Rabbi Jonah Wise would call "the most valuable citizen Oregon has ever had," Thomas Lamb Eliot.[25]

Like Reed, Henry W. Corbett, the Ladds, and much of the Portland elite of his time, Eliot was a New Englander. Unlike them, he was from a very long and distinguished family line, the line that also produced his nephew, T. S. Eliot. Thomas Lamb could trace himself back to the original Puritans and earlier, to a well-known English family that included, among others, the martyr for civil liberties who died in the Tower of London under Charles I, Sir John Eliot. Thomas's father—the name full of status resonance—was Reverend William Greenleaf Eliot, founder of

the first Unitarian church west of the Mississippi and almost sole founder
of Washington University, both in St. Louis. Thomas was the eldest son
and one of a minority of fourteen children who survived into adult life.
Like so many others he would be a sickly yet long-lived person. A member
of the first graduating class at Washington University (1862), a graduate
of Harvard Divinity School (1865), and then an apprentice minister under
the elder Eliot, Thomas left for Portland to found the Northwest's first
Unitarian church in 1867. Thanks to the opportunity afforded by frontier
fluidity he had broken with his father in a constructive way. Newly married to Henrietta Mack and finding himself in a town of 7,000 souls thirsty
for institutions, he was equipped to act in a region that offered boundless
scope for it. Eliot's activities in the next thirty years included work with
"juvenile delinquents," with Indians, foundlings, the insane, and crimi-
nals, as well as support for a galaxy of key progressive causes of his time—
a child labor bill, temperance, prison reform, equal suffrage, and educational expansion.

By organizing lecture series with featured speakers like William S.
U'Ren, Eliot played a part in bringing the Australian ballot and direct
primary to Oregon. He also brought in lecturers on controversial subjects
such as cremation. He was one of the founders of the Portland Arts Association and of the Oregon Humane Society, a director of the Portland
Library Association, and the prime inspiration for the building and stock-
ing of the Public Library. He served on the Park Commission and was in
close contact with the famous Olmsted brothers. Then there were his many
sermons and lectures, his articles for *The Oregonian*, his missionary trips
and visits to the poor, and of course his own family responsibilities—he had
eight children. And Reed College. The founding of Reed College—"the
Reed Institute," as Amanda's $2,000,000 will labeled it—was indeed
Eliot's pet project, and the growth and functioning of the college his main
concern in the latter part of his life. The progression was significant; from
1867 to 1892 he had been a pastor, and from then on his focus shifted to
education. The religious drift toward and its ultimate dilution in education
is one of the important themes of modern intellectual history.

One can, in fact, place Eliot within an intermediary generation that
renounces religious dogma and espouses liberalism, yet which holds onto
high moral standards. French positivists and Spanish Christian anarchists
of his time are equally within the same generation. It would be a mistake,
therefore, to equate Eliot's viewpoint with the modern liberal temper. The
latter may still be devoted to improvement, but improvement meant
mostly in the clinical sense—within what Phillip Rieff calls a therapeutic
society or, at his most exaggerated, a "hospital-theatre," what I sometimes
call a "helpocracy."[26] In such an atmosphere there is no overarching moral-
izing intent. To be fair, the idea of what is moral has radically changed and

no modern liberal would express, as Eliot did, a faith in the Indian's "capacity for enlightened, useful citizenship," nor say that "The final object is to make the Indian an American citizen, merging him into the mass [meaning the mainstream]."[27] It is also fair to say that these are somewhat loaded quotations; much more symptomatic of Eliot's "intermediary" tenor of thought is his view of education—at once progressive and deeply moral. He writes, "No greater mistake can be made than that of supposing that non-religious institutions are therefore irreligious. The atmosphere of schools ,strictly secular, can be charged with the highest morality."[28] To be liberal-secular on the one hand and religiously moral on the other is a configuration only a man of Eliot's time could achieve. That time is no longer with us.

In the setting up of what John Scheck refers to as "pattern states" in the West, education was obviously a prime instrument of culture formation. But Thomas Eliot wanted not only to replicate but to move forward with the times. So he touted the methods of Pestalozzi in the Northwest of the 1870s, sponsored phonetic and musical instruction, and became a fierce admirer and partisan of Dewey in the early 1900s. Education would civilize, it would socialize, as we now say, but it would also find new progressive answers to human problems while remaining within an ethical rubric.

Eliot's own classical education, harmonizing with religious training, also constituted a claim to Northwest moral leadership in an era before such credentials became hollow. His sermons, some of which were reprinted in *The Oregonian*, are full of quotations from his favorites like Homer or Cervantes, the latter's Don Quixote a character with whom Eliot identified. On trips away from home he carried around Homer, once exulting, "I am reading my *Odyssey* and it never seemed finer, it is full of the sea itself."[29] And of the *Iliad* on another occasion: "That is the greatest book ever written."[30] This love of great books, then, suggests a relationship to the classics very different from that which prevailed among many nineteenth-century orators, lawyers, and politicians. Classics, for Eliot, were not simply one more piece of a conventional snob artillery; rather, he enjoyed a genuine European culture, once again in the transitional period (the period of Henry James's quaint travel accounts) before this culture would become routine among America's growing educated class. Eliot loved symphonies and could play at the piano. He could quote Trollope and Walter Scott, Ibsen and Zola, and even Oswald Spengler after the appearance of *Decline of the West*. Plutarch was another favorite, and Shakespeare was as dear to him as to Harvey Scott.[31]

It is interesting to linger on this reverential attitude toward books. A very long, almost manic sermon (or lecture?) Eliot wrote in June of 1895, called "A Plea for the Old Authors," is a defense of serious reading that can be read unironically today.[32] He says first that he had always loved old things since he was a boy. Reading old books, particularly on vacation in the country, was Eliot's attempt to "atone for the hours I have wasted within the city with the daily Morning Convulsion, or the Monthly Cataclysm—in vain attempts to keep up with the times." Contrasting Plutarch or the Bible with "whole libraries of ephemera," not to mention the products of journalism, he wonders whether too much bad will drive out the good; "whether we are not breeding a whole race of mental dyspeptics and imbeciles, upon the prodigious indiscriminate diet of written words—a surfeit in quantity and quality of mental food." Eliot goes on, bursting with energy and riddling his prose with Dreiseresque dashes, to deplore

> the congested imaginations, the crowded consciences—of this reading herd. This means more than mischief. It is disease—It means intellectual putrefaction or dry rot. Does it not augur for our children the loss of mental fibre, the lapse of healthy imagination,—the access of morbid feeling—the total inability to think . . . distaste for the healthy thoughts and emotions of natural life[?]

So the old books are supplanted by more accessible diversions, and minds themselves become "like the newspapers—a hash—a kaleidoscope—a sewer." Himself? Eliot stays back with his classics, rereading them carefully and considering them part of the family. He approves Charles Lamb's attitude that one must say grace before reading as well as before eating meat. He would probably have been interested to know that Heine read *Don Quixote* to the trees or that St. Jerome slept with a copy of Aristotle by him. With such company can Eliot be ranged.

To label Eliot a rereader does not mean that he always did the reading himself. From his teens on Eliot was plagued with eye trouble, and by the last half of his life as he grew blind had to have his daughter or friends read to him frequently. It is not, of course, how much one reads but the quality of reading one takes to heart that reflects true education. Eliot from this standpoint was truly educated, and this was a part of his notability in Oregon.

So, more obviously, was his physical image. Extremely handsome and noble-looking, his mien connoted ethical direction: he had a fine, chiselled face, cropped white hair escaping in curls, a beard, a sturdy build, and of course the august clothes of his station. Due to overwork he was a victim of endemic ill health, but the serene look of self-mastery never left him. One of the oratorical delights of the region, he thoroughly captivated his auditors, whether urban or rural.

His sermons were usually not so frenzied as "A Plea for the Old Authors" cited above; more typical and orthodox is "To the Worship of God," delivered in San Francisco and in Portland. He did, however, speak on subjects like "Modoc Murder Victims" (first given April, 1873) and on

women's rights (first delivered in October of 1871). The latter sermon, as
befitted a friend of Abigail Scott Duniway, noted "nothing extraordinary
in the request of individual women to be physicians, professors, ministers
or lawyers. It seems to me only the legitimate widening of the circle."
And in one of those statements that unknowingly undermined the patri-
archal ground upon which the Eliots themselves stood, he added, "We
owe it to our daughters to make them independent of the necessity of
marriage."[33]

Eliot's relations with his own wife were rather romantic for the time, as
one discovers from their letters to each other. Certainly absence can make
the heart grow fonder, and Thomas always acquired a peculiar exuberance whenever he left on one of his camping or fishing trips in the wild
places he enjoyed. From the top of Mary's Peak near Corvallis he wrote
an enthusiastic letter home, wishing his wife Henrietta were there beside
him. Then his mind instinctively raced to his children, "Every trout stream
I cross, I think of Willy, every good fat cow, I think of Mick and Don.
Every new flower, of Nelly 'your little flower wild,' Every lamb, of Grace,
and Every chipmunk of little Etta. The doves and quail with their broods
—big Etta!"[34] To "big Etta" (sometimes "my darling wife") he confessed
his depression when he visited the less fortunate or diseased, writing, for
example, from a hospital near Olympia in August of 1883: "I am so over-
cast by their condition, at times, that words seem a mockery."[35] And
whenever Henrietta herself felt ill he seems to have been kind and protective toward her. The same modern capitalist impulse of chivalry toward
the spouse, present in Reed, is also to a lesser extent one of Eliot's own
traits. In a letter of 1887 he mentions holding onto some viewfront property that will increase in value, hoping "some day, maybe, our ship will
come in, with a moderate load, against our old age."[36] (He would unload
at considerable profit in 1906.) From the other side Henrietta wrote in a
fashion somewhat bold for her age, "My own dear Tom," but she would
also apologize for the supposedly inferior quality of her letters compared to
her husband's.[37]

Eliot, like Simeon Reed, was an indefatigable worker. He rose at seven
o'clock every day of the week and often worked late at night, doing with
little sleep, sometimes because of insomnia. When he visited other areas
of the Northwest he would routinely ride horseback thirty-five miles a day.
His hiking trips were no flat two-milers, but often uncharted and difficult
climbs in the Cascade glaciers, one of which was named for him. He also
loved to fish in the Hood River. These vigorous outdoor trips were a response to a work load that took him several times to the brink of breakdown. His conscience seems to have been a constantly-running motor, as
even his bedtime prayer suggests: "Dear God, help me to be thoughtful,
and helpful, and unselfish," but it did not prevent him from acting effi-

ciently nor from noticing the trees in life's forest.[38] On board ship to Japan in 1903 he wrote some of his highest letters to Henrietta: "A splendid breeze, blue sky and indigo sea with white caps. It is inexpressibly exhilarating to me."[39] Each morning at 6:30 a.m. he took a salt bath on board and then he lit into a hearty breakfast where he met with great interest travellers from Boston, Philadelphia, San Francisco. A stern moralist, a crusading teetotaler, a sponsor of antitobacco legislation, a disciplined, over-conscientious man, Eliot still found ways to channel the exuberance beneath in a human way.

He could not delegate that pitch of elation to his successors, even though he was the father of eight children, seven of whom survived him. He had three sons. The eldest, William Greenleaf, took over at the Portland Church in 1906 after three other pastorates; Samuel, one of the first Rhodes scholars, went to Pittsburgh to work with the poor; and Thomas became a professor of sociology at Northwestern University. The daughters were all married, and one of them, Dorothea Dix, became the spouse of the Unitarian churchman Earl Morse Wilbur, who was Eliot's first biographer. Eliot would also have many grandchildren, although four died between 1919 and 1934, among them a Thomas Greenleaf Eliot and a Thomas Eliot Wilbur. (Other names included a Mather Greenleaf Eliot, a Rosemary Anna Henrietta Greenleaf Eliot, and a Thomas Lamb Eliot Wilbur.)[40]

Here then are portraits of business notable and moral notable of the nineteenth- and early twentieth-century Pacific Northwest. Well before Eliot's death in 1936, the advent of mass media spelled the demise and devaluation of such notables—both in the Northwest and in the western world generally. They had helped build up a civilization, but that civilization would no longer need them. No individual could quite measure up to the collective sources of power in our time, or at least not in the same way. Even if there were a Unitarian minister of Eliot's stature today—and there is not—it is doubtful he could command the attention that Ann Landers or Merv Griffin now receive. Perhaps the reason is that Eliot was both an educationist-intellectual and a religious moralist, and these two functions have progressively parted company. The great intermediary era was supplanted by the era of abundant expertise. There is now no one educator who can guide our lives, nor teach us to be cultivated and virtuous human beings, as Aristotle did for Alexander the Great, or as Seneca failed to do for Nero. Many voices resound in the academy and many in the churches and clinics, but increasingly these are voices confined within high walls.

The academy, however, was the positive point of confluence between the two notables discussed, for Reed College resulted from their combination of financial and intellectual-spiritual funds. This was to be the ideal college—the Johns Hopkins of the Pacific Northwest. Its first president, the brilliant William Foster, a Keynesian economist before his time, wanted liberal education at Reed "to meet new situations, analyze them, discover the issues involved, and develop new solutions in new crises."[41] Students were asked "to share in a high adventure"—to participate in the government of the university, live in the same dormitories as teachers, share the same activities. When Dorothy Johansen wrote a play on Simeon Reed for students in 1937, the romantic ideal belonged to the Swing era, but the optimism about education still reflected the tail end of the Enlightenment and a certain sense of tradition.[42] The contemporary scene at Reed is another matter. Reed and Eliot appear on the masthead of the college newspaper, there is still pride in learning, even snobbery, and there is fine work being done, but at Reed, as elsewhere, few today believe the contents of the stacks will help create a better world. It is ironic to read the letters of Eliot on this lovely campus, letters spiced with an optimistic wit, and then to juxtapose the wit of contemporary graffiti reflecting our own age. The comparison is unfair but will serve to show the advent of a cynicism in the educational world that Eliot could not have predicted; from some of the better talents:

> In the land of the mindless the Halfwit is King
> Marcuse is the Methadone of the intellectual classes
> Marijuana makes me menstruate.[43]

It is not clear, finally, how consciously regional men like Eliot and Reed were. They helped build our section, they enjoyed working in the area, they were definitely Northwestern, but to call them regionalists in the modern sense would be anachronistic distortion. Regionalism today is a pulling away, a reining-in process—whether one studies Brittany, Wales, or Tom McCall's Northwest; but nineteenth-century Oregon notables were expanding, forming, amalgamating. The contemporary regional impulse—which deserves more critical definition than it has gotten—does not seem to be a part of that outlook. To further distinguish between these two periods, one might adapt the Hindu idea of *Kitra* eras and *Kali* eras, perpetual alternations in history. In the *Kitra* era aristocracies or elites are being produced, this denoting a rising civilization; in a *Kali* period elites (in India, castes) degenerate, but no new elite appears to take its place. Regionalism today may be tainted—one hesitates to be firm on this point— by its inward-looking character, a character that does not embrace and sustain renewing achievement.

In the last analysis our sympathies go out to Eliot. There is really not much that excites us in Reed's balanced books and records of acquisitions. Most right-thinking, modern, university-oriented Americans would laud Eliot's victory; and America's "spokespersons" will be the many heirs of

Eliot's kind—diluted heirs, more caught up in a culture than directing it—me, you, all the right-thinking, right-wine-drinking, yogurt-eating, Europe-visiting, *Beowulf*-citing, *Four Hundred Blows*-watching, politics-reviling Americans who today constitute a formidable contingent, even a style, made up of many fine and decent people, but of people perhaps not quite possessing the finish, or, given the sea of competition, the voice to steer us through this century's poised pile of hardware. Such an estimate may be pessimistic and styles do change; it may be safest to chronicle another era only, an era of notables, as I have tried to do here.

1. Alan Hynding, *The Public Life of Eugene Semple, Promoter and Politician of the Pacific Northwest* (Seattle: Univ. of Washington Press, 1973); Robert C. Nesbit, *"He Built Seattle"* (Seattle: Univ. of Washington Press, 1961), on Burke. Nesbit calls such men "business pioneers."

2. André Tudesq, *Les Grands Notables en France (1840-1849)*, 2 vols. (Paris: Presses universitaires de France, 1964); Barnett Singer, "The Village School-master as Notable in Brittany 1880-1914," *French Historical Studies*, 9 (1976), 635-59, among other papers published and unpublished on this theme.

3. On Curry, see Leslie W. Dunlap, "The Oregon Free Press," *Pacific Northwest Quarterly*, 33 (1942), 171-85. On similar kinds of careers, see Ann Briley, "Hiram F. Smith, First Settler of Okanagan Country," *PNQ*, 43 (1952), 226-33 and W. A. Katz, "Public Printers of Washington Territory, 1853-1863," *PNQ*, 51 (1960), 103-14.

4. A convenient biographical sketch is Dorothy Johansen's "Mr. and Mrs. Simeon G. Reed," in *Reed College Pioneers*, Reed College Bulletin, Vol. 15 (Portland: Reed College, 1931). I have also used Miss Johansen's unpublished manuscript, as yet untitled, on the history of Reed College; hereafter cited as "Manuscript."

5. On the various technological "mini-revolutions" that changed American history see Daniel J. Boorstin, *The Americans: The Democratic Experience* (New York: Random House, 1973), much more materially-oriented than the title suggests, and Howard Mumford Jones's overview of the period, *The Age of Energy: Varieties of American Experience 1865-1915* (New York: Viking Press, 1971).

6. Dorothy Johansen, "Capitalism on the Far-Western Frontier: The Oregon Steam Navigation Company," Diss. Univ. of Washington 1941, pp. 19-31. On Portland, see Joseph Gaston, *Portland, Its History and Builders*, 3 vols. (Chicago: S. J. Clarke Publishing Co., 1911).

7. Johansen, "Oregon Steam Navigation Company," pp. 89, 90, 191, 218.

8. Johansen, p. 202. This was when Oregon Steam was dickering with Northern Pacific to take over some of its stock.

9. Reed to A. Onderdonk, November 11, 1884 in "The Letters and Private Papers of Simeon Gannett Reed," typed version, prepared by Reed College Project, Division of Professional Service Projects, WPA, Portland, 1940; in Reed College Library, vol. 16, p. 124; hereafter cited as "Letters."

10. Reed to M. H. Cochrane, January 18, 1885, "Letters," Vol. 16, pp. 154-55.

11. Reed to John Fowler and Co., March 4, 1872, "Letters," Vol. 2, p. 177; Reed to Hugh Stevenson, May 12, 1890, "Letters," Vol. 31, p. 89; Reed to A. Onderdonk, October 8, 1883, "Letters," Vol. 16, p. 65.

12. Reed to V. P. Despierres, July 8, 1864, "Letters," Vol. 2, p. 5.

13. P. Pohalski to Reed, January 21, 1885, "Letters," Vol. 18, p. 15.
14. Some of the personal detail on Reed comes from a conversation I had with Dorothy Johansen at Reed College, May 6, 1976.
15. Conversation with Dorothy Johansen; Johansen, "Manuscript," Chapter I, and her *Anniversary Play*, Reed College, given June 6, 1937.
16. Reed to Arthur, October 12, 1883, "Letters," Vol. 16, p. 71.
17. Reed to Williams and Corbett, December 9, 1867, "Letters," Vol. 1; also cited in Johansen, "Oregon Steam Navigation Company," p. 207.
18. Reed to E. C. Darley, February 8, 1890, "Letters," Vol. 30, pp. 47-48.
19. Reed to H. Villard, February 12, 1890, "Letters," Vol. 30, p. 54. Villard was the chief buyer of Oregon Steam in 1879. That sale alone made over a million dollars for Reed. See Johansen, "Oregon Steam Navigation Company," p. 277.
20. W. S. King to Reed, November 24, 1872, "Letters," Vol. 5, p. 19.
21. Edward Reed to Reed, February 16, 1873, "Letters," Vol. 5, pp. 62-63.
22. See Johansen, "Mr. and Mrs. Simeon G. Reed," p. 5; Reed to Jas. H. Beatty, January 9, 1891, in "Letters," Vol. 30, p. 173.
23. On blackmail, see Reed to Mr. Mills, September 24, 1884, "Letters," Vol. 16, p. 111; on granting of monopoly to Villard, see Reed to Villard, December 21, 1889, Vol. 30, p. 27, mentioning "the exclusive right to cross *both* bridges with The Motor and Electric franchises on the other side of the river, *in connection* with the water power of the O.I. & S. Co. at Oswego . . ."; on rents and reputation, see Martin Winch to Phillip Wasserman, November 21, 1889, Vol. 30, p. 2, averring that Reed "now has the reputation of being one of the fairest and most just landlords in Portland."
24. The will is cited in Johansen, "Manuscript," Chapter I.
25. Jonah Wise in *The First Quarter Century: Retrospect and Appraisal 1911-1936* (Portland: Reed College, 1936), p. 24. This book gives details on the founding of Reed. Biographical details that follow on Eliot are found in Earle M. Wilbur, *Thomas Lamb Eliot 1841-1936* (Portland: privately printed, 1937) and John Frederick Scheck, "Transplanting a Tradition: Thomas Lamb Eliot and the Unitarian Conscience in the Pacific Northwest, 1865-1905," Diss. Univ. of Oregon 1969.
26. See Rieff, *Triumph of the Therapeutic: Uses of Faith after Freud* (New York: Harper and Row, 1968).
27. Cited in Scheck, "Thomas Lamb Eliot and the Unitarian Conscience," pp. 281, 284.
28. From a report of 1876, cited in Johansen, "Manuscript," Chapter II. On the "intermediary generation" and education in France see my "Jules Ferry and the Laic Revolution in French Primary Education," *Paedagogica Historica*, 15 (1975), 204-25.
29. Eliot to wife Henrietta, March 12, 1903, in Thomas Lamb Eliot Papers, Reed College Library; hereafter cited as TLE Papers.
30. Quoted in Wilbur, *Thomas Lamb Eliot*, p. 111.
31. Scott's writings on Shakespeare are found in Leslie Scott, ed., *Shakespeare: Writings of Harvey W. Scott* (Cambridge, Mass.: Riverside Press, 1928).
32. In TLE Papers.
33. He goes on to describe "the courageous woman who dares to have an opinion, and is not ashamed that she studied Greek. It seems to me that there is no more significant evidence of the progress of our race, than that women are rapidly obtaining the same facilities of education that men have had." Sermon in TLE Papers.

34. Eliot to Henrietta, July 21, 1881, TLE Papers.
35. Eliot to Henrietta, August 17, 1883, TLE Papers.
36. Eliot to Henrietta, September 30, 1887, TLE Papers.
37. For example, April 14, 1901: "This is a very stupid letter, but it comes from a very stupid woman." TLE Papers.
38. In Wilbur, *Thomas Lamb Eliot*, p. 103.
39. Eliot to Henrietta, March 12, 1903 in TLE Papers. The letters and postcards from Japan testify to a continuing interest in new things and in people.
40. See Wilbur, *Thomas Lamb Eliot*, pp. 99-104 and the Eliot genealogy at the end of Wilbur's book.
41. Cited in Johansen, "Manuscript," Chapter III.
42. See the hortatory *The First Quarter Century* which has a series of appreciations. The quote on a "high adventure" is in this book, p. 5. Significantly, the student newspaper was called *The Quest*. I want to thank Dorothy Johansen for showing me a copy of her play.
43. Reed College Library, men's toilet, lower level.

In sharp contrast to Professor Singer's treatment of a pair of Portland leaders, Stanley Scott turns to the isolated Kootenay area of southeastern British Columbia and traces the impact of English, Italian, and Russian immigrants attracted by opportunities in mining and farming. The result, Scott argues, has been neither assimilation nor congealed ethnic identities but rather an evolving multicultural society. Stanley H. Scott received his Ph.D. in history from Texas Christian University in 1973. He has taught courses in United States history, expansion of the American West, and Pacific Northwest/ British Columbia history at Notre Dame University in Nelson, British Columbia, where he chaired the history department, and at Boise State University. One of his published works is *A Giant in Texas: A History of the Dallas-Fort Worth Regional Airport Controversy*. Professor Scott's interests are about equally divided between the Pacific Northwest and the Southwest Borderlands.

The Origins of Kootenay Society, 1890-1930

Stanley H. Scott

Removed from the influences of coastal British Columbia, the West Kootenays in the southeastern interior of the Province form a unique microculture of the larger society; yet at the same time, the region displays characteristics that defy Canadian, British Columbia, or Pacific Northwestern generalizations. Dominated by two major river systems, the Columbia and the Kootenay, the area snugly conforms to what nature so grudgingly has conceded for settlement. River benches, cut from the "sea of mountains," as David Thompson described the Selkirks, allow for small cities, extractive industries, and the occasional farm plot, while the higher ranges harbor rich mineral veins—some found, others not—and thick evergreen forests. Pure mountain streams, high pocket tarns, three large, natural mountain lakes, and of course, the rivers, seemingly fill most available valley land. These surface waters, resulting from mild and snowy winters, wet springs, and warm summers, drive the turbos of numerous hydroelectric dams, furnishing power for the prairies, the interior, and the coast.[1]

Although scenic to the tourist and pristine for those seeking "to get away from it all," the West Kootenays have been, and remain, one of the unknown areas of the Pacific Northwest—and despite arguments from environmentalists, one of the most undeveloped. Although the 1971 census reported a population of 44,790, isolation—both aesthetic and physical—has been the most profound environmental force in a land of almost 20,000 square miles. The southern-flowing rivers, now partially tamed by technology, have been difficult, almost impossible, routes to outside markets, supplies, and cultures as late as 1950. The numerous falls and downward steps made frequent portages necessary even for the lightly equipped trappers of the 1840s; miners and loggers fifty years later found the waterways worthless as avenues to prosperity. Sternwheelers early plied the lakes, transporting many settlers from Colville, Washington, upstream on the Columbia to a landing near the confluence of the Kootenay. Inevitably, however, people or goods moving by water had to load and reload countless times before completing most trips. East to west travel across the maze of mountains, canebrakes and swamps was both hazardous and expensive as late as 1960; neither the Dewdney Trail of the 1860s nor the Southern

Trans-Canada Highway one hundred years later provided much east to west relief. Railroads, often instruments of great and rapid change in other areas of the North American West, did little to change these patterns of isolation. Although the Canadian Pacific Railway (C.P.R.) began operations in 1892, service was spotty, time-consuming, and dangerous. To reach Vancouver, B.C., for example, 300 miles directly west, meant a four-day trip, including delays, transfers on two feeder lines, and two ferry trips across the lakes. And to avoid the most precarious months of the winter, officials as late as 1955 simply cancelled service to the Kootenays from December until April.[2]

Other twentieth-century innovations have been only partially successful in lifting the isolation. It was 1950 before road replaced sternwheeler on Kootenay Lake; some villages lacked even a wagon path until that time. In every direction from the West Kootenays, surface transportation still meant travel over a mountain pass. Nor has commercial aviation helped, for flights arrive less than thirty percent of the time from October to May. Radio came in the early 1930s from Salt Lake City and in 1956 from the Canadian Broadcasting Company. Some parts of the region, in fact, still do not receive television signals. The physical environment, while typical of the Mountain West, has inhibited the development of national insights, even serving as a barrier between the West Kootenays and the rest of the Pacific Northwest.[3]

Despite these patterns of physical isolation, human geography has also molded the West Kootenays. Numerous natives and mountain men criss-crossed the region during the early nineteenth century. The local Indian populations, primarily Kootenai and Flathead, had been living off the abundant game for approximately 2,000 years. Generally friendly to the new intruders, they and their culture were aptly described by the structure of their name—Ko (water) and Tinneh (people). After the arrival of David Thompson in 1807, trappers exploited the wildlife resources; when Dr. John McLoughlin ordered a Hudson's Bay Company post constructed at Fort Colville in 1824, trapping and trading reached its height. Although these activities continued sporadically for over forty years, neither group—native nor trapper—left significant imprints on the Kootenay society today.[4]

In September, 1867, however, miners hurried to the area, responding to news of a strike at Forty-Nine Creek, nine miles west of Nelson. Soon Fort Colville, now controlled by Americans in the Washington Territory, buzzing with rumors, began to attract Americans "off to the diggins" and became the center of a frenzied, but brief gold rush. Expectations outstripped reality. Obvious concerns of the colonial government about the sudden and unexpected invasion of Americans led to the construction of the unsatisfactory Dewdney Trail and several attempts to control the

unruly miners; alarmists in Victoria were relieved when the strikes expired
and the newcomers moved on. By 1882 only eleven registered voters remained in the area. Even the Hudson's Bay Company withdrew, thereby
failing to maintain its trading posts in the Kootenays.[5]

But that same year numerous discoveries of silver and lead around
Kootenay Lake attracted permanent settlements. On the eastern shores at
Riondel, the Bluebell Mine opened; five years later in 1887 the Silver King,
near Nelson, began operations; between 1887 and 1891 strikes in Rossland
and in the Slocan Valley made the region well known. And while George
Buchanan, a settler from the United States in 1888, recalled that he
saw "no signs to show that a human being had ever entered the valley
[of Nelson]," by 1891 another newcomer, Englishman R. T. Lowery,
complained that Nelson was

> new and short of frills, boiled shirts, parsons, lawyers, and prohi-
> bition orators. It had plenty of whiskey, a few canaries, and other
> birds, even several pianos. All the rest of the population were
> mule skinners, packers, trail blazers, remittance men and pro-
> ducers, with a slight trace of tenderfeet. The police only slept in
> the daytime.[6]

Indeed, Lowery might thus have described most mining camps in the
West. Initiated by Americans, the West Kootenays soon attracted hundreds to mine for gold, silver, lead, zinc, and coal. Arriving by foot or
canoe at first, they usually packed all their belongings. Some were veterans
of another rush, others were not. Towns, hastily constructed, lasted only
as long as the local boom, often burning once or twice. Since no Canadian
model was available, society conformed to the typical American mining
frontier. Claims, for example, were lost if the prospector was absent for
seventy-two hours without official title. Frontier justice was sometimes
sudden and violent. An assassination, a dubious trial, and a hanging that
made headlines in the distant *New York Tribune* occurred during these
turbulent days. In fact, while the region was Canadian and therefore osten-
sibly governed by Canadian laws, as late as 1896 the *Rossland Miner*
pointed out that only Americans would take the "necessary risks while
everyone else sat on the sidelines." Bemoaning reliance on the cheaper
supplies of the United States rather than on goods from British Columbia
or the rest of Canada, the newspaper noted that eight-five percent of the
Kootenay trade was across the border as late as 1900. With an unstable and
partially unknown population, only 1,307 voters were listed as eligible in
1894; these lists, of course, excluded "women, children, immigrants, orientals, and Americans," according to the *Rossland Miner*. Apparently
"immigrant" referred exclusively to non-British Europeans.[7]

Naturally such a supply of minerals attracted the railroads and the
steamers. First to arrive was the Great Northern. Crossing the border to

exploit the lucrative deposits and ample forest products, the railroad provided sporadic and unreliable service; soon, in any case, the C.P.R. replaced the American company. Arriving in 1892, the Canadian railroad received numerous grants from the provincial and federal governments, bought up several unprofitable feeder lines, and provided the first links with Canadian markets. But the giant Canadian Corporation was not content to provide merely service and almost immediately became directly involved in the economy of the region. In 1898 the C.P.R. purchased a small smelter at Trail Creek on the Columbia that F. A. Heinze had constructed two years earlier; in 1904 the plant was incorporated (with fifty-one percent C.P.R. control) as the Consolidated Mining and Smelting Company (Cominco).[8]

Obviously human needs and ambitions had changed the nature of the West Kootenays. By 1900 the C.P.R. needed settlers to maintain a profit margin; the Government of British Columbia also needed to expand the region's population to achieve a sufficient tax base for expected services. Hardrock miners—not prospectors, adventurers, and entrepreneurs—were needed for the heavy extractive industry; soon Cominco would demand legions of skilled and unskilled workers. Farmers to feed and loggers to house these newcomers were also in demand. Thus great expectations greeted the twentieth century. Although hardly more than forests, a few mining camps, fewer still supply centers, and the C.P.R. existed in 1900, shortly the Provincial and Federal Governments, independent agents, churches, intellectuals, and, most important, the C.P.R. would begin an immigrant recruiting program that would change forever the "American" nature of the West Kootenays. By 1930 this second wave of settlers had created a multicultural society, occasionally representative of Canada, more typically West Coast, but primarily and uniquely different from both regional and national generalizations.

In 1900 Canadians were actually not favorably disposed to "differents." "British" Canada preferred to remain just that—British; surely "French" Canada presented enough problems. Yet the "foreigners," who entered in ever increasing numbers after 1900, were the central and southern Europeans and not members of the charter groups of Canadian society.[9] Firmly following the dictates of Social Darwinism, citizens believed that "poor stock"—central and southern Europeans—could dilute "superior breeds" of British and northern Europeans. In 1881 British and French Canadians made up ninety percent of the population; Germans, another seven percent. By 1931 these groups had dropped to eighty percent, while the new immigrants increased from less than one to eighteen percent.[10]

The increases did not pass unnoticed by the older nationals, who subtly opposed these new "tides" of immigrants. Rumors circulated widely: The newcomers were diseased ("trachoma was practically unknown before the immigration from southern and eastern Europe"), crazy ("statistics show that the foreign-born furnished two and one thirds times their normal proportion of insane"), criminal ("the highest rate [of prisoners] occurred among the foreign born"), impoverished ("in 1900 the English at port of entry possessed $38.90, as opposed to the southern Italian's $8.84"), and uneducated ("English illiteracy was 1.2 percent in 1904; while among the southern Italians, 54.2 percent, even in *their* language").[11]

Yet assimilation, not restriction, seemed the answer to many in the early twentieth century. And education and language provided the keys. "Ignorance of our language is a barrier," one Canadian writer maintained, "that isolates these peoples from us and our institutions; behind their language is a foreign mind and training which still further separates them from us." Schooling in English and Canadian ways, therefore, became the goal for many societies—the various churches, the Masons, the Y.M.C.A. "If compulsory education can be generally enforced," P. H. Bryce, Head of the Medical Division of the Department of Immigration, claimed, "we have in such races not only an individual asset of great value but also the assurance of a population remarkably free from the degenerative effects seen of those classes."[12]

Persisting in their first view of the new immigrants, other Canadians disagreed with the humanitarian educators. Italians easily became "wops;" orientals, "slopes;" Russians, "doukies." All immigrants—with the exception of the British—were simply "foreigners." Some violence occurred, particularly in the West. Anti-oriental riots broke out in Vancouver and soon orientals were universally believed "unassimilable." Russians were often and indiscriminately jailed; a group of Italians was nearly lynched in Alberta in 1906 after attacking a native Canadian who had taunted them. J. S. Woodsworth, soon to become the organizer of the Cooperative Commonwealth Federation, discredited most ethnic groups; typically, he maintained that the southern Italian's "intelligence is not higher than one could imagine in the descendant of peasantry illiterate for centuries."[13] Robert England, a "scholar of immigration," wrote that "if we mean by assimilation a process that molds racial stocks into something else we are flying into the face of what every stock-breeder knows . . . no melting pot can make a Slav, or an Italian, an Anglo-Saxon. Racial qualities, vices, and instincts remain."[14] Stephen Leacock, noted Canadian humorist and economist, wrote in 1930 that "I am not saying that we should absolutely shut out the Oriental. But we should not facilitate his coming. Not for him the free land, the found job, nor the guaranteed anything. He is lucky if he is let in 'on his own.' "[15]

Why and how, then, did the West Kootenays differ from Canada in general? Several distinctions are apparent. The lateness of settlement, the slowly developing lines of economy and transportation, the prevailing isolation partially blocked these Eastern and West coast ethnic attitudes of superiority. No social structure was entrenched by 1900 that might have been defined as typically Canadian. With a large influx of American miners during the last decade of the nineteenth century, the area did not conform to the normal patterns of systematic settlement. There was, however, another significant and unique difference in the social stratification of the developing region. By 1930 three important immigrant groups had arrived; besides the normal Canadian migration and the remnants of the American mining frontier, large numbers of British, Italian, and Russian newcomers settled in the area. Attracted by economic or religious reasons, eventually none of the groups dominated the others. Although discrimination and abuse certainly existed—Nelson had its Bogustown for Chinese, Trail had its Dago gulch, Castlegar had its peasant Czars—a multicultural society, in any case, emerged by 1930.

Canadians foremost sought newcomers from the British Isles, and by 1900 the trade in immigrants had become quite sophisticated. Naturally the "sturdy Britishers" were first choice, since they were "members of one great empire, inheritors of a common tradition, accustomed to the more or less successful operation of democratic institutions . . . and speak a common language."[16] Two large horsedrawn exhibition vans constantly toured the agricultural districts of rural England, Wales, Scotland, and Ireland, generating interests and recruiting immigrants. In 1903 Canadian officials distributed free textbooks and 25,000 maps throughout the British Isles. The results were astonishing. Over 50,000 settlers came that year from Great Britain alone, 4,000 more than the total entries from all countries just four years earlier. Between 1900 and 1931, over 1,500,000 British immigrants came to Canada; certainly most Anglophiles had much to admire in these developments.[17]

Many Britons settled in British Columbia; some 23,000 came to the West Kootenays.[18] Most had been lured by C.P.R. agents or propaganda, stressing a "genteel" career in fruit ranching—thereby providing settlers with an "idyllic life" and the railroad with bulk cargo. Booklets such as the *Resources and Climate of the Kootenay, Boundary, and Okanagan Districts of British Columbia* (1906) noted the advantages to the man of "small means who is steady and industrious. Everywhere there is a great demand for labor—skilled and unskilled at high wages."[19] Recently retired army and navy officers were advised to sell their pensions and invest in Kootenay Lake lands—$5.00 per acre for first class agricultural holdings and $2.50 per acre for lands that only needed irrigation. Other disfranchised commodities of the British upper classes—the younger sons and daughters—were also encouraged to bring their "remittance money and use it for the limited capital needed in the planting of an orchard and four years of survival." After that period, the recruiters continued, "it was mainly a matter of watching the fruit ripen in the sun." "The fruit-grower will find here an ideal home," James Johnson, President of the Nelson Agricultural and Industrial Association, claimed. "The climate, as you know, is perfect, the soil very rich and productive, and the market the best. He will be surrounded by beautiful scenery, and the shooting and fishing is the best." An American from West Virginia, Johnson also doubled as the local agent for the C.P.R. "The transportation companies," he concluded, "are willing to assist the Fruit Growers' Association at all times to place the fruit in the consumer's hand in the best possible condition."[20]

Upon arrival, expected conditions strangely bore little resemblance to the Garden of Eden. Somehow land speculators had beaten the British to the Lake; by 1908 lands sold minimumly for $100 per acre. One young immigrant recalled that her father had a chance to buy some land "for about five dollars per acre or $200 for the whole lot [of 160 acres]. Only trouble was, it happened to be on top of a mountain." Ferried and paddled across the lake, she and her family "were dropped into the wilderness" at Crawford Bay. "Father paid $3,000 for eighty acres of the wildest, most isolated land you would ever see. Mother said 'good heavens!' but father rather enjoyed roughing it. We had no knives, no forks, certainly not the silver that mother was accustomed to. We were in a bit of a pickle since mother had never done any cooking at all . . . . We didn't even have an idea where we'd get food!"[21]

Nor did other expectations materialize. The "perfect" and cold climate took many Britons by surprise. Few were prepared for the snow; fewer still had any notion of the black flies, mosquitoes, or swamp fever; none were prepared for the rigors of fruit ranching. "My father grew fruit, that's true," Margaret Draper recalled. "Called them golden apples! Golden apples, my eye! More the size and shape of a prune."[22] By 1922 demands for West Kootenay fruit had dropped disastrously; "after shipping and handling charges are deducted from the price received for your crop," the C.P.R. notified one rancher, "we find that you owe us a sum of ninety-seven cents."[23] Some British settlers even found themselves victims of fraud. The President of the British Tourist and Colonization Society arranged—for a fee—for twenty Scots and their families to buy land near Fruitvale in 1907. When they arrived, they found that the land was not for sale nor were any jobs available. The "real" and "best" British also suffered sneers from local residents and in novels such as the *Call of the West* (1917).

> Look at that group of Englishmen who keep so much to themselves. They are obviously fruit ranchers returning from a day in Nelson. Two of them are retired army officers, the others are young fellows who have never done anything since they left college . . . . There is one with a supercilious air, who has no damned

> use for this beastly country, don't you know! He was sent out by
> his people, and is maintained by them, being a remittance man.
> He had tried his hand at several things out here, but finds one has
> to work in order to earn a living, and that doesn't suit him . . . .
> "No, this is a rotten country; it is not a fit place for a gentleman,
> and as soon as I can get my mother to send me the fare back I am
> going straight home!"[24]

Locals equally disdained British laborers, viewing them with suspicion, jealousy, and fear. Workers (who could arrange for the necessary $25.00 required on arrival) often found storefronts with "no British need apply" signs. Wages were low, but room, board, and clothing deductions left workers with even less. Edmund Kirby, manager of the War Eagle Mine in Rossland, preferred instead illiterate eastern and central Europeans to Britons. "How to head off a strike of muckers or laborers for higher wages, without the aid of Italian labor, I do not know."[25] Although many British had arrived by 1920, English accents were not necessarily received well within the West Kootenays.

The charter group thus failed to establish domination. Many immigrants returned to England to fight in World War I, never to come back. Most that remained disappeared into the Canadian mosaic. Margaret Draper, for example, married a "Canadian" while she was in Saskatchewan working as a farm laborer during the War. Although her father held several Cambridge and Oxford degrees, she had little more than a grade school education. Hitching freights and drifting about the countryside at the height of the depression, she retained few English characteristics, becoming instead an example of the environmental impact of the frontier. Her son never thought of himself as British, resented "uppity" Englishmen, disliked England during the Second World War; her granddaughter claimed that she "never thought about being English, not even English-Canadian," concluding, she was "just 100 percent Canadian, like all her friends." No family tales, heirlooms, nor mannerisms reminded the visitor of the Draper heritage—coffee, not tea came at 3:00 p.m.[26]

And while the occasional eighty-year-old former fruit rancher still flies his "Union Jack" in defiance of the changing Canadian society, the British immigrants, at least in the West Kootenays, seemingly retained less of their culture than the other newcomers. Round and clipped "rathers," "old boys," and "mother and father" have given way to "aye?," "mum," and "pop;" "Yanks" became "Americans," cousins in the old country became "Brits," and the British immigrants became "Canucks."[27]

During the same era, however, recruiters also crisscrossed the Italian peninsula, seeking new sources of labor. Since unification in the 1870s, the local conditions more and more had stimulated immigration. One popular legend recounted that the mayor of an Italian village, while greeting a national official, gave the following salutation: "The 5,000 members of my town greet you—the 2,000 that are in North America and the 3,000 presently preparing to leave." Indeed, soaring unemployment, stifling taxes, the continued struggle between North and South, droughts, floods, and overpopulation each played an important role in driving Italians from their homes and across the ocean to North America.[28]

Immigration had begun in the 1880s, reaching a height in 1914, when 24,722 Italians entered Canada. Labor contractors, agents from the C.P.R. and steamship companies, even local priests, teachers, and officials helped distribute handbills, circulars, and other pamphlets. But word-of-mouth discussions and letters proved the most powerful inducement. Normally the elder sons first went to neighboring European countries to augment the meager family incomes. Some of these early immigrants migrated as many as twenty times, always returning or, at least, sending back money to aid those that had remained.[29]

Most Italians entered Canada through Montreal. Eager to accept any work—for any work was better than none at all—they usually lacked the language skills that could have provided better access to the job markets. Often they took jobs requiring far less skill than they possessed. Wholesale labor contractors provided the connections. Antonio Cardasco, for example, boasted in the early 1900s that he could place, or displace, 10,000 Italian workers a day. Crowned on a cold winter day in January, 1904, as "King of the Italian Workers," he was special assistant to George Burns, Director of the Special Service Department of the C.P.R. Montreal, in fact, was the headquarters for the expanding railroad; hence it readily employed these new immigrants, exploiting their newness to the country, their lack of language, and their genuine desire to work. Italians, like their counterparts, the Irish on the Union Pacific, built most of the railroad west.[30]

But the C.P.R. also owned a copper smelter in Trail, British Columbia, an attractive lure to these immigrants. For there, full-time, stable work was available. Far removed from the frozen wastelands of the prairies and the uncertainties of labor contractors in Montreal, British Columbia seemed ideal. Word-of-mouth reports quickly spread. Luigi Tognotti, for example, heard about the smelter from his sister's husband, who had signed on with the C.P.R. in 1896 and had come to Trail in 1899. Tognotti, who had been a part-time orderly in Luca, a small city in Northern Italy, left the temporary work and arrived in Trail in 1901. Dutifully shipping money home, soon he had saved enough for his wife and three sons. Surprisingly entering through Ellis Island at the Port of New York, the family followed in 1909. Speaking no English, with little more than the money for passage and entry, they left only the elderly grandparents behind. By the time they reached Trail, their money, homemade bread, and

cheese were gone. But Gino, then nine, recalled that the "gulch was beautiful; not only was it Canada, but it was full of Italians and was home."[31]

Indeed, the gulch became home for 2,652 Italians by 1931. Ninety-five
percent of the immigrants lived there. "If at night you wanted to go for a
beer," Allan Tognotti recalled, "the parlor was only a two minute walk.
If you wanted a game of Italian cards, or play some pool, it was also two
minutes." Language and communication varied. An Italian newspaper and
radio station flourished, for many first-generation immigrants—including
Mama Tognotti—never learned to speak English. "She talked with her
hands," Gino reminisced, "and she was at her best with the Chinese vege-
table man. Neither one speaking any English, but away they would go.
Didn't seem to matter. We always got our vegetables for dinner." Homemade wines and liquor, card games, bocci, black bread, lodges, and
churches (Roman Catholic with Irish priests) began to appear. Allan,
Luigi's grandson, spoke "English at school, Italian at home, and Canadian
on the streets."[32]

Most of the Italians worked "up on the hill" at Cominco. The smelter,
in fact, dominated the town. Almost all the time everybody was happy.
Only two strikes, one in 1917 and another in 1974, disturbed the company
town and the Cominco plant. During the 1917 unrest, the Italian Counsel
traveled from Winnipeg—at C.P.R. expense—to speak to the workers; the
strike was broken in less than a month and blamed on "white union radi-
cals." Gino worked there from 1917 to 1964, never missing a day. The mill,
in fact, was his life. His brother, Rico Tognotti, was once replaced for his
vacation period by Herb Draper, who quit after a day, claiming that "no
white man would work in the zinc plant." Slowly the Italians became floor
bosses, then foremen at the plant; by 1940 they had proved their loyalty,
and many became workers in the production of heavy water for the American nuclear tests during the Second World War.[33]

Much has changed for the Italians of Trail since 1900. Ethnic foods,
games, language and relationships seemingly have been replaced by many
Western alternatives. While still in his teens, Gino preferred, in order,
"hockey, girls, cars, and clothes." Often he traveled; Los Angeles, New
York, and Italy were but a few of his vacation spots. Allan Tognotti, third
generation, has since moved out of the Gulch into East Trail, owns a
grocery store and has a swimming pool in his backyard. During his birthday, in fact, he served Scotch whiskey, roast beef, whipped potatoes and
corn. One of the most respected local officials in Trail, he prefers baseball,
hockey, hunting, and fishing as hobbies. Few Italian artifacts decorate
either Gino's or Allan's home. The community, in fact, looks prosperous,
pleasant, and North American.

Yet much remains of the Italian past in Trail. The Columbo Lodge still
attracts large numbers. Italian, as a language, while no longer a chief

vehicle of communication, is growing in both the schools and the homes. A real affection still exists for the family unit. The local history club now proudly stresses the ethnic background of Trail, while just twenty-five years ago a reputable account did not even use the words, "Italian," or "Italy." Proud of their accomplishments and successes, the Italian immigrants look back with curiosity to examine their past. Well aware that they have changed, they also realize that they have contributed to the culture of the Kootenays. "It is a different life here," Gino points out, "different altogether. But it is different because we made it that way. We wanted a better life when we came. Now we have it, and the Kootenays have their Italians. I love Canada," Gino concludes, "because I come over when I was a little kid. Now I'm seventy-six and Trail is the only place for me." "I'm a Canadian, that's true," Allan firmly contends, "but an Italian-Canadian."[34]

Other non-British immigrants, however, equally contributed to the mosaic of the West Kootenays. Driven from their homeland by persecution, discrimination, and prosecution, the Russian Doukhobors began to arrive in Canada in 1898. Mostly simple farmers, they were gentle pacifists who rejected the Bible, the worship of idols, and the religious ceremonies of the church, including marriage, baptism, communion, and other doctrines. "Marriage," explained Tom Oglow, a faithful Doukhobor for eighty-nine years, "is God's law. If you love her, she loves you that's God's witness. No need for anything else. Then you got to look after one another." They believed, in the words of Leo Tolstoy, one of their sympathizers, that "the Kingdom of God is within you." Not only did they disagree with the conventional Russian Orthodox Church, they also disapproved of certain governmental practices. Specifically they refused to comply with conscription in the 1890s, destroying and burning instead all the weapons issued by the government. Exiled to the Georgian Caucasus, many died of undernourishment, dysentery, and malaria; others simply deserted the cause; most remained as staunch as ever in their beliefs. Headed by Tolstoy, worldwide pressure eventually led to a Czarist decree in 1898, permitting the Doukhobors to leave Russia.[35]

At that time Canada was advertising to extend the prairie frontier. People, willing to work and of "sturdy stock," could settle the virgin lands and, in turn, stimulate trade with the eastern provinces. Clifford Sifton, Federal Minister for the Interior, had offered a grand scheme of "free land for new immigrants." But results had been discouraging; prairie-bound immigration dropped from 82,000 in 1891 to 23,000 in 1895. C.P.R. cars rushed eastward half empty; something had to be done. Since Russian Doukhobors seemed exceptional candidates to reverse the trend, almost 750,000 acres were offered to them near Yorkton, Saskatchewan. The C.P.R., realizing that most of the Doukhobors were arriving almost penniless, reduced rates west—the prosperity and expansion of the railroad depended on settlement of the prairies. "We had just the bare necessities," recalled Oglow, then thirteen, "a teapot, a couple of dishes, and one or two wooden spoons apiece."[36]

Energetic and ambitious, the Russians did not remain impoverished for long. With young and able-bodied men away working for money, older men, women, and children built sod houses, cleared the lands, planted the crops. Soon sixty-one villages were in place; brick factories, sawmills and flour mills dotted the countryside.

At first other settlers viewed the Doukhobors with curiosity; quickly, however, interest turned to distrust, then resentment. Claims that the Russians were "peculiar," "strange but polite," "different but industrious," became cries for education, loyalty oaths, and citizenship. David J. Goggin, nationally noted educator, demanded assimilation: "Gather the children of different races, creeds, and customs into the common school and 'Canadianize' them . . . though they may enter as Doukhobors, they will come out Canadians." When an Edmonton editor, Frank Oliver, who had originally opposed the Doukhobors in Alberta, stating that "the introduction of inferior settlers simply means the exclusion to a far greater degree of superior settlers," became Federal Minister of the Interior, he demanded that the Doukhobors sign an oath of allegiance to Canada. If they refused, he warned, within two months they would be deprived of their land. Although some of the Russians complied, most did not; so in 1907 eviction and foreclosure cost them 256,800 acres valued at over $11 million.[37]

Seeking isolation like the Mormons of Utah, the Doukhobors found the West Kootenays ideal for their needs; and too, British Columbia did not demand the loyalty oath. Beginning in 1908, over 6,000 Doukhobors came to the region by 1931. Again prosperity returned. Under the leadership of Peter Verigin, they bought 15,320 acres, built villages, sawmills, a large jam factory, and several brick factories. Cultivating the rich river benches and planting trees, they also built their own roads, ferries, and bridges. Collectivism, first tried in the West Kootenays, provided the group protection and unity. "We formed into a communal life," Oglow recounted, "in order to survive."[38]

By 1931, however, disruption and conflict had begun to divide the Russians. Education, a problem on the prairies, also resurfaced in British Columbia. Many settlers disagreed with public schooling. "I was never anti-education," Oglow pointed out, "but I'm very much anti-school system; the end result is always the same—assimilation." His son, however, remembered that "our family always insisted that you must have an education, as long as it didn't involve military service."[39] But other Russians did not leave the question up to the individual. The Sons of Freedom, a radical minority wing of the Doukhobors, sought through violence the retention of the status quo. Fires and bombings, in addition to nude protest parades, brought arrests, enforcement, and disapproval by the non-Russian community. All Doukhobors became equated with the radical camp; editorials, books, and articles universally condemned them collectively. "I remember passing Freedomite homes on the way to school," Paul Oglow recalled, "and they would turn their dogs on me, just a little kid." The death of Verigin, mysteriously killed in a train bombing in 1924, also significantly damaged solidarity. The depression forced the jam factory into bankruptcy; slowly the communal Christian Community of Universal Brotherhood began losing members—forty-three percent by 1940. And education also proved disruptive. "I went to public school," Paul noted, "unfortunate part was, it was always hard to get much education because on an average, every second year the school burned down." By selecting guards from among the community for twenty-four hour watch, school continued. "School was a luxury for us," Paul went on. "I didn't want to stay a farmer, so I tried to learn something."[40]

Much has changed in the Russian settlements of the West Kootenays. Many Russians no longer practice the rigors of the Doukhobor faith. They have left the land, preferring instead the business community, trades, or teaching. Some have joined other religious groups; marriage outside the faith or ethnic group, always a damaging force for such a religious sect, has also become more and more common. Prosperity too has altered the Doukhobor way of life. "Life-styles change," claimed Paul. "Even the way of life now is different—people don't deserve to be called Doukhobors any more. That's why I call myself Russian." "When the commune died," Tom conceded, "so did the Doukhobor ideal. The outside world came in and we went out."[41]

Yet similar to the Italian retention, much has also remained of the Russian culture. Tom Oglow, Doukhobor settler of eighty-nine years, has never eaten meat, has never strayed from the beliefs that brought him to Canada, has become famous for carving the same kinds of wooden spoons he brought from Russia in 1898. Now his grandson wants to learn the art. The Doukhobor Ladies Choir, singing always and only in Russian, is perhaps the most popular and most requested "folk" group in the Kootenays; they represented the area, in fact, at the Spokane World's Fair in 1974. An historical society dedicated to the preservation of the Doukhobor culture attracts many, while a Doukhobor Museum, funded by the Province, draws large numbers of guests—locals as well as tourists. There is a remarkable alliance, for example, between the American antiwar communalists and the Russians in the Slocan Valley who together seek an "alternative free school" for their children. On a more pragmatic front, Paul Oglow, second generation and in his fifties, has just begun to read Russian, a language that was introduced into the schools first in 1934. Successful as a businessman and gently urbane by character, Russian Paul Oglow (not Doukhobor) typified his people when he reflected on his youngest daughter's life-style: "She's more Doukhobor than me. Like her grandpa, she lives commonlaw, speaks of peace, eats no meat. Someday she may realize she's as Russian as she is Canadian."[42]

Society in the Kootenays, then, has been shaped and formed by diverse elements. Other groups—German, Scandinavian, and Ukrainian—also are representative here. While the popularized American "melting pot" myth certainly has not existed, neither has the equally popularized Canadian "vertical mosaic."[43] Assimilation, as defined by sociologists, is the "process by which different cultures, or individuals, or groups, are merged into a homogeneous unit. Ordinarily, the modifications must be made by the weaker or numerically inferior group."[44] Certainly the Canadians had attempted to weld the West into a single unit. Education seemingly became the universal tool for such a process throughout the region, pushed by both professionals and the public. Yet one important factor did not exist in the West—a large and overwhelming percentage of English and French citizens, members of the charter groups of Canadian society. Educator Goggin in his exhortations for assimilation proved both correct and incorrect. True, many of the ethnic children entering schools emerged as Canadians; what he failed to consider, however, was that Canadian was not necessarily synonymous with English. Perhaps Michael Novak, executive director of the Ethnic Millions Political Action Committees best summarized the West at the Second Canadian Conference on Multiculturalism when he poined out that "the culture here belongs to none of our ethnic groups. But nor does it belong to the English or the French."[45]

Such a modified Canadian society certainly has existed in the West Kootenays. While retaining many of their individual and group customs, the ethnic groups have also consciously and unconsciously merged many characteristics. Chinese restaurants serve borsch and spaghetti under the label of Canadian or Western foods. Golf foursomes, baseball teams, and hockey teams are composed of representatives of many different groups. Friendships, courtships, and professional occupations follow peer and scholarly mandates rather than ethnic ambitions. Perhaps the best example of multiculturalism, however, is Multifusion, the largest folk festival in Western Canada which annually occurs in March. Local poets present their work, while local artists stock a gallery. Ethnic images, despite the similarity of objects, still emerge from the canvas. Other artisans demonstrate immigrant crafts such as pottery, spoonmaking, and weaving—side by side work individuals of various heritage. Each evening, first special ethnic meals are served; then music follows—Scottish bagpipers and dancers, the Doukhobor Ladies Choir, Italian quartets, English madrigal singers, Oriental soloists, Canadian and American folksingers patiently take their turns. Then together they try a tune or two, finally joining in a Canadian version of Woody Guthrie's classic "This Land is Your Land." This is perhaps as close as these people come to demonstrating a regional identity.

So in spite of time and tremendous social and economic pressures, these groups have retained their churches, their clubs, their dances, and often their language. Proud of their heritage, they have maintained their cultures in a strange land that seemed determined to strip them of their past. What has emerged instead is a new social structure, neither ethnic nor English, but rather an evolutionary multicultural society. After years of pressure and intimidation, the residents of the West Kootenays have begun to recognize the diverse elements of their past. And that recognition inevitably will enhance the community in the years to come.

1. The best geographic survey of the West Kootenays remains International Joint Commission, *The Kootenay Valley: A Report on Certain Cases Involving Reclamation and the Development of Water Power in the Valley of the Kootenay River* (Ottawa: King's Printer, 1936).

2. For more information on the early isolation and development of the Kootenays, see John Fahey, *Inland Empire: D. C. Cobin and Spokane* (Seattle: Univ. of Washington Press, 1965), and Ronald Howard Meyer, "The Evolution of Railways in the Kootenays," M.A. Thesis Univ. of British Columbia, 1970.

3. For more information on the development of communication during the twentieth century see Donald E. Spritzer, "Waters of Wealth, The Story of the Kootenai River," report prepared for the U. S. Corps of Engineers (Washington, D.C.: U.S. Government Printing Office, 1973).

4. Wilson Duff, *The Indians of British Columbia* (Victoria: Provincial Museum of British Columbia, 1964); John S. Galbraith, *The Hudson's Bay Company as an Imperial Factor, 1821-1869* (Berkeley: Univ. of California Press, 1957); Richard Glover, ed., *David Thompson's Narrative, 1784-1812* (Toronto: Champlain Society, 1962).

5. Isabel M. L. Bescoby, "Some Social Aspects of the American Mining Advance into Cariboo and Kootenay," M.A. Thesis Univ. of British Columbia, 1935, pp. 32-40.

6. See the *Nelson Daily News*, June 15, 1943, and July 7, 1947; and Paul Phillips, *No Greater Power, A Century of Labour in B. C.* (Vancouver: Boas Foundation, 1967) pp. 11-45.

7. See the *Rossland Miner*, Nov. 10, 1894, and Sept. 16, 1896; Bescoby, "American Mining Advance," pp. 40-42; and David Scott and Edna Hanic, *Nelson: Queen City of the Kootenays* (Vancouver: Mitchell Press, 1972), pp. 11-23.

8. F. W. Howay, W. N. Sage, and H. F. Angus, *British Columbia and the United States* (Toronto: 1942), pp. 244-47; Martin Robin, *The Rush for the Spoils: The Company Province, 1871-1933* (Toronto: McClelland and Stewart, Ltd., 1972), pp. 20-25; George A. Tripp, "Transportation and Lead Smelters in the Kootenays: A Reconsideration," B. A. Honours Thesis Univ. of British Columbia, 1970, pp. 59-96.

9. The various groupings of Canadian society are described in John Porter, *The Vertical Mosaic: An Analysis of Social and Class Power in Canada* (Toronto:

Univ. of Toronto Press, 1965). While Porter's analysis has been challenged, debated, even refuted, it still provides an acceptable, if somewhat general and eastern, view of Canadian social stratification. The two "charter," or leading ethnic groups are British and French; all other groups are significantly below these two in economic gain, power, and status, according to Porter.

10. *Census of Canada, 1951,* Vol. X, Table 1; Porter, *Vertical Mosaic,* pp. 62-65.

11. R. H. Coates, *The Immigrant Program of Canada* (Toronto: Ryerson Press, 1926), pp. 177-94; Committee on Immigration and Colonization, *Canada's Child Immigrants* (Ottawa: King's Printer, 1925), pp. 3-11.

12. P. H. Bryce, *The Value to Canada of the Continental Immigrant* (n.p.: n.p., 1928), p. 138, as quoted in Porter, *Vertical Mosaic,* p. 64; Coates, *Immigrant Program,* pp. 181-83.

13. Coates, *Immigrant Program,* pp. 188-94; Howard Palmer, *Land of the Second Chance: A History of Ethnic Groups in Southern Alberta* (Lethbridge: The Lethbridge *Herald,* 1972), pp. 180-81; J. S. Woodsworth, *Strangers Within Our Gates* (Toronto: Missionary Society of the Methodist Church, 1909), p. 61.

14. Robert England, *The Central European Immigrant in Canada* (Toronto: Macmillan, 1929), p. 174; see also "British Immigration," *Queen's Quarterly* (Winter 1929), 131-44.

15. Stephen Leacock, *Economic Prosperity in the British Empire* (Toronto: Mac-Millan, 1930), p. 196.

16. W. C. Smith, *A Study in Canadian Immigration* (Toronto: Ryerson Press, 1920), pp. 54-71, 178-83; Committee on Immigration, *Child Immigrants,* pp. 1-26; England, "British Immigration," pp. 133-38; Stanley C. Johnson, *A History of Emigration from the United Kingdom to North America, 1763-1912* (London: Frank Cass and Co., 1966), pp. 63-66.

17. *Census of Canada,* 1931, Vol. III, Table 39; Johnson, *Emigration from the U. K.,* p. 63.

18. The exact numbers are difficult to locate, since the *Census of Canada, 1931,* reported all Britons in the Kootenays—first or fifteenth generation—under the same columns. The 23,000 figure, however, was a guess of the *Nelson Daily News,* June 26, 1937.

19. Canadian Pacific Railroad, *The Resources and Climate of the Kootenay, Boundary, and Okanagan Districts of British Columbia* (Calgary: Herald Co., 1905), pp. 9-10.

20. Canadian Pacific Railroad, *Resources,* pp. 11-14, 35-36; Scott and Hanic, *Nelson,* p. 101.

21. Interview with Margaret Draper, June 26, 1976; W. F. Teetzel, *British Columbia Commission of Inquiry: Report of the Commissioner Appointed to Make An Inquiry Into the Claims of Certain Persons Who Entered Upon Crownlands in the District of the Kootenay Under Reserve for Reclamation Purposes* (Victoria: King's Printer, 1908), pp. 8-12.

22. Interview with Margaret Draper, July 6, 1975.

23. Scott and Hanic, *Nelson,* p. 106.

24. C. F. J. Galloway, *The Call of the West* (n.p.: n.p., 1917), p. 17.

25. Robin, *Company Province,* pp. 42-47.

26. Interviews with Margaret Draper, June 26, July 6, Aug. 8, 1975; Interviews with Herb Draper, July 9, 16, 23, 30, 1975; Interviews with Gervane Draper, July 5, 6, 15, 1975.

27. Interviews with Margaret and Herb Draper, 1975. Observations, of course,

are equally important sources of information during the interview sessions. The author has included some observations throughout this paper.

28. For the conditions in Italy, 1880-1930, see H. Hearder, ed., *A Short History of Italy, From Classical Times to the Present Day* (London: Cambridge Univ. Press, 1966); John A. Crow, *Italy: A Journey Through Time* (New York: Harper and Row, 1965); and Muriel Grindrod, *Italy* (London: Ernest Bern, Ltd., 1968).

29. Andrew F. Rolle, *The Immigrant Upraised* (Norman: Univ. of Oklahoma Press, 1968), pp. 27-31; A. V. Spada, *The Italians in Canada* (Ottawa: Italo-Canadian Ethnic and Historical Research Center, 1969), pp. 8-15.

30. Spada, *The Italians in Canada*, pp. 9-14; H. A. Citroen, *European Emigration Overseas, Past and Future* (The Hague: Nighoff Co., 1951), pp. 3-8.

31. Interview with Gino Tognotti, July 10, 1975; Interview with Allan Tognotti, Aug. 3, 1975.

32. Interviews with Gino Tognotti, July 10, July 16, 1975; Interviews with Allan Tognotti, Aug. 3, Aug. 10, 1975; *Census of Canada, 1931*, Vol. I, Table 47.

33. Interview with Herb Draper, July 23, 1975; Interviews with Gino Tognotti, July 10, July 16, 1975; Interview with Allan Tognotti, Aug. 3, 1975; *Trail News*, Dec. 14, 1975.

34. Interviews with Gino Tognotti, July 10, July 16, July 26, 1975; Interviews with Allan Tognotti, Aug. 3, Aug. 10, Aug. 12, 1975.

35. John P. Zubek and Patricia A. Solberg, *Doukhobors at War* (Toronto: 1957), pp. 7-15; P. N. Maloff, "The Doukhobors, their Life, History, and Struggle," Manuscript in the Possession of the Doukhobor Historical Society, pp. 14-23; Koozma J. Tarasoff, *A Pictorial History of the Doukhobors* (Saskatoon: Prairie Printers, 1969), pp. 2-14; George Woodcock and Ivan Avakumovic, *The Doukhobors* (Toronto: Oxford Univ. Press, 1968), pp. 11-40; Interview with Tom Oglow, July 18, 1975.

36. Tarasoff, *Doukhobor Pictorial History*, pp. 14, 67; Zubek and Solberg, *Doukhobors at War*, p. 21; Interview with Tom Oglow, July 8, 1975.

37. Tarasoff, *Doukhobor Pictorial History*, pp. 19-87; Robert S. Patterson, ed., *Profiles of Canadian Educators* (Toronto: D. C. Heath, 1974), pp. 175-80; Palmer, *Land of the Second Chance*, p. 203; *Victoria Daily Times*, Sept. 13, 1907, March 16, 1908, May 23, 1908.

38. *Census of Canada*, 1931, Vol. I, Table 47; *Victoria Daily Times*, June 6, 1925; Tarasoff, *Doukhobor Pictorial History*, pp. 114-17; Interviews with Tom Oglow, July 8, July 15, 1975.

39. Interview with Tom Oklow, July 15, 1975; Interview with Paul Oglow, July 25, 1975.

40. Interviews with Paul Oglow, July 25, Aug. 5, Aug. 8, 1975; Christians of the Universal Brotherhood, "The Message of the Doukhobors," undated pamphlet, pp. 45-55.

41. Interviews with Paul Oglow, July 25, Aug. 5, Aug. 8, 1975; Interviews with Tom Oglow, July 8, July 15, July 18, 1975.

42. Interviews with Paul and Tom Oglow, 1975.

43. For critiques of the popular statements on acculturation, see Nathan Glazer and Daniel Patrick Moynihan, *Beyond the Melting Pot* (Cambridge: M.I.T. Press, 1963), and James L. Heap, ed., *Everybody's Canada: The Vertical Mosaic Reviewed and Re-examined* (Toronto: Burns and MacEochern, Ltd., 1974).

44. Henry P. Fairchild, ed., *Dictionary of Sociology* (Ames: Littlefield and Adams, 1959), pp. 276-77.
45. Government of Canada, Minister Responsible for Multiculturalism, *Multinews*, April/May, 1976, p. 3.

Literary Interpreters

Examining the claim that the Pacific
Northwest has failed to evolve a distinctive
regional literature, George Venn here
demonstrates that a more searching study
of the treatment of physical environment
by Northwest writers may lead to different
conclusions. In addition, the essay presents
a fresh and insightful means of surveying
and classifying Northwest literature
from its historical beginnings to the
present. George Venn did his graduate
work at the University of Montana and
now teaches writing and literature at
Eastern Oregon State College in La
Grande, where he provides a strong
regional and historical perspective for his
students. In addition to encouraging their
creative efforts, Professor Venn himself
publishes critical essays and poetry.

Continuity in Northwest Literature

George Venn

Two recent commentators on regional literature in the Northwest assert that no identifiable regional literature has emerged in the country drained by the Snake, Columbia, and Fraser Rivers. Writing in 1972, Robert Cantwell concludes that the recognized writers of the region do not "possess any sharply defined characteristics that identify them as belonging to the region." This view finds another spokesman in Richard Etulain, who states he can not "find a group of writers in the Northwest whose writings reveal common characteristics which may be expressive of their regional background."[1] Similar statements have also been made by other writers and critics; although their arguments and evidence diverge, they all converge on the fact of an apparently amorphous literature.

At the same time that these writers and critics define their doubts about regional literature, many of them also agree on a point which is generally touched in passing. For instance, Cantwell's penultimate sentence reads: "It is possible that a new examination of the history of the old Oregon country will reveal that its overlooked educational power—the scenery—has been exercising its influence from the start." In his "Preface" to *Five Poets of the Pacific Northwest* (Seattle: University of Washington Press, 1964), Robin Skelton writes that "the poets have all been deeply affected by their physical environment. It is obvious that, in this area, the landscape must have a powerful influence upon the art created within it." In a recent interview, Richard Hugo, one of the poets included in Skelton's volume, states explicitly, "I think maybe in the Northwest poets there is a tendency to use more landscape. . . . There's just less of the outside world gets into Eastern poetry."[2] If such statements are coupled with a reading of the writing about exploration and settlement, a study of Northwest poetry, and a cursory examination of Northwest literary history, it may be that environment and the human response to it will emerge as one source of continuity in the region's literature that cannot be easily dismissed. Although I am not yet prepared to say such a source of continuity is the distinctive characteristic of writing in the Northwest, I believe a survey of Northwest literature might describe a more continuous regional vision than writers and critics here previously claimed and might also serve to describe how a literature evolves under frontier conditions. In such an effort at survey, criticism, and synthesis, I believe I am following up on suggestions made by the contributors to V. L. O. Chittick's volume, *Northwest Harvest* (New York: Macmillan, 1948), especially those of Harold G. Merriam in his paper "Does the Northwest Believe in Itself?"

I. 1781-1868

In this period, from the time of the first journal kept by a sea explorer describing the Oregon country up to the year of publication of Joaquin Miller's first collection of poems, most of the people who held pencils or pens in their hands in the Pacific Northwest were not what we would today call writers or poets. But what they wrote in journals, diaries, autobiographies, and letters constitutes what may be called a collective folk epic—not of going home—but of discovering, coming to, and settling in a new home. When read as a body, this literature is replete with *mythos,* heroes, a transcendent God, unknown country, dangerous terrain, mystical Indians, and hazardous passages. Read continuously for two weeks or a month, this literature constitutes a full document of "the mythic beginning," and what its writers chose and avoided can be seen as the roots for a future tradition. Writers during the period of exploration and discovery, such as Robert Stewart, were generally charged with recording the physical facts of the region—flora, fauna, natives, weather, and terrain—and usually thought of themselves as wandering reporters or alien observers sojourning in the wilderness. Journey is their obvious form and ordeal in profane space is their frequent theme. The dominant tone in many writers is often a combination of gloom, nostalgia, and depression varied occasionally by writers like David Thompson and Theodore Winthrop, who celebrated the beauty of the Promised Land, and Simon Fraser and Alexander Mac-Kenzie, who are both known for their sophisticated reporting. Generally, explorers moved through a new land they had to name and map, and most had neither the time nor the inclination to interpret or discover the spirit of the place or the people who inhabited it. Writers of Oregon Trail diaries and journals, another source of this collective folk epic, also focus most frequently on the facts of environment—how far they traveled, if they had water and grass, and where tomorrow. A number of these writers also praise the fertility of the new land or mourn its desolation. Like the style of many exploration journals, emigrant diaries tend to be terse and do not investigate interior life. In general, they all report the physical details of wilderness that would allow themselves and others to orient themselves in the new space. Thus, the environment and their response to it—as something to be endured while it was discovered—became their major subject.

I believe we can claim that large body of original writing as a collective folk epic and see it as the beginning of a Northwest literature. The November 12, 1805, entry in the journal of William Clark illustrates the points I am making about form, subject, style, and tone, and demonstrates how accessible such prose still is today:

> A Tremendious wind from the S.W. about 3 oClock this morning with Lightineng and hard claps of Thunder, and Hail which Continued untill 6 oClock a.m. when it became light for a Short time, then the heavens became suddenly darkened by a black cloud from the S.W. and rained with great violence until 12 oClock, the waves tremendious brakeing with great fury against the rocks and trees on which we were encamped. Our Situation is dangerous. we took the advantage of a low *tide* and moved our camp around a point to a Small wet bottom, at the Mouth of a Brook, which we had not observed when we came to this cove; for its being verry thick and obscured by drift trees and thick bushes. It would be distressing to See our Situation, all wet and colde our bedding also wet, (and the robes of the party which compose half our bedding is rotten and we are not in a Situation to supply their places) in a wet bottom scerecely large enough to contain us our baggage half a mile from us, and Canoes at the mercy of the waves, althou Secured as well as possible.[3]

To dismiss Clark's writing as simple historical artifact or to say that all this was simply written for Jefferson is to miss what it expresses about the human condition in new space: the environment was upon Clark and his men, even intimidating them. Clark writes without specific names because he is new and not at home. He did not know what was out there, how it could be used, or how he and his men would have to change in order to survive. For settlers, diaries and journals show that in some cases men and women went mad under these conditions in which language, culture, and history had not yet established relationships between people and the environment that would allow them a greater chance of survival. Although the literal facts of such experiences seem to be their only significant dimension, what those facts *express* about the human condition in new space also needs to be understood.

This need to understand such writing on a symbolic level is particularly important because of the attraction of the folk epic to later novelists and poets who constantly return to it in much the same way that writers in other cultures constantly return to their epics and myths—as sources of expression for the true human condition at the origin, at *the beginning*. The presence of this epic in *Tale of Valor* by Vardis Fisher, *The Land is Bright* by Archie Binns, *The Big Sky* by A. B. Guthrie, *The Earthbreakers* by Ernest Haycox, *Swift Flows the River* by Nard Jones, and *Trask* by Don Berry—to name a few novelists and novels—demonstrates that this epic is one of the most productive sources of recent literature. That contemporary poets in the Northwest have used two of the stances from this epic—the journal of traveling through unknown territory in search of sacred space as seen in William Stafford, and the autobiography of discovery in profane space as found in Richard Hugo—attests to its usefulness and durability.[4] The epic of man moving across unknown land and writing out his encounter with it continues in the books of such recent Northwest visitors as Edwin Way Teale in *Autumn Across America*, in Robert Cantwell's *The Hidden Northwest*, and in the recently published journal titled *The Pacific Crest Trail*. Understood symbolically, the epic of discovering new space and the act of writing out the human response to that new space has defined and directed much of our literature.

II. 1868-1919

If the early collective folk epic shows that the environment and the human response to it were the requisite materials for writing in the region, what followed in this next period was an extended naming and cataloging of environment. Such an impulse, which found national expression in the poetry of Walt Whitman, was carried on with difficulty here because of a transplanted set of literary techniques and attitudes that allowed description and inventory of the new place to continue, but without any new perception of it. For instance, the Columbia "murmurs plaintively," the moon is a Queen, the sun is Venus, the west is purple. British topographical terms like *wold*, *mead*, *glen*, *dale*, and *brae* appear throughout the poetry. Seas have breasts, rivers have silver tongues, brooks babble and winds whisper. Unlike their predecessors, who had probably not been reading the publications of the Hakluyt Society or exploration diaries, these writers were bound to a preconceived poetic vision that was designed to embody the facts of a settled agrarian territory.[5] Such a poetic vision could not encompass the environment and lives of settlers on a frontier where the Cayuse were still feared and where people were surrounded by millions of acres of wilderness.

Tied to such a preconceived vision, most poets could only write out their predictable jargon of an idyllic pastoral landscape and then try to find an audience for their poetry in places like London, as Joaquin Miller did, where the British still believed in their own poetics. But in the Northwest, I sense that no matter how many times Joaquin Miller wrote

> As proud Columbia frets his shore
> Of sombre, boundless wood and wold,
> And lifts his yellow sands of gold
> In plaintive murmurs evermore,[6]

and no matter how many times he described Oregon, "The Great Emerald Land" in these terms—

> I heard their shouts like sounding hunter's horn,
> The lowing herds made echoes far away[7]

—I doubt that anyone in the Northwest believed that such writing embodied the Northwest experience of environment. The terms and perceptions are clearly British, and we expect to see Squire Thomas Gray riding through the sagebrush after rattlesnakes and coyotes with his hounds. Juxtaposed with this entry from Robert Stewart's *On the Oregon Trail*, the contrast between pastoral England and the Northwest experience of wilderness is clear:

> The sensations excited on this occasion and by the view of an unknown and untravelled wilderness are not such as arise in the artificial solitude of parks and gardens, for there one is apt to indulge in a flattering notion of self-sufficiency, as well as a placid indulgence of voluntary delusions; where as the phantoms which haunt a desert are want, misery, and danger, the evils of dereliction rush upon the mind; man is made unwilling acquainted with his own weaknesses, and meditation shows him only how little he can sustain and how little he can perform.[8]

In the first two periods of Northwest literature writers made the environment and their response to it their recurring subject. While the writers of the collective epic were creating the first verbal maps of new space, the first generation writers could not, basically, front the facts of wilderness frontier experience in language. Instead of deriving their language from the environment confronting them, they took language, imagery, and vision from the historical poetic tradition of a settled country. The inability of that tradition to embody the Northwest experience of and response to environment was intensified by an even greater inadequacy in the Genesis *mythos* which separated man from his environment.[9] Coming to new space with a "mythology that married us to rock and hill" (as Yeats said it in *The Trembling Veil*), first generation writers brought instead a mythology that declared our divine right to exploit, conquer, and subdue the environment and the people in it for exclusively human purposes. While the writers of the folk epic could focus on the physical facts of new space, the first generation writer had not only to continue to map and inventory but also had to interpret that space in order to be at home in it. With only a mythology of conquest and without a language of terrain or a tradition that could embody wilderness frontier experience, they could only grope backward for British terms, Greek and Roman gods and goddesses, and a pastoral tradition.[10]

III. 1919-1946

In 1919, H. G. Merriam at the University of Montana founded what began as a campus periodical but later became the first major Northwestern regional magazine, *The Frontier*, and in Portland in 1923, Col. E. Hofer founded *The Lariat*. As *The Lariat's* patron and editor, Hofer described his magazine's mission:

> *The Lariat* might be called a volunteer captain in the lists of literary militancy. The fight is for undenatured nourishment to the popular mind, that the "conscience of the people" may be such as a free country may depend on. The past decade has been one of political and literary swindle. Hot air has been blown into everything, giving distention and inflation to every living avenue. A people with a conscience will react against this, and safety to the world of common good (not democracy) depends on how large a percent of the thinking humans are thinking for truth and beauty and brotherhood.[11]

In his editorial for the first regional issue of his magazine (1927), H. G. Merriam articulated the vision that he brought to the editorship of *The Frontier* for nearly 20 years:

> The Northwest is industrially alive and agriculturally alive; it needs to show itself spiritually alive. Culturally, it has too long accepted uncourageous, unindigenous "literary" expression of writers too spiritually imitative and too uninspired. We in this territory need to realize that . . . the roots for literature among us should be in our own rocky ground, not in Greenwich Village dirt or Mid-west loam.[12]

These two magazines and their contrasting editors and editorial policies embody the continuing tension between the collective epic and the transplanted poetic vision. In contrast with *The Lariat's* uncritical publication of anything that seemed "poetic," Merriam could not accept a poetry in which the preconceived vision of environment was dominant, and his editorial clearly expresses his opposition to the tradition of mimicry and easy pastoralism.

However, certain changes soon began to occur, as a reading of Merriam's 1931 anthology will show. Most of the old Briticisms for terrain have been replaced by more concrete local language. Black bears, lupin, sagebrush, hop-vines, moose, seagulls, crows—these and other similar nouns appear consistently in *Northwest Verse*. And the babbling brooks and murmuring rivers, the hunting horns and kings and queens have disappeared. Although the movement away from the transplanted tradition has begun, most of the poems in the anthology still only describe environment. In fact, Merriam declares in his "Preface" that he was overrun with poems that were descriptive "especially of the sea and of the sky with the sun and moon and stars and clouds." Thus, the style and language has begun to change, creating a kind of hybrid of the folk epic's language of immediate experience of environment written in the prosody of the transplanted vision which found such popularity in Portland.

But two writers who had grown up in the region were impatient with this hybrid and the dominance of the first generation tradition of mere description in pretty phrases. H. L. Davis and James Stevens blasted that imported tradition in their 1927 pamphlet, *Status Rerum*, which begins in this rhetorical fashion:

> The present condition of literature in the Northwest has been mentioned apologetically too long. Something is wrong with Northwest literature. It is time people were bestirring themselves to find out what it is . . . . Is there something about the climate, or the soil which inspires people to write tripe? Is there some occult influence which catches them young, shapes them to be instruments out of which tripe, and nothing but tripe, may issue?[13]

In a later issue of *The Frontier*, Davis identifies in a guest editorial the problem's source more succinctly: "We began here with a new way of life, new rhythms, new occupations. We have failed to make that freshness part of ourselves." (By extension this applies, of course, to the environment remaining outside the language of poetry and fiction.) James Stevens also blasts the literary establishment of *The Lariat* in a scathing satirical article published in *The American Mercury* in 1929. His objections to *The Lariat* are formidable, but most of his attack is aimed at the poetic practice of mere description of environment, or a frivolous or trite treatment of it, that do not join man and the space around him. Stevens illustrates the discontinuity among language, experience, and environment by writing about his first reading of the magazine:

> My first encounter with the *Lariat* occurred when I was laboring on the green chain of the sawmill at Westport, Oregon. I was on the night shift, which ended at three in the morning. At the end of one night of labor, when a wet wind hammering up from the Columbia River bar had made work under the open shed of the green chain an infernal misery, I discovered a copy of the *Lariat* in a chair of the hotel lobby. . . . As I gnawed my plug for a heartening chew, I idly turned the pages of the pretty publication.

Stevens finds the following poem by Col. E. Hofer, "Madonna of the Poor"—

> She ne'er beheld the birth of day,
> Or saw the infant morn born softly forth
> On noiseless pinions of the air,
> Laid in the pearly shell of dawn
> And carried joyous on the shoulders of the sun.
> She ne'er lived through a radiant day
> When all the earth with feeling thrills
> Beneath caresses of her lover bold. . . .

—and writes: "I quit there, partly because I felt myself blushing, but mainly because I had swallowed my chew."[14] In both style and statement, Stevens shows how clearly language, experience, and environment did not meet, as earlier they had not met in Joaquin Miller and others. The facts of weather and work built into Stevens's language instead echo the language of the folk epic and make the poem seem silly and affected.

The impatience of H. L. Davis with the poetry and standards of *The Lariat* is easier to understand when juxtaposed with his own poetry because it shows clearly a new relationship with and response to environment in Northwest literature. His poem "The Rain Crow" illustrates his advance:

> While women were still talking near this dead friend,
> I came out into a field, where evergreen berry vines
> Grew over an old fence, with rain on their leaves;
> And would not have thought of her death, except for a few
> Low sheltered berry leaves: I believed the rain
> Could not reach them; but it rained on them every one.
> So when we thought this friend safest and most kind,
> Resetting young plants against winter, it was she
> Must come to be a dead body. And to think
> That she knew so much, and not that she would die!
> Not that most simple thing—for her hands, or her eyes.
>
> Dead. There were prints in the soft spaded ground
> Which her knees made when she dug her tender plants.
> Above the berry leaves the black garden and all the land
> Steamed with rain like a winded horse, appeared strong.
> And the rain-crow's voice, which we took for a sign of rain,
> Began like a little bell striking the leaves.
> So I sat listening to this bird's voice,
> And thought that our friend's mouth now, its "Dead, I am
>   dead,"
> Was like the rain-crow sounding during the rain:
> As if rain were a thing none of us had ever seen.[15]

Like many of Davis's poems, which began to appear in *The Frontier* shortly after it was founded, "The Rain Crow" begins with environment, as did the collective epic. But Davis then moves beyond mere description; rain, berry leaves, crows, allow the poet to objectify in language the experience of human life and death in an immediate locale. Such writing becomes possible when the poet has internalized environment, taken it as part of himself, and watches and listens and feels for the truth it expresses about the spirit of place, the moment, and the people. The image of mortality is fresh and the language is fresh because Davis is willing to name and name again and again; thus through environment he becomes articulate. His language touches the place because the place has been taken personally. It is fair to state that Davis's poetry shows, for the first time in the Northwest since the folk epic, that naming is more than mapping an external environment; such externals are also a means of binding environment to the internal universe of human experience.

In fact, Davis is the first Northwest poet literally to pack his poems with local nouns as he does in these lines from "After Love":

> Here I would invent praise, and have learned no other than
> to name
> the kinds of grass here: the great bunches of blue
> windflowers that leak shining water; big-stemmed vetch;
> yellow and black snapdragons; wild strawberry runners;
> Cheat-and-ribgrass with white pollen rimming its dark
> heads
>
> . . . .
>
> And I am not ashamed praising by count this grass
> standing in the wind.[16]

As Gertrude Stein has said about other writers, Davis was "drunk with nouns." Having learned how "to name earth sea and sky and all that was in them was enough to make him live and love in names, and that is what poetry is it is a state of knowing and feeling a name," and by extension, a place. This immediate and specific unity of poet, environment, and language is the dominant presence in Davis's poems. By saying these names, Davis is showing us what *The Lariat* poets could not show us—that he had seen the Northwest and touched it with language that would make it possible to interpret human experience in new space.

In *The Frontier* and the writing of H. L. Davis and James Stevens, it is again clear that environment and the human response to it were the sources and materials for literature, while in *The Lariat* it is clear that the sources and materials for literature were the conventions of an imported literary tradition. This tension between the folk epic and the transplanted vision fostered numerous literary quarrels, and I understand that the repercussions of *Status Rerum* are still audible today in certain circles. Certainly, the imported tradition can still be found among the newspaper column poets and various local and state poetry societies, and also, no doubt, in schools and colleges. But the larger disagreement between the two magazines arises here quite clearly. In response to the most demanding questions of our literature—"Where are we?" and "How shall we live here?"—*The Lariat's* reply was basically to perpetuate and even exaggerate a poetic tradition of man separated from environment and bound exclusively to a historical past. In contrast, *The Frontier* responded by advocating a literature that would unite man and environment through a language of the new place.

IV. 1946-present

With the arrival of four new literary immigrants between 1947 and 1949 —Theodore Roethke, William Stafford, Leslie Fiedler, and Bernard Malamud—these questions and the continuous and conflicting answers to them were more sharply defined. In the pre-Northwest poems of Theodore Roethke, his affinity for the tradition of Davis, Stevens, and Merriam is stated quite explicitly. For instance, these lines in "Feud"—

> There's canker at the root, your seed
> Denies the blessing of the sun,
> The light essential to your need.
> Your hopes are murdered and undone.[17]

—articulate Roethke's consciousness of the inadequate *mythos* of a people separated from their environment and trying to be at home by conquest alone. He resolves this dispute personally in another pre-Northwest poem, "In Praise of Prairie," with these final lines:

> Here distance is familiar as a friend.
> The feud we kept with space comes to an end.[18]

This, I believe, declares a posture where subject and object coalesce as they had in some of the poems of H. L. Davis.

William Stafford's alignment with Davis, Merriam, and Stevens is built into many statements and poems, but his most recent published statement on how the material for art and unity with self and place emerge appears in an article, "Having Become a Writer: Some Reflections":

> The world was conspiring to teach me the lesson that is upon us now in the current literary scene: a new poem or story or novel or play can be traced back through earlier poems etc., and endless games can be played with analyses of influences from literature; but the plain truth of the matter is that any literary work must rely for its effects on bonuses and reverberations that derive from the original resonance between human beings and their total experience, not from that little special tangent that comes from the Literary Succession . . . the way toward a fuller life in the arts must come by way of each person's daily experience. To deny that experience—even to veer from it in a minor way—is a false step.[19]

This is the kind of statement that H. G. Merriam was making throughout his nineteen-year editorship of *The Frontier* and also the kind of statement, setting aside the pamphleteer's rhetoric, that Davis and Stevens were making in *Status Rerum*. This confluence of Stafford and Roethke with *The*

Frontier, Davis, and Stevens, all favoring what Stafford himself had earlier called "an immediate relation to felt life" was an important contribution because it made the sources of mature art more local—hence more universal—and moved attentive regional writers even further from the traditions of Colonel Hofer and *The Lariat*.

In contrast with Stafford and Roethke, Leslie Fiedler and Bernard Malamud acted out in both criticism and fiction the most recent statements of the very *mythos*—man is bound only to human history, not to place—that *The Frontier* had challenged. In his essays on Montana, Leslie Fiedler more or less declared his condescension to the Northwest by assuming that local philistines could not see the mountains because of the movies, and we could not see ourselves except in Rousseau's mirror. (It was this kind of critical stance that later prompted W. H. Auden to note that Fiedler had no sense of landscape.)

In Malamud's *A New Life*, we see Levin's inability to respond to the environment or engage it in any significant way as the earmark of his non-Northwest status and his derivation from a homocentric *mythos* that could not include man's unity with environment as part of its ethical structure. Levin's preoccupation with an exclusively human world exemplifies the tradition later Northwest writers have explicitly rejected, as may be seen in the work of Gary Snyder, who is the direct antithesis of Levin. It is a hallmark of Malamud's artistic acuity that he could see that even in Corvallis in the 1950s the major drama was not exclusively human. Even though *A New Life* cannot address the spatial and environmental questions that concern Gary Snyder, the novel remains an excellent description of what might be a developing distinctive quality in Northwest literature —namely, that literary material cannot be derived here from exclusively human relationships in time; our literature must also include the presence and influence of space and our responses to it.

It is also important to recognize that Roethke and Stafford both inherited a territory and a milieu from Davis, Stevens, and Merriam where the need for new teachers who could bring memorable language and local environment together had been expressed. It should be remembered that the second prong of the attack in *Status Rerum* was made against teachers of poetry and fiction in the regional universities who had been drawn into supporting the transplanted vision and who even encouraged writers to imitate the hack western and grind out the "snowflake school" poem. By example and by emphasis on technique, Roethke unknowingly provided what Davis and Stevens had described as lacking twenty years earlier. And the work of William Stafford in regional writers' conferences continues to provide a similar contribution. Walter Van Tilburg Clark and Vardis Fisher offered comparable, three-dimensional teaching at the University of Montana during the years they were in residence there, and the Rocky

Mountain Writers Conference and the University of Washington Writers
Conferences initiated by Roethke began to fill that pedagogical void.
There was substantial confluence between the conditions of regional poetry
and culture and the arrival of Stafford and Roethke. I doubt, however, that
the same case could be made for either Fiedler or Malamud, although their
influence also has been continuous as both poets and teachers.

Although I can describe only a small part of Theodore Roethke's contribution to Northwest literature—Richard Hugo and John Haislip have
written excellent articles on this subject already[20]—I want to declare briefly
what I believe his contributions were to this continuous tradition of making
the environment and the human response to it the recurring subject of
Northwest literature. His first contribution—that language is a means to
unity with place—is fully articulated in his poem "The Rose" (1964)
which begins,

> There are those to whom place is unimportant,
> But this place, where sea and fresh water meet,
> Is important—
> Where the hawks sway out into the wind,
> Without a single wingbeat,
> And eagles sail low over the fir trees,
> And the gulls cry against the crows
> In the curved harbors,
> And the tide rises up against the grass
> Nibbled by sheep and rabbits.[21]

To place this poem in a Northwest context, I want also to quote an H. L.
Davis poem from *Proud Riders* (1942) which opens in nearly the same
way on a comparable scene:

> ### New Birds
> Now all of the snow's gone from the high desert, now
>   the frost
> Lets go of the ground in the deep draws, we find
> And recognize and enumerate new birds.
> The blue bird's the first comer back to the dead grass range.
> Out of some waterless gray rock-break, his low voice
> Utters a song almost tuneless; but his blue wings
> Are bright like gay innocent music. The brown thrush,
> Colored like old hay weathered in the rain, then sings
> At evening, when all's darkened except water. Then concealed
> Among dark pastures of the desert, he sings his hurt.
> The loud-voiced little yellow-hammers shine by day,
> The color of new sagebrush blossoms. Red-winged blackbirds

Blazing at the wing-joints with scarlet like the blaze
Of naked red willows in the black creek-beds, flock and talk.
The thorn-brush jolts with hundreds of bright black-bodied
Birds joking over their new country. Then come swans.
Dark wild swans come from the cane marshes in the south,
And pass, long-throated and still-mouthed. Then white geese
Trail, reaching across the dark sky, broad-winged as eagles,
But flapping their broad wings. Silence follows them.
No other new birds follow after these.

Both poets have perceived the function of naming as a means of establishing unity with place; the place is important, must be seen, and is a means to metaphor. For Davis, the return of spring birds creates a mood of qualified hope, while for Roethke, the scene begins to engage him at the beginning of his journey out of himself. Davis's opening lines are not indicative of his subsequent intention or mood, while Roethke's are indicative, and Davis seems to be much more interested in the process of naming (getting the names right) while Roethke seems to be interested in both the external objects *and* the music of the language which names them. As the poems develop, Roethke continues another full stanza of naming shore birds while Davis introduces a contrasting stanza about birds that have wintered over on the high desert. In the third stanza, Roethke opens with his second statement—"I sway outside myself / Into the darkening current."—thus intensifying his impulse toward unity with environment through naming the external landscape. In the same pivotal, transitional position, Davis says of the winter birds, "Without their presences, / I'd have been too lonely to live on this bare plain." Roethke then continues to catalogue and expand the dramatic confluence between poet and environment for some ten additional stanzas until, in the fourth section, he comes to the end of swaying and articulates his unity with place:

Near this rose, in this grove of sun-parched, wind-warped
   madronas,
Among the half-dead trees, I came upon the true ease of
   myself,
As if another man appeared out of the depths of my being,
And I stood outside myself,
Beyond becoming and perishing,
A something wholly other,
As if I swayed out of the wildest wave alive,
And yet was still.
And I rejoiced in being what I was:
In the lilac change, the while reptilian calm,
In the bird beyond the bough, the single one

With all the air to greet him as he flies,
The dolphin rising from the darkening waves;

And in this rose, this rose in the sea-wind,
Rooted in stone, keeping the whole of light,
Gathering to itself sound and silence—
Mine and the sea-wind's.

To this point, it would appear that, with the exception of attention to music in the language, there is an appealing similarity. Naming of the environment has led Roethke to transcendence in the same way that winter birds have led Davis away from self-consciousness and loneliness during the bleak winter. But the comparison ends there because Davis continues for another five lines of simile that apply his catalog of new and old birds to an unidentified woman:

It is the same with my beloved as with new birds.
Old thoughts, that were my company when I lived alone,
Under her beauty's and youth's energy, have been lost.
I strive to recover them, to put them all in words,
Thinking they'll help me again, when she is gone.[22]

What began years apart in the Northwest as a similar act of naming the external environment, and what appears to be leading both poets to unity with environment, has suddenly turned dissimilar with Davis's ending. While Roethke's ending expands, intensifies, and dramatizes his achievement of unity with place, Davis spins off into abstractions and rhetoric that close off possibilities of transcendence, exclude the reader from the poem, tack on a new question of interior life, and reduce the catalog of birds to a simple comparison. Although Davis has carefully attended to the environment and its names and has achieved a kind of metaphor with the first two stanzas, he is unable to bring together interior landscape and the exterior environment in his ending. In Davis's best poems, like "The Rain Crow," he shows he is capable of binding together man, environment, and language throughout the poem, but he was unable to achieve that unity here because he could not bring his entire internal life to the entire poem. When "New Birds" gets too self-revealing, Davis pulls back and the voice goes soft. For Roethke, the poet of "Open House," moving back was impossible. Instead, he simply moves more and more into the music of names, the voice remains strong, and he becomes what is around him.

I hope this comparison illustrates Roethke's first as well as his second contribution. While his language becomes the obvious means of unity with environment, Roethke also shows that external landscape must be balanced with attention to internal landscape if the poem is to avoid collapsing on itself. This was a major contribution to a developing literature that was still, by and large, dwelling on the physical and external details of environment as the writers of the folk epic had done. For example, the following poems, one by Roethke's predecessor at the University of Washington and one by a Montana poet, show the prominence of the descriptive tradition with the removed poet's voice reporting.

Philipsburg

An old man lives in a little grey town
Where, in his dreams as night slips down,
Creaking ore carts laden high
And strings of dusty mules go by
And men who heard the outlands cry.
But dreams grow pale in the morning sun,
And memories vanish—one by one.[23]

John Frohlicher

from *Rain on Orcas*

Rain in the islands,
With the black clouds flying,
And the last faint spots of sunlight fading on the sea.
Changing, hurrying, shifting of shadows,
And the high grey fan of rain-streaks in the east.

Darker, darker,
With the wind rising and falling more loudly in the trees,
The waves' slap sounding stronger and quicker on the sand,
Where the driftwood,
Sad, spent, weather-weary travelers of the deep
Lie grimly, white and naked to the rain
When it shall come.[24]

Glenn Hughes

Although both poems are clearly attempting to move beyond the language and posture of the folk epic, neither seems to escape it and achieve any unity between external and internal space. I believe this consistent dominance of "setting" or "nature" is less a result of an impoverished imagination than a result of first, an intimidating physical environment; second, an inadequate *mythos* of space; and finally, an inadequate poetic tradition. Hence, writers could only describe unless they, like Davis, and now Roethke, interiorized environment and brought to it their full internal landscape.

This emphasis on the necessity of internal landscape in the poem—on a voice that would not go soft, merely descriptive, or abstract when confronted with environment—was also a major contribution to future Northwest writers (I think here of Richard Hugo and David Wagoner) because it freed them from the deadfall of a strictly physical poetry and made them intensely conscious of the importance of *voice* as the binding and significant presence in a Northwest poem. Although this contribution has not been acknowledged, I believe that the first books by both poets show the influence of this contribution. From *A Run of Jacks* to *What Thou Lovest Well Remains American*, Richard Hugo shows that equal attention to the music of language and to interior life are the only means of escaping tedium and inertness in a poetry where place and the naming of place and thing are the means of objectifying and discovering personal interior. Even though his experience in profane space may be gray, rainlocked, and desperate, the presence of Hugo's shaping, strong musical voice carries the poems and the poet through the journey to another temporary stay against confusion. Although David Wagoner's vision is generally less bleak and more charged with intellect, Wagoner is often taking the task of animating a universe through voice alone, as can be seen in a poem like "Guide to Dungeness Spit."[25] It is possible that both of these poets, and others whose work I do not know, have learned the balance that Roethke taught between environment, interior landscape, and music. Instead of simply describing or feuding with environment in a mythos of detachment and conquest, Roethke showed future writers how articulate they could become if they simply united themselves with the space around them in a balanced fashion. To see how dramatically this has transformed Northwest poetry, compare Hugo's "Degrees of Gray in Philipsburg" from *The Lady in Kickinghorse Reservoir* with the poem about Philipsburg by John Frohlicher. The differences between them are attributable, in part, to the example of Theodore Roethke.

In the poetry of William Stafford we can see a final expression of the continuity in Northwest writing. Although there is much more to Stafford's poems than can be discussed here, the poems do generate responses to those two enduring questions of Northwest literature. To the question, "Where are we?", Stafford's reply seems to be that we have come to and are still traveling through a territory (both literal and metaphoric) where we must engage in the continuous act of discovering the unknown. Like the writers of the folk epic of discovery, Stafford sends back messages to Kansas and the East, makes reports on Oregon, writes many poems about traveling while he develops the ability to "hear the wilderness listen." His means to such a continuous process of discovery is articulated through environment in many poems; "Starting With Little Things," seems to illustrate how he proceeds:

> Love the earth like a mole,
> fur-near. Near-sighted
> hold close the clods,

their fine print headlines.
Pat them with soft hands—

But spades, but pink and loving: they
break rock, nudge giants aside,
affable plow.
Fields are to touch:
each day nuzzle your way.

Tomorrow the world.[26]

Taking the perspective of the mole and binding it to himself, Stafford can articulate his unwillingness to abstract or generalize his love for new space. To be at home here, Stafford seems to say we must establish a comparable immediate and personal unity with environment, as he has through the mole, through acts of the imagination that bridge with language and *mythos* the easy (or most difficult) barriers we have erected to separate man and environment. Instead of thinking of the environment as an exclusive arena for man and his work with machines, Stafford asks us to consider the mole's relationship to the environment where "Fields are to touch" and where clods have headlines we probably can't read because we haven't looked at their "fine print." In short, Stafford's voice encourages us to see the potential power in a vision of environment that includes the nonhuman universe.

In contrast with Theodore Roethke, who dramatized his journey out of himself in "The Rose," Stafford begins many of his poems where "The Rose" ends. With his nearly a priori imaginative achievement of unity with environment, Stafford accomplishes in the first three lines of "From Eastern Oregon" what Roethke dramatized for the entire poem:

Your day self shimmers at the mouth of a desert cave;
then you leave the world's problem and find
your own kind of light at the pool that glows far back
where the eye says it is dark. On the cave wall
you make not a shadow but a brightness; and you can feel
with your hands the carved story now forgotten or ignored
    by the outside, obvious mountains.

Your eyes an owl, your skin a new part of the earth,
you let obsidian flakes in the dust discover your feet
where somewhere drops of water tell a rock.
You climb out again and, consumed by light, shimmer
full contemporary being, but so thin your bones
register a skeleton along the rocks like
an intense, interior diamond.

You carry the cave home, past Black Butte,
along the Santiam. The whole state
rides deep, and the swell of knowing it makes
yearning kelp of all you can't see.
For days your friends will be juniper, but
never again will material exist enough, clear—
   not any day, not here.[27]

Although I hesitate to explicate what has already been said so well, Stafford
seems to be building into this poem one of his replies to the second enduring question of our literature—namely, "How shall we live here?" First, it
is obvious that we must move beyond a literally reported, surface realism
universe; we must move beyond the pretty descriptions of *The Lariat*. Even
though he is nearly uninterested in the "outside, obvious mountains" of
external landscape, and even though he states that surface material will
never "exist enough" after this kind of encounter, his language is still the
language of place as we saw it first appear in the folk epic and later emerge
in the poetry of H. L. Davis. Like Davis, Stafford's perceptions in the
poem are gained through the eyes of an owl, and the cave is a place that
must be perceived through this medium because so much of what its dark-
ness contains is not available to the human eye. After such an encounter
with place, the poet interiorizes it ("You carry that cave home"), and that
act of becoming what was around him literally transforms his entire per-
ceptual process and himself as well. All this suggests Stafford's reply is
that we must "live by imagination," our only means out of the shimmer-
ing homocentric consciousness to unity with places inside and out of ourselves. Such unity replaces the need to simply and superficially describe,
dominate, or conquer the cave; in fact, the cave itself becomes a means to
a celebration and illumination of both the resources of environment and the
imagination's ability to respond to environments it discovers or creates. If
the imagination can separate man from environment and declare all life
as subservient to human will, the imagination as Stafford shows can also
restore man to a place within environment and document the *genius loci*
of desert caves.

   Although this analysis and survey of Northwest literature ends here, it is
clear that the process needs to continue, since a great many excellent writers and poets—Vi Gale, Vern Rutsala, Kenneth Hanson, David Wagoner,
Robin Skelton, John Haislip, Henry Carlile, Gary Snyder, Don Berry,
Ken Kesey, William Kittredge, Madeline DeFrees, Vardis Fisher—need
to be present in any complete study of Northwest writing. The absence of
such writers and poets here makes it clear that a complete literary history
of the Pacific Northwest needs to find an author who is not subject, as I
am in these pages, to the limits of a professional paper. Such a literary his-

torian would be obligated to trace other sources of continuity in our literature which have been omitted here: in the presence of the Indian, the experience of women, regional magazines and presses, regional folklore, the influence of the universities, Northwest expatriates, the current literary situation, and so on. For such a history to be complete, it would have to include an analysis of that interface between environment and literature which, as I have tried to show, has become an obligatory locale, perhaps a unique territory, for Northwest writers and poets.

1. Robert Cantwell, *The Hidden Northwest* (Philadelphia: Lippincott, 1972), pp. 280-81; Richard W. Etulain, Comment on "A Symposium: The Pacific Northwest as a Cultural Region," by Raymond D. Gastil, *Pacific Northwest Quarterly*, 64 (October 1973), 159.
2. William Stafford and Richard Hugo, "The Third Time the World Happens," *Northwest Review*, 13, No. 3 (1973), 43.
3. *The Journals of Lewis and Clark*, ed. Bernard DeVoto (Boston: Houghton-Mifflin, 1953), p. 282.
4. In my essay, "The Search for Sacred Space in Western American Literature," *Portland Review*, 22 (1976), 6, I define *sacred space* as "implying home, a heterogeneous landscape in which man has both privileges and responsibilities. It contains enduring qualitative differences. It has fixed points, centers, from which all human activity takes its meaning. It endures beyond any particular individual as a source of objective reality. In sacred space, there is continuity between internal and external space; man seeks that continuity and binds himself to it. He claims space as part of himself, he identifies with it. Hence, man is part of the landscape and knows his place in it. He knows what the mountains mean, and he knows their names. Sacred space is constructed through a prolonged period of orientation. . . . In sacred space, man tends to be at home, at rest, more concerned with being than doing."

   On p. 8 of the same essay, I define *profane space* as "implying a territory in which man believes he has all privileges and no responsibilities. It is homogeneous and neutral, hence without any enduring experiences of qualitative difference. Profane space appears and disappears as a result of expediency and necessity. It is a space to pass through more than a space to call home. In profane space, man feels a profound discontinuity between internal and external reality, and confronted with that discontinuity over a period of time, man is emptied of himself and confronts absolute 'other.' In profane space, things have no names, or only the most general names. In it, man is an alien, an orphan, a wanderer, a stranger; he belongs nowhere and must keep moving to get somewhere but when asked, he does not know where that somewhere is. Man does not know what the mountains mean or their names. It is a spiritless world and all is relative in it. In part, it produces what has been described in Peter Berger's book, *The Homeless Mind* (New York: Vintage Books, 1973)."
5. See Aldous Huxley, "Wordsworth in the Tropics," in *Do What You Will* (London: Chatto and Windus, 1929), pp. 113-29.
6. Joaquin Miller, *Songs of the Sierras* (New York: Putnam, 1923), p. 147.
7. Joaquin Miller, "The Great Emerald Land," in *Oregon*, ed. John B. Horner (Corvallis: The *Gazette-Times* Press, 1919), p. 389.
8. *On The Oregon Trail*, ed. Kenneth A. Spaulding (Norman: Univ. of Oklahoma Press, 1953), p. 109.

9. Ian G. Barbour, ed., *Western Man and Environmental Ethics* (Reading, Mass.: Addison-Wesley, 1973) provides an introductory discussion of this *mythos* and the debate about it.

10. See H. L. Davis, "The Old Fashioned Land—Eastern Oregon," in *The Frontier*, 9 (March 1929), 201. Davis comments further about the classic pastoral in confrontation with the western experience: "The nearest approach to Vergil's conception of the trade was a little, falsetto-voiced runt I met once in the Blue Mountains, who lent me his library. It was the complete works of Zane Grey. And he wasn't a good sheepherder, either. His flock was always counting in about thirty or forty short. Vergil's shepherds may not have had more than that many woolies to bother with, all told. An Eastern Oregon sheepherder has charge of 1,000 heads, often more. No wonder he can't find time to cut pastorals on the back of trees. If there were any trees to cut them on."

11. Colonel E. Hofer, "Western Literary Militancy," *The Lariat*, 2 (Feb. 1924), 43.

12. H. G. Merriam, "Editorial," *The Frontier*, 8 (Nov. 1927), 1.

13. H. L. Davis and James Stevens, *Status Rerum: A Manifesto, Upon the Present Condition of Northwestern Literature* (The Dalles, Oregon: privately printed, 1927), p. 1.

14. James Stevens, "The Northwest Takes to Poesy," *The American Mercury*, 16 (Jan. 1929), 68. (I am indebted to Professor Glen Love for drawing this article to my attention.)

15. H. L. Davis, *Proud Riders and Other Poems* (New York: Harper and Brothers, 1942), p. 14.

16. Davis, p. 29.

17. Theodore Roethke, *The Collected Poems of Theodore Roethke* (Garden City, N.Y.: Doubleday, 1966), p. 4.

18. Roethke, p. 13.

19. William Stafford, "Having Become a Writer: Some Reflections," in *Northwest Review*, 13, No. 3 (1973), 90-91.

20. John Haislip, "The Example of Theodore Roethke," in *Northwest Review*, 14, No. 3 (1975), 14-20; and Richard Hugo, "Stray Thoughts on Roethke and Teaching," *American Poetry Review*, 3, No. 1 (1974), 50-51. [*Kermit Vanderbilt's essay in this volume is a further addition to the topic—Ed.*]

21. Roethke, p. 202.

22. Davis, p. 33.

23. John Frohlicher, "Philipsburg," in *Northwest Verse*, ed. H. G. Merriam (Caldwell, Idaho: Caxton Printers, 1931), p. 140.

24. Glenn Hughes, "Rain on Orcas," in *Northwest Verse*, p. 196.

25. I propose that David Wagoner is even conscious of this tradition, as he shows in the restraint of "The Poets Agree To Be Quiet By The Swamp," and in the vocabulary of "The Words." See his *Collected Poems 1956-1976* (Bloomington: Indiana Univ. Press, 1976), pp. 20, 53, 67.

26. William Stafford, "Starting With Little Things," in *Northwest Review*, 13, No. 3 (1973), 83.

27. William Stafford, *The Rescued Year* (New York: Harper and Row, 1966), p. 65.

Something of the conflict between outside influences and Northwest conditions
which George Venn discusses in the
preceding essay can be seen in the writings
of the British Columbia author, Frederick
Niven. Marvin Singleton here evaluates
Niven's contribution to Northwest
literature above the 49th parallel. Professor
Singleton has a doctorate in English from
Duke University and also holds the
Doctor of Jurisprudence degree in law
and legal history from the University of
California at Berkeley. He has taught at
several universities in the United States
and Canada, and was visiting Fulbright
professor at the University of Oslo in
1967-68. He is the author of *H. L.
Mencken and the American Mercury
Adventure* and many other studies on
literary, historical, and legal topics.

Frederick Niven *Redivivus:*
A Scots-Canadian's
Pacific Northwest

M. K. Singleton

"There is a place I have made here—a little, little place—with olive trees. And now they have grown, and it looks something like that country, if you stand in a particular position. I will take you there to-morrow. I think you will understand what I mean."

"Another resemblance!" said the volatile and happy Gaston.

Owen Wister, "Padre Ignazio"

A modern lover of paradox has pointed out how we jest at the serious when it is very serious. . . .

Frederick Niven, *Cinderella of Skookum Creek*

I. Frederick John Niven (1878-1944):
"I live the life I write."

Frederick John Niven, who was born in 1878 to Scottish parents resident in Chile, and who died in Vancouver in 1944, remains, as William New has observed, "a paradox," his many books "difficult to assess."[1] That Niven declared: "I live the life I write," as much as the fact that he is now almost forgotten, makes a short sketch of his life doubly useful. Indeed, though Niven's family returned to Glasgow before Frederick was six years old, the author, who prided himself on his memory and who used many of his adventures as materials for his prose, used his early Chilean impressions as well.[2] And Niven exemplified his own theory of character—that family upbringing was determinative—a theory that affected his delineation of character in both his Scots and his Western novels.

In Glasgow he grew up with a mercurial father who encouraged his son to read books such as *Tristram Shandy*, *Don Quixote*, and *Gil Blas*; and the New World was made vivid by Catlin's *North American Indians* and

McLean's *The Indians of Canada*, Ballantyne and Butler (as, *The Great Lone Land*), and Hudson's Bay narratives.[3] Frederick's mother, however, was made of sterner, more dour, stuff, as was the nurse who set the boy to reading, in addition to Holy Writ, Defoe's *Journal of the Plague Year* to burn out the untrue fairy stories into which the lad had fallen. The mother intended young Niven for the Presbyterian ministry, but she was disappointed when a youthful escapade made the vocation seem inapt; and she was further disappointed when he shrank from the family muslin business. By his mid-teens, Frederick dreamed of being an artist; by his mid-twenties, of being a writer; and his mother was chagrined when in 1911 he married Pauline, the willowy daughter of an ex-actress and influential Fleet Street journalist, Isobel Thorne. Niven, in *Ellen Adair*, indicated his milieu and some youthful unhappiness when he wrote of Scottish families over which hang "the curse of Calvin and a misconceived Christ. The children of such families, if they love beauty, either love it very tenderly, with a minor key in their voices, or are carried off their feet, and are as moths around a candle." Although Niven's mother used Carlyle's epithet ("sugared nonsense") to score her son's interest in Keats's paradoxy, Niven was less granitic than Carlyle. He became something of an Anglican, something of an esthete. And he remained something of a boy throughout his life, though his mother left a sober print on her son.[4]

Still, the father's enthusiasms were the ones that controlled. The elder Niven's romantic hobbyhorses led the youth—through the magic of the old dolphined atlas charting the Mauvaise Terre of Dakota, the Great American Desert, the British North America—into a lifelong search for the true West. The father equipped the son with an overwhelmingly persuasive myth—that all Canada was Nova Scotia. Findlay, and Fraser, Stewart and Mackenzie, Livingston and MacDougal, Angus Shaw and Donald McTavish and David Thompson—these were only the start of the Scots New World heritage. Niven knew why the Douglas fir was so named, and he knew of Lord Selkirk's Red River settlement for evicted Scots, and he saw the Indians as romantic counterparts in their own eviction—there was no significant Anglo-Saxon racism in the Niven panorama. And the myth came to be confirmed, in the way large-scale myths do. His father taught him that wherever in the New World there was machinery—whether in mine or in ferry—if you called out "Jock," out would climb the inevitable Glasgow machinist or mechanic. Niven eventually reinforced the myth by British Museum and Provincial archival research, but equally important was his experience of meeting innumerable Sandys and Scottys who were guides, prospectors, and cowpunchers in the West of United States and Canada. Their talk, as much as that of the other exotic talkers of Niven's British Columbia, the remittance men, fed with pawky dialogue and anecdote Niven's myth of the Scot as the True Westerner.[5]

Niven early was a lover of the literary word as well as of life, history, and map. The discovery by Frederick as a boy of Edward L. Wheeler's *Deadwood Dick* Dime Novels was important. This series provided a deep and private place for the young Niven; and the continuing impact on his Westerns of the *Deadwood Dick* series, and tributes until the close of his life, showed one sense in which Niven was a hero-worshipper.[6] The young Niven at play in Scotland was, he fancied, in Rocky Mountain House, and there on one hand were the Sioux, here, the Blackfeet, the Crees, the Stoneys. And he kenned as well the appearance of the noted chiefs and warriors.[7] But romance for Niven spanned Homer to Norris, belles lettres as well as pulp. Owen Wister remained his main source of the Western Code. But he read Twain, Bret Harte, Joaquin Miller, Emerson, Hergesheimer, Cabell, and other Americans as well as Stevenson, Scott, the romantic and metaphysical poets—these two groups influenced the most insistently, if occasionally superficially, "literary" writer yet, if frequency of explicit allusion and quotation be the standard.

Most important of all was his deep regard for the poet, classical translator, and romancer, the Scots Victorian Andrew Lang.[8] To the extent that Niven's vision and sensibility are truly integrated, to the extent he was able to achieve harmony within himself and his works, the central influence of Andrew Lang must somehow be reconciled with the influence of *Deadwood Dick*, Wister's *The Virginian*, and Niven's Scots mythology. Surely there can be no reconciling these aspects of Niven's viewpoint without using the language of paradoxy.

To resume our biographical sketch, we should note that Frederick was sent, in 1897, to British Columbia's Okanagan Valley to improve his health. He had hoped to follow Hutcheson's Boy's School with Glasgow School of Art, but poverty and an eye defect directed him into the workforce, and he continued to support himself after he had arrived in British Columbia. His various Canadian work experiences gave him something to write about when he returned from the Okanagan (with improved health) and began newspaper work for Scottish and English newspapers; and further visits to Canada before World War I kept fresh his sense of Canadian life. In 1908 Niven's future mother-in-law helped him to publish *The Lost Cabin Mine*, and by 1911 he intensified his steady output as an independent writer, in support of his new bride, Pauline. Niven's work in one of the War ministries did not interfere with steady publication throughout the First World War (a heart ailment prevented more active war service). During this period, Niven learned that his fictional abilities were not well suited to the short story, whether Western or otherwise.[9]

By the time of the Nivens' decision of 1920 to move permanently to British Columbia, the forty-two-year-old author could look back on a successful career. Praised by British and American critics had been several novels, especially two Scots novels, *Ellen Adair* (1913) and *Justice of the Peace* (1914). And three of five other books set in the Pacific Northwest, *Wild Honey* (1911), *Cinderella of Skookum Creek* (1916), and the *Lady of the Crossing; a Novel of the New West* (1919), could have been recognized as original, and perhaps all three as Westerns of the "New West." In any event, by 1920 Niven had actually been listed along with James Joyce as a possible contender when the older novelists (Bennett, Conrad, Galsworthy, Hardy, and Wells), might vacate the lists.[10] Why then did the hardworking Niven's reputation gradually subside, even before his death?

II. A Critical Issue

The critical weakness which Niven partly conceded in 1923—that his "weak point seemed to be construction"—was not the problem seen by Hugh Walpole in Walpole's preface to the 1923 edition of *Justice of the Peace*. Walpole believed that Niven's strength was in the Scots novels, but he asserted that critics had been put off from looking at Niven's work carefully because of Niven's romantic indulgence "for sheer enjoyment and the fun of the thing, [in writing] a series of cowboy Western romances that are jolly and gay and unimportant [though] better than most cowboy romances." And a distinction between the Scots novels and the Westerns is implied in Lionel Stevenson's opinion of 1926 that "the most distinguished novels written in Canada are those of Frederick Niven which describe the Scotland of his youth." Because this view provides an interface with a crucial judgment by Edward McCourt, Stevenson's point should be kept in the context of his overall exposition, which noted with some approval Niven's use of British Columbia ranching and industry as dramatic matter for his novels,[11] and in the context of Stevenson's commitment to the view, already evident in 1926, that only old and complex civilizations can engender and sustain the novel.

A split between those who saw Niven as, say, the Scottish Chekov, and those who saw him as one who loved the Canadian land in fruitful ways erupted after Niven's death.[12] This division was intensified when Edward A. McCourt's *The Canadian West in Fiction* (1949) influentially faulted Niven's writings set in Canada. After asserting broadly that Niven's earlier Westerns were simply thrillers,[13] McCourt passed on to an exploration of Niven's three-volume trilogy on the development of the Canadian West: *The Flying Years* (1935), *Mine Inheritance* (1940), *The Transplanted* (1944). *Mine Inheritance* started the saga with an account of the founding of Selkirk's Red River settlement, and *The Flying Years* continued the saga by following the life story of Angus Munro past the First World War and westward into Western Alberta. *The Transplanted*, which tells of the success of of another Scots-Canadian, Robert Wallace, in developing Elkhorn, B.C. mines and ranches, was found by McCourt to be so poorly written as to warrant no discussion; and this view makes rather scathing McCourt's name for the chapter on Niven: "The Transplanted." McCourt basically saw in the books evidence that Niven's lateness in coming to Canada ("he did not settle in Canada until middle age") meant that Niven knew Canada only through books and experience, but could not be a part of Canada, could not "feel" Canada. He could feel for Scotland, wrote McCourt, but he did not really know Canada, so he relied on book knowledge: "after many years of residence in Canada Niven was still spiritually an alien, as perhaps all must be who pass from one country to another comparatively late in life. . . . Niven to the end of his life was a Scot."[14] (This, given the high percentage of immigrants into the Pacific Northwest region, and the region's tendency to rely on many immigrants for culture, and even self-images, might be a broadly important issue.) And Desmond Pacey, writing in 1952, followed much of McCourt's thrust. Pacey found the main defect in Niven's novels was "their tendency to be overweighted with theme and history," and the characters were not "living beings, and no amount of verisimilitude . . . can make up for this fundamental lifelessness." Pacey also found weakness in the "episodic nature of [the novels'] structure . . . scarcely ever is a scene 'arranged. . . .'" Desmond Pacey does, however, find the scenery and landscape in the books to have succeeded extremely well, but even in the area of setting a recent critic has objected to Niven's "laziness" in salting place-names throughout his narratives—again, verisimilitude is not enough.[15] And this critical issue must be recognized, even though both McCourt and Pacey overlook various pre-1920 visits and sojourns by Niven, as well as his youthful erudition.

After the above criticisms consolidated the view of a Scottish high road and a western low road in Niven's writing, William New has been the main voice suggesting lines of revaluation for Frederick Niven. New has asserted that Niven "knew well" the western Canadian landscape, as well as that of Scotland. William New appreciates Niven's style, and he has noted the need to read the Scots books together with the Western ones.[16] (New's suggestion that Niven might have been slighted by the London *literati* because of his removal to Canada, is, of course, difficult to prove.) But New has not directly challenged the McCourt/Pacey verdict, nor has he undertaken the extensive demonstration that Niven is the sort of "paradox" that makes sense. Proposed here is an interpretation that the landscapes of Niven's books are reinforcing, rather than dividing and alienating; that we "know" only comparatively; and that, to come to particulars, *The Transplanted* is, while not a perfect novel, an important, useful, and moving close to Niven's trilogy, and to his life.

III. Old and New in Niven's "New Westerns": The Machine in the Pastoral

Niven's full-length Westerns set in the Pacific Northwest include *Wild Honey* (1911), *Hands Up!* (1913), *Cinderella of Skookum Creek* (1916), *The Lady of the Crossing; a Novel of the New West* (1919), *The Wolfer* (1923), *Treasure Trail* (1923), and *The Transplanted* (1944). The setting of *The Lost Cabin Mine* (1908) is diffusely Wild West, but elements suggest Pacific Northwest terrain. All of these books are essentially "Westerns" in that, as John Cawelti words the formula, their emphasis is on " 'symbolic landscape,' " a "field of action that centers upon the point of encounter between civilization and wilderness, East and West, settled society and lawless openness," and that at this moment individual actions can tip the balance; hence, something of the tragic and epic inheres in the form of heroism displayed.[17] The books show free use of the codes, conventions, stereotypes, and formula paraphernalia, and the chief sources for these in the first *(Lost Cabin)*, and most of the other books, are the *Deadwood Dick* Dime Novels, Bret Harte's stories, and Owen Wister's writings. *Lost Cabin* and *Hands Up!*—both of which feature a hero named Apache Kid—are cluttered and overwritten. Both feature moments when the narrative appears to subside into "pulp," when "incident takes precedence over plot," and the excitement inheres only in unrelated episodes.[18] Both books, however, show some original Niven qualities: Apache Kid is erudite, and, by the close of *Lost Cabin*, even world-weary in the high Victorian tenor. At the moment of his success, he sighs, "One grows weary of patronage" (p. 285); and earlier the Apache Kid, bewildered by a West on the verge of hanging up guns, advocated the open carrying of guns (p. 78)—the hero mentions an intent to look up Carlyle's remark to the effect that the backwoods are where manners flourish; and he believes that Carlyle was not being sarcastic, that Carlyle recognized that when guns go out, manners disintegrate. Otherwise, the Apache Kid expounds explicitly the Western code of the gentleman, including absolute gallantry when women are concerned.[19] *Hands Up* confirms the typings and formulae, adding Niven's respect for the Dime Novel (pp. 141, 240). *Hands Up!* is set near the Canadian border, and it is not only dedicated to an ex-Royal Northwest Mounted Policeman, but it contrasts that Force to venal American troopers (p. 137), noting the shooting of Sitting Bull (p. 138); and in one other instance, Canada is shown as the "freedom" route (p. 204).

The two other Westerns most like *Lost Cabin* and *Hands Up!* are the pair published in 1923: *The Wolfer* and *Treasure Trail*. These are better books than the earlier El Dorado stories, *Lost Cabin* and *Hands Up!*, partly due to the author's ability to dovetail formulae and characterization, or to contradict such conventions as the "strong, silent" hero—Niven in these books develops the most garrulous heroes since Cooper's Natty Bumppo.[20] The explicit commentary on formulae in these El Dorado books makes understandable Walpole's belief that Niven enjoyed writing such stories.[21]

The remaining Westerns, while they add to our knowledge of Niven's use of formulae and types, are most immediately drawn from Niven's own experiences; and *Wild Honey*, *Cinderella of Skookum Creek*, *The Lady*, and *Transplanted* are more reflective, slower-moving narratives. *Wild Honey*, a thoughtful story of a vagabond idyll by three friends, traces a number of lifestyles in the Thompson River, Okanagan, and Grand Forks areas. *The Lady* and *Transplanted* both chart the growth of small cities—in *Lady*, Nelson, B.C.; in *Transplanted*, Elkhorn, B.C. Both these novels feature political themes and socioeconomic problems, and they are all three novels of the New West more pervasively than were the El Dorado books. (*Cinderella of Skookum Creek* combines the vagabond, "new city," and "New West" themes and thus is transitional between *Wild Honey* and *The Lady*.) Niven's major contribution to the Western was his recognition of the simple fact that, in his part of the Pacific Northwest, the frontier had, during a thirty-year period after the closure of the lowland frontier, re-opened "aloft" in the Upper Country. This meant that simple fidelity to fact saw cities founded, "wide open," then respectable and electrified, all within a few years. For example, candles in the mines were almost immediately replaced with carbide lamps, then lamps almost immediately by electricity (*Transplanted*, p. 136). That Niven's "New West" books covered the 1905 to 1925 period meant that modern technology accompanied the frontier. Thus one character, named Movie Bill, often carries an automatic instead of the Colt Thumbuster, and heavies, after they have been disarmed externally, are carefully frisked for "gats" too. At the close of *Wolfer*, the eponymous hero trudges back into a small city dazzlingly lit by electric streetlamps, and he remarks, "We're in suburbia." This same hero wears glasses, and he will polish them after shooting you if you call him "four eyes." When the auto stage will not slow for some frightened horses, the hero reaches over and turns off the ignition, though he must then vindicate his kindness by a fist fight with the churlish driver (*Wolfer*, p. 64). The wholesome characters prevail by shrewd use of the new "party line" aspects of the telephone, and the author provides a footnote on telephone argot (*Wolfer*, p. 73, n.1). In *Trail*, when one character shows possible boxing ability, another wonders whether he's been trained, or he's seen a "Charlie Chaplin film" (*Trail*, p. 103). When the same character displays an ability to make a canoe, it is pointed out that he once worked in Peterboro' before coming West (*Trail*, p. 159). Cowpunchers are not too proud to make hay, or to put up fences.[23] They use flashlights to check the cows, and they prefer peep sights on their rifles. For all of Kipling's delight in describing machinery in his books, Niven's unironic exploitation of the automobile in his 1916 *Cinderella* for "nomadic-hearted" joyriding surpasses any Kiplingesque kinetics.

More important for those who suspect that nature imitates art was the fact that Niven's New West frontier was preceded by the Wild West Show, Bret Harte and Owen Wister, and the *kitsch* of the West. This meant that Niven's heroes (invariably also heroes of sensibility) saw and confirmed reality in terms of these cultural clichés. In *Honey* (p. 166), the hoboes see a ranch house that looks like a Remington drawing, and the mountains are beautiful to the point of looking like a Wild West Show backdrop. When they enter an abandoned cabin high in the mountains they see (p. 174) an advertisement picture of Fuji-Yama with the caption, "Why not go West to the East?" When Wolfer (whose Christian name is Dewar) wishes to warn those who would presume, he says, " 'When you call me that, smile' " (p. 256). In *Treasure Trail*, when the Scot hero marveled at whether he had misjudged a friend, he reviewed the friend's *bona fides*:

> He had travelled with observation and affection for the land. He knew its history—the history of the Old MacLeod Trail, the Oregon Trail, the Sante Fe Trail. He knew the land of Wister's "The Virginian" and of Norris's "The Octopus." He had placer mined on the Pend d'Oreille in Idaho, and punched cattle in the Little Missouri country.

Moving to his heartfelt climax, the Scot recalled that his friend could understand and sympathize with the Indian, and had a photograph from Seattle of Old Red Cloud, and had brought to Angus a bronze buffalo from Calgary, "cast in Yokohama, maybe, but a souvenir of the Old Plains days." And he was *personally* acquainted with a number of Indians, and not simply from "cigarette box cards" (pp. 179-180). Robert Wallace, the hero (of action and sensibility) of *Transplanted*, elaborately tracks parallels between Elkhorn and Bret Harte's Roaring Camp, Poker Flat, and Red Gulch (pp. 18, 20).

A third aspect of the New West featured in Niven's Westerns arises from the modern awareness of social and economic problems. Physical and mental disease, especially mental derangement from excessively lonely lives, was a grim fact of the landscape.[24] The ability of labor unions to help their members is frequently alluded to in the Westerns, and the pro and con of socialism is debated by characters.[25] The need for fruit marketing cooperatives is also mentioned,[26] and there is considerable discussion of what is sometimes called by other writers "the problems of ideology."[27] The problem of racial and ethnic minorities is explored with increasing humanity and thoughtfulness by the novelist: the Chinese in British Columbia,[28] the remittance men of the Province,[29] venal politicians and civil servants,[30] women,[31] Indians,[32] animals.[33] Niven's concerns with people are as richly present as his depictions of the landscape, or of heroic action.

But this attempt to weave, without parody or distorting self-conciousness, the Old West into the New West would not seem to advance the solution of the critical problem posed by McCourt and Pacey. Yet the preference for serious jesting and other paradoxy, and for open structures, after Sterne and Cervantes, follows a tradition that New Critics must appreciate. And Niven's use of quotations from literature to express the considerable sentiment of all of his Western heroes—as shown in the quotations of the transcendentalists by Wolfer (previous to his unmistakable revelation as a transcendentalist)[34] and in the grand fusion of sensibility and action in Robert Wallace or Angus Macpherson. These combinations express a paradoxy sufficient to elevate the Western into literary significance.[35]

And Robert Wallace, the central character of *The Transplanted*, is identified as "a paradoxical person" (p. 192). What are the largest elements in the paradoxical equation? First, he is sensitive to beauty, including the landscape,[36] but he is also practical and energetic: he is, as was Wister's Virginian, alert to economic opportunity.[37] Moral and ethical dilemmas, though he feels them, are transmuted into energy, not guilt. A sharp business transaction is redeemed,[38] and even the decision to perjure himself so that a friend is acquitted of murder does not infect his relationship with his sensitive wife. He combines something like opportunism with profound musings, lives gracefully with culture and with *furor*. His wife's ability to lead Robert to see the reality of Elkhorn history enables Robert to become a transnational hero, not simply a local tycoon. Niven's baroque characterization of Wallace in this novel is developed firmly (using interplay between Jock and Robert, Marion and Eleanor), and Wallace founds a small civilization, becomes an Aeneas.

The key paradox, overlooked by McCourt and a central clue to the *genius loci* in issue,[39] is the simultaneous understanding by Robert Wallace that his experience was truly "all history" (p. 144), and that his memories of the Scottish landscape sharply intensified his feeling for his Canadian landscape. He has an ecstatic sense that the place-names reinforce,[40] and he experiences this as keenly in Scotland as in Canada. At this point, the friendship doctrine, the syncretic sense of place, and his universal yet purely Scot identification with all history, allowed Niven to evoke the most substantial "Look homeward, Angel" since Milton. As the great formalist critic of Yale, Geoffrey Hartman, has suggested in his essays on *genius loci* in Virgil, Milton, and the Romantic poets, the bonding power of "place" paradoxy, in welding the laminated ideology characteristic of myth-based civilization, is immense.

IV. Conclusion

There are, of course, no mute, inglorious Miltons . . . but there
are the mute and inglorious who are aware that they are not
Miltons, despite all the lyric or threnodic impulse in their hearts.
Frederick Niven, *Ellen Adair*

" 'Tis a long road that has no turning,' Gove'nuh," said F. Jackson
Gilet, more urbanely. . . . He too arrived on a mule, but could at
will summon a rhetoric dating from Cicero, and preserved by
many luxuriant orators until after the middle of the present
century.

Owen Wister, "The Second
Missouri Compromise"

   The critical problem set (namely, the justice of the severe criticisms
McCourt and Pacey leveled at Niven's Westerns, including *Transplanted*)
led, after a description of Niven's unique depiction of the unsentimental
truth that "A new country makes its beginning with the inventions of its
day" (*Coloured Spectacles*, p. 227), to a consideration of the ways in
which the hero of *Transplanted* was a paradoxical person. The hero of the
posthumously published final volume of Niven's trilogy of the Scots
achievement in Canada was shown to become, not only intensively bi-
national, but international, in a way comparable to Virgil's Aeneas.
Achieved in the novel is the sense of nationhood whose loss was the subject of George Grant's well-known *Lament for a Nation*. Thus to find
Niven other than the perfected Canadian is most ironical. Niven's great
myth that the Scots, with their appreciation for the Indian, their Theocri-
tan sensibility,[41] their prowess as explorers and settlers, really are *the* Canadians ("from lieutenant-governors in the land to breakesmen on the
trains rolling through it" [*Coloured Spectacles*, p. 73]), seems validated
by a coherent vision. Moreover, Niven's view that the Interior represented
the truer Canada, rather than the Coast of British Columbia, indicates
his wisdom in ending his trilogy where he did.[42] In any event, Niven's
Westerns can now enable us to see ourselves, in that they are articulate: the
non-immigrant is frequently mute, in that perception and expression are
the outgrowth of comparative strategies.

---

  1. "A Life and Four Landscapes: Frederick John Niven," in *Articulating West:
     Essays on Purpose and Form in Modern Canadian Literature*, ed. W. H. New
     (Toronto: New Press, 1972), p. 3. New's essay originally appeared in *Cana-
     dian Literature*, 32 (Spring 1967), 15-28.
  2. Pauline Niven, Pref., "When I Was a Child," unpublished MS. by Frederick
     Niven (Niven Collection, Univ. of British Columbia Library), p. 1; Frederick
     Niven, *Triumph* (London: Collins, 1934). Niven's *The Flying Years* (Lon-
     don: Collins, 1935) depends for its effect on a doctrine of memory expressed
     briefly in his *The Story of Their Days* (London: Collins, 1939), pp. 424-25.

3. Frederick Niven, *Coloured Spectacles* (London: Collins, 1938), pp. 69-74; and cf. *Two Generations* (London: Nash, 1916), pp. 134-35, and *Justice of the Peace* (New York: Boni and Liveright, 1923), pp. 89, 339.

4. Niven was a communicant, after his settlement at Willow Point on the West Arm of Kootenay Lake, in the Anglican Church (St. Andrews) at Willow Point. The view of Niven as "the eternal boy" is set down by Mrs. Niven, in the preface for "When I Was a Child," p. 2. Niven was a mild monarchist, and weighted his historical romance, *Under Which King* (London: Collins, 1943), accordingly. The quotation from *Ellen Adair* (New York: Boni & Liveright) is from page 119 of the 1925 edition; the nurse's addition to his reading is noted in *Coloured Spectacles*, p. 44; the interpretation of the author's mother is indebted to Ellen Hodgson, "Frederick John Niven," unpublished essay (written Summer, 1975), p. 2; and I acknowledge the assistance of Ms. Hodgson's extensive bibliographical work with Niven as she continued in the Summer of 1976 her Professions-for-Tomorrow project.

5. Frederick Niven, *Old Soldier* (London: Collins, 1936), p. 249; on remittance men as good storytellers, see Stewart Holbrook, *Far Corner: A Personal View of the Pacific Northwest* (New York: Macmillan, 1952), pp. 39-53, and on Niven's use of remittance men in his Westerns, see n. 22 below. On the Anglo-Saxon racists, Niven goes out of his way in *Canada West* (London: J. M. Dent, 1930) to hold Canada open for non-Scots, non-English (p. 42). Guides Niven knew are extolled individually, and as a neglected class, in his and Walter Phillips' *Colour in the Canadian Rockies* (Toronto: T. Nelson and Sons, 1937), pp. 57, 60; and other sources note Niven's horse-packing trips into the High Country to enjoy not only the scenery but also talltale contests with guides.

6. *Coloured Spectacles*, pp. 105-13; "Epistle Dedicatory," *The Wolfer* (Toronto: Dodd, Mead, 1923), pp. v-vii (on Richard Bullock, the original Deadwood Dick); and see *Hands Up!* (London: Martin Secker, 1913), pp. 141, 240.

7. *Coloured Spectacles*, pp. 142, 298.

8. *Coloured Spectacles*, pp. 90, 95, 113. In *Ellen Adair*, Niven used opinions of Lang in scenes revealing characters' worth (pp. 106-07). Evidence of other Lang influence is noted in the Niven Collection, Notre Dame University Library.

9. *Above Your Heads* (London: M. Secker, 1911), was made up of short stories rejected by magazine editors; and *Sage-Brush Stories* (London: Nash, 1917) was similarly unsuccessful.

10. Compare Rebecca West, "Notes on Novels," *The New Statesman*, 16 (Oct. 9, 1920), 22, with W. L. George's listing, as noted in Edward A. McCourt, *The Canadian West in Fiction* (Toronto: Ryerson Press, 1949), p. 39.

11. *Appraisals of Canadian Literature* (Toronto: Macmillan, 1926), pp. 261-62. (Stevenson's initial tribute appeared on p. 137.) The Walpole quotation is from Preface I, *Justice of the Peace*, p. x.

12. Representative are, on the one hand, Gretchen Gibson, "Frederick Niven Had Novelist's Memory and Loved His West," *Saturday Night*, 59 (Apr. 1, 1944), 25, and, on the other hand, Alexander Reid, "A Scottish Chekhov?," *Scotland's Magazine*, 58 (March, 1962), 45-46.

13. "Wild West thrillers intended for an audience more interested in action than in art," McCourt, p. 41.

14. McCourt, pp. 42, 44, 51-54. Actually, McCourt's approach could well be extended to challenge the authenticity of the Scots books: Niven's Scots land-

scapes are often shown to be haunted by his or a character's sense of the
Canadian scene. (As will be shown, this writer does not advocate this view of
"authenticity," but the logic should be noted.) It should be noted further
that McCourt allowed his analysis of Niven to stand in his 1970 revision of
The Canadian West in Fiction.

15. Desmond Pacey, *Creative Writing in Canada: A Short History of English-
Canadian Literature* (Toronto: Ryerson Press, 1952), pp. 159-60. The reservation about Niven's use of place-names is set down by Hodgson, "Niven," p. 11,
but the point is made only in connection with *Treasure Trail*, a novel of 1923.

16. New's "Individual and Group Isolation in the Fiction of Frederick John Niven:
Setting as a Basis for a Study of Conflict and Resolution," M.A. Thesis, Univ.
of British Columbia 1963, cross-analyzed the two "types" of Niven works in
illuminating ways. See especially pp. 140-44. Other information is from "A
Life and Four Landscapes," in *Articulating West*, pp. 3, 4, and ff.

17. Quotation from John G. Cawelti, *Adventure, Mystery, and Romance: Formula
Stories as Art and Popular Culture* (Chicago: Univ. of Chicago Press, 1976),
p. 193. A companion study is Cawelti, *The Six-Gun Mystique* (Bowling
Green, Ohio: Popular Press, n.d.); and occasionally useful is Will Wright,
Six Guns and Society (Berkeley: Univ. of California Press, 1975); and vari-
ously helpful has been Richard W. Etulain who with Michael T. Marsden has
deepened our reflections on Western literature by editing *The Popular Western:
Essays Toward a Definition* (Bowling Green, Ohio: Popular Press, 1974).

18. Definition from Cawelti, *Adventure*, p. 211.

19. Apache Kid rebukes any ridicule of "any gentleman's religion"—see *Lost
Cabin* (New York: Dodd, Mead, 1929), p. 144; shows "quiet courtesy"
(*Cabin*, p. 231); appeals to a "sense of propriety. . . for which our western
country is famous"; notes that in the West no one is ever forced to take liquor
when he does not want to, no one forces anyone to disclose his history when
he does not want to (*Cabin*, p. 274); gallantly protects Miss Pinkerton from
knowing unpleasant aspects of life (*Cabin*, p. 279).

20. On atypicality of garrulous heroes, see Cawelti, *Six-Gun*, p. 61.

21. For example, Niven attaches, as an epigraph to *Treasure Trail* (New York:
Dodd, Mead, 1923), p. 1, a quotation from Frank Norris's "The Passing of
Cock-eye Blacklock" indicating that stories must be about the "discovery of
hidden wealth." But Niven prided himself on his freedom from use of hack-
neyed formulae, using more notably the odd idea (as, "the romance of reality,"
a favorite Niven phrase [*Trail*, p. 84]) or the literary idea of Don Quixote
and Sancho Panza character pairings (notable in *Trail*, pp. 131, 220, 235). At
the close of *The Wolfer*, the hero jests, as the romantic accompaniment to the
heroes' property gain approaches, that the quest for the mine calls for "a
stereotyped ending" (*The Wolfer*, p. 311).

22. In filling out the type-groupings set down in Cawelti, *Six-Gun*, pp. 56-63,
Niven used types common in United States Westerns; but he also used types
he noted north of the border: remittance men are failures, roués, and woman-
izing cads; prospectors are frequently somewhat demented due to isolation or
mania for gold; whores are shrill and cadaverous and very tough; miners (or
"moles," as the cowboys call them) are rough and rude; one newspaper reporter, though cynical, is kind (*Lady*, pp. 219-20). The most sustained and
thoughtful musing on "types" is in *Wild Honey* (New York: Dodd, Mead,
1927), on the "types" at the railway workers camp (p. 9); on the merits of
lumberjacks, miners, and cowpunchers (pp. 131-32, 228); on redeeming In-

dians from the stereotypic view that they do not laugh (pp. 202-03); on tradesmen "who live for making money [being] mean as hell" (p. 240); and, throughout, on vagabond/hobo life and lore.

23. *Treasure Trail*, p. 53; *The Transplanted* (Toronto: Collins, 1944), p. 45.

24. Syphilitic Indians are shown in *Wild Honey* (pp. 91-92); and the toll in insanity for sheepherders, prospectors, and some others who dwelt alone, is noted even in *Lost Cabin*.

25. Hank, the Wobbly-figure in *Wild Honey*, is rendered sympathetically by Niven. In *Lady*, p. 200, the effort by the Mayor to use chain-gang labor was limited by the strong union to unskilled labor projects.

26. As in *Lady*, p. 305; but also note Niven's alertness to economic realities, including fruit growing, in the Far West.

27. The character Sam Haig in *Lady*, though he "held no theory regarding the discrepancy between the average man's creed and his life," astutely competes with a Darwinian whose "creed or obsession" leads him to court the same girl (pp. 131, 140). Along with his elegiac sensibility, Haig has an ability to unravel local politics, despite the adage that "Nobody expects any visible means of support to touch invisible politics" (p. 241). Though Niven once wrote that, "whatever the material base of it, and the many inventions of men —steam-ploughs on the prairies . . . the spiritual base of Canada is not in steel and sky-signs any more than the quintessential England is only in London," his statement is on behalf of the land, rather than ideology as false consciousness. For although Niven could, as in *Mrs. Barry* (London: Collins, 1933), p. 226, show a deep compassion for persons enthralled by religious services, Niven ultimately avoided, according to his own lights, such use of art, patriotism, or even the scenic beauty of British Columbia, as "enough" (as, Eleanor in *The Transplanted*: is landscape beauty enough? [p. 164]). It is unfortunate that Ezra Pound, that deep student of ideology, could not have made contact with Niven: they were, after all, the two main twentieth-century appreciators of Andrew Lang.

28. Niven's first books are very unfavorable to the Chinese characters in the novels, but gradually he develops an appreciation for the Chinese, and he informed himself of their culture.

29. Two exceptions to the remittance man type indicated in note 22 above are of interest: the story "Abyssinia" in *Above Your Heads* attempted the only West to East (from Vancouver) movement into the Interior; and it also makes the character Abyssinia into a reverse "remittance man" in that he commences sending money back home. This double inversion of the convention can not be explored, however, because Niven ends the story when Abyssinia falls under a train in an attempt to hitch a ride. The other exception is the character Harker in *Transplanted*, who, though a man exploitative and caddish towards women, refuses remittance support and is allowed considerable humanity before he is killed.

30. *Lady* traces the venality of elected municipal officials in a setting commonly conceded to be Nelson, B.C. *Transplanted* shows Robert Wallace protecting tourists from drunken and abusive officials.

31. Niven would nowadays be found to have stereotyped women into the good/ bad categories: whores are ghastly; promiscuous girls come to grief; and good, clean girls are, if pretty, marriageable. (The motherly hotelkeeper's wives are permitted some robust honesty, of course.) A key problem within *Transplanted*

is the character Marion; but Marion is for some a credible, deeply moving, character; and Eleanor, the intelligent mate of Robert, is an independent and engaging character, as are several female characters in *Lady*. And in *Cinderella of Skookum Creek* (London: Nash, 1916) Niven sympathetically offsets a "homely" girl against the pretty but selfish Dulcie, allowing educational and moral sensitivity to "bloom" over the stereotypic cold "beauty."

32. Indians are treated with great respect in all Niven's books, though, especially in *The Flying Years* and *The Transplanted*, realism based on Niven's extensive knowledge of Indians prevents any suspicion of excessive sentiment. Niven, always welcome to visit Indians in British Columbia and Alberta, learned sign language and was accepted into one tribe. Before his death, Niven had accumulated a valuable collection of Indian artifacts. Archer, the hero of *Cinderella*, completes valuable scientific studies of the various Pacific Northwest tribes in the Columbia River area. He spoke to Indians in their own language, disdaining Chinook (p. 54).

33. Wister's Virginian would have recognized the trait (" 'When a man is kind to dumb animals, I always say he has got some good in him' " [*The Virginian* (New York: Macmillan, 1902), p. 266]): Niven's love of horses, as indicated in his novels and by Mrs. Niven's remarkable statement in the preface for "When I Was a Child," p. 3, was a lifelong commitment. Although the genteel poverty of the Nivens prevented his owning a horse, he was an able rider and used every spare cent in going on trail rides into the mountains.

34. Wolfer's extreme capability is matched only by his love of Thoreau, Burroughs, Muir, and Emerson. Towards the close of the novel, Wolfer sees abandoned placer camps as "symbols of the transience of man"; and this shortly leads to a transcendental epiphany: the "visible world" he scorns; and when mundane details loom, he quotes the words of Emerson, " 'We must attent to [the matter] as if it were real' " (p. 296).

35. Cawelti's wording (*Adventure*, pp. 11, 12) for success within formulaic art limits is: employment of "stereotypical characters and situations in such a way as to breathe new life and interest in them," yet without "departing very far from the typical situation his audience has come to expect"; and the final "test of a truly vitalized stereotype is the degree to which it becomes an archetype," thereby transcending its particular cultural moment; and the commentator notes the role of "human complexity" and even "frailty" in the process. And Cawelti notes the need to "express contemporaneous concerns" for those who would revitalize convention and stereotypes (*Six-Guns*, p. 86). But these wordings, while I believe they fit *Transplanted*, and, to a considerable extent *Cinderella*, *Lady*, *Wolfer*, and *Wild Honey*, are difficult to apply.

36. Wallace can fancy David Thompson smelling the landscape; and Niven, throughout his Western novels and nonfiction books, stresses the odor of the Upper Country as compellingly beautiful.

37. Just as Wister's Virginian ended up with coal land and a concern in various business enterprises, so too did Wallace move into ranching, as suited the market opportunity, and he became a director of the Smelter.

38. Wallace, though he pays the ignorant prospector all that he asked ($5,000) for the rich claim, and he felt that he had served his employer well, felt the ethical problem throughout most of the novel. But by allowing the prospector to work at well-paid jobs, and, after the prospector returned penniless from squandering his "fortune," by arranging a pension, Wallace exemplifies a

certain *noblesse oblige*, and a rather conservative social philosophy seems to have been vindicated.

39. Two novels mention *genius loci*, one set in Canada (*Lady*, p. 205); the other set in Scotland (*Justice of the Peace*, p. 338—between quotations from *Lycidas*, and mention of Deadwood Dick, Jack Harkaway, and Ching Ching.)

40. The term "ecstatic" is frequently used by Niven in fiction and nonfiction to indicate the quality of feeling generated by sight and smell of the Upper Country or the High Country. This word might be used because of Arthur Machen, whose pre-World War I book *Hieroglyphics: A Note Upon Ecstasy in Literature* (London: M. Secker, 1910) found ecstasy basic to true literature.

41. Niven mentions Theocritus in several of his Westerns, to underline either some intense quality of friendship or some elegiac moment. Niven, who had memorized many of the poems of Andrew Lang, was familiar with the Idylls, and this partly explains why Niven could allow modern technology in his books of the New West—the original idyll or pastoral had no quarrel to pick with technology. The friendship theme explains the perjury on behalf of Jock Galbraith in *Transplanted*, though Jock had considerable community sympathy for killing his wife's lover. Again and again in Niven's books, when the sensitive hero become moved by some elegiac sense, or some Rip Van Winkle sense that time flees, out of the musings come effective assertion in the world, and financial success.

42. Niven, although he had worked in Vancouver, and had visited there (often with little money), never revised upward his low estimate of the city on the salt chuck. In his *Far West*, Niven left the entire Coast area to the last twenty pages of his book. He sees Vancouver as lurid, sinister, and corrupt, and he ridicules the excessive rain (p. 170). He points out that the seaport is, "to a great measure," supported by the "Upper Country" (Niven's term for the Interior). Nor does Niven's attitude towards Victoria show much more enthusiasm: he uses up most of his space allocated to Victoria telling of an English woman, "who had given her heart to the Upper Country," after a short time in Victoria moving back to the Interior because she wished "to return to Canada" (p. 173). And when Jock Galbraith travels to Vancouver's seedier areas to find his dying, runaway wife, he notes "a coyote look" about the characters in the back streets (*Transplanted*, p. 256).

As Frederick Niven worked with the formula Western north of the border, so Ernest Haycox became perhaps the leading practitioner of that form in the United States. No writer from the Pacific Northwest has had a larger readership than Haycox. Yet, as Richard Etulain makes clear in this essay, very little of Haycox's work is evocative of the region. Haycox's mastery of the formula Western returned such substantial financial reward that he did not attempt, until late in his career, the kind of serious regional treatment that Northwest novelist H. L. Davis achieved. Haycox's effort in *The Earthbreakers* was impressive but, as Etulain points out, fell short of the mark. Richard Etulain has a Ph.D. in history from the University of Oregon and teaches American history and American literature with an emphasis on the trans-Mississippi West at Idaho State University. Professor Etulain has published extensively in the field of his special interest. He has compiled a useful reference tool in *Western American Literature: A Bibliography of Interpretive Books and Articles*, and in the Western Writers Series he wrote the volume on Owen Wister. He is currently at work on a guide to western American literature and an edition of Jack London's tramp diary.

Ernest Haycox:
Popular Novelist
of the Pacific Northwest

Richard Etulain

Historians and literary critics in search of a regional culture often overlook a writer who lives in a region but who generally exploits themes that transcend his surroundings. Such is the case with Ernest Haycox (1899-1950). Although he lived in the Pacific Northwest for nearly fifty years and was a resident of the region during most of his thirty-year writing career, Haycox was not primarily a regional writer.[1] His major contribution was to the Western, a popular genre more closely tied to formula fiction than to the matters of regional literature: dialect, local customs and character types, man-land relationships, and a sense of place. At the same time, he is a significant figure because he became a nationally known writer and because his career in the pulp magazines of the 1920s and the slicks of the 1930 and 1940s parallels the experiences of several other writers living in the Pacific Northwest.[2] Only in his last novel, *The Earthbreakers*, did Haycox work to weave regional influences into his writing. In the process he nearly achieved a work genuinely of the Pacific Northwest as opposed to one simply set in the region.

Ernest Haycox began to write early in his career. His first essays were for his high school publications; later he wrote for campus papers at Reed College and the University of Oregon. While at the University, he enrolled in the creative writing classes of W. F. G. Thacher, who encouraged him to study and imitate, if necessary, the short stories and serials appearing in popular magazines. Before he was graduated in 1923, Haycox had sold several yarns to *Sea-Stories* of the New York-based Street and Smith company.[3]

After a brief stint as a reporter for *The Oregonian*, Haycox went east in 1924 to be near his markets. At first he was unsuccessful in placing his work, but by 1926 he was selling fiction to *Western Story*, the best-known pulp Western magazine of the Street and Smith fiction factory. Two years later, he was publishing regularly with the more prestigious *Adventure* and the Doubleday and Doran magazines, *Short Stories* and *West*. By the end of the twenties, Haycox had served his apprenticeship and was considered a leading writer of pulp Westerns.

Research for this essay was made possible through grants from the Idaho State University Faculty Research Committee and the American Philosophical Society.

Most of Haycox's first stories were set in the Pacific Northwest and dealt with occupations that were familiar to him: logging, homesteading, and fishing. In this fiction, however, setting was less important than action and character conflict. Haycox also wrote about the American Revolution in the Street and Smith pulp magazines, but in the middle twenties he made an important decision that shaped the rest of his career. On the advice of Frank D. Blackwell, editor of *Western Story*, he decided to concentrate on the Western. This popular genre with its format of action, romance, and stereotyped characters already firmly established by such authors as Owen Wister, Zane Grey, and Max Brand, was an ideal fictional type for Haycox, a man of cautious temperament and limited talents.[4] He abandoned his contemporary settings, retreated to the era of the cattle kings, and began to write about cowboys. For the next fifteen years the man on horseback would be the central character in most of his fiction.

His extensive treatment of the cowboy began with *Free Grass* (1929). In describing his first novel to his former teacher, he wrote, "It is slightly historical, in which I find I do my best, though the history won't impede the skip and run reader any. It's a trail herd from Texas to Dakota."[5] One week after the publication of *Free Grass*, Charles Alexander, an Oregon author and a friend of Haycox, claimed the book had a "Western plot with no new variations." "But," he added, "there is a variation in style and in treatment. This variation that lifts the book above what one reads in the wild west magazines is the author's careful reproduction of the cattle range as it was." In essence, Alexander pointed out that Haycox's novel was better than most Westerns because it contained a credible historical background on which a romantic story was superimposed. Haycox concurred with his friend's critical opinion; he knew that the "thin part of the book [was] the plot." And, he said, "this will continue to be the thin part of my stories until I can afford to wean myself from serial rights in the pulps." But, he continued, "within the limitations of the pulp market . . . I still have plenty of elbow room to fill out and richen my stories."[6]

The plot of *Free Grass* centers on Tom Gillette, a Texan who went east for schooling and has returned to the West. Soon after his return, he is quickly reborn under the stern but beneficent forces of the West. When he left for the East, he was a boy. Now he returns a man, but he must learn the demands of the western code. He must be quiet and reflective and voice his opinions only when they are needed. The West, his father says, is a place where you " 'Play your own hand, ask no favours, ride straight, shoot fast. Keep all obligations.' "[7] The West is a land where a man can be neither soft physically nor loose morally. He has to follow the code that fuses southern gentlemanliness and frontier individualism.

But Tom is more than a young man who lives by the western code; he is also a man with a memory. He cannot forget completely Christine Ballard, an alluring but selfish and proud eastern girl. When he meets Lorena Wyatt, the warm and vivacious daughter of a Texas rancher who has come to the Dakota territory, tension arises in the mind of the hero as well as between the two women. This struggle between Christine (who comes west for a visit) and Lorena parallels the conflict between East and West in Tom's experience. Only when the West and Lorena gain the upper hand is he able to forget Christine.[8] The two women epitomize their environments, and they help to aggravate the problem of Tom's indecision. In utilizing a part to symbolize the whole, Haycox portrays his theme on two levels and thereby enlarges its possibilities. This structural device is an outstanding feature of the novel.[9] The well-conceived structure, along with the author's terse style and his attention to historical atmosphere, lifts the work several notches above the level of the typical Western.

The setting is also important in *Free Grass*. It is not merely a backdrop for the action, such as one finds in most Zane Grey Westerns. Here the characters feel its influence directly. Kit Ballard cannot accept the West; she says, " 'It's too raw, it's ungenerous. There's no sport to it. It's cruel.' " And again, " 'It's a brutal land! I hate it' " (pp. 154, 160). Blondy Lispenard, who comes west with Tom, fails to withstand the sheer force of the West, nor can he live up to the demands of the western code. On the other hand, Tom, Lorena, and Quagmire, the taciturn foreman, respond to the West, and it in turn seems to invigorate them. The West, in short, is a catalyst—changing others but remaining unchanged itself.

All in all, Haycox's first novel was an important step in his writing career. He proved to himself that he could write a full-length Western, and the reactions of readers and reviewers indicated that Haycox had a promising future in the pulps. But his contribution should not be overestimated. Haycox was tied to the format of the Western, and his characters and plot were all too typical of the popular genre. For Haycox the aspiring artist, the Western would be restrictive; but for Haycox the craftsman, there would still be a future in writing Westerns. The framework of the popular type could be enlarged and its essential characteristics refined. For more than a decade Haycox accepted the role of a craftsman and established a reputation as a writer of superior Westerns.

Bugles in the Afternoon (1944) illustrates the second stage of Haycox's literary career (which commenced with his appearance in *Collier's* in 1931) and epitomizes his gradual development as a western historical novelist. During the late thirties and early forties, Haycox based some of his Westerns on historical events. *Trouble Shooter* (1937) dealt with the construction of the first transcontinental railroad; *The Border Trumpet* (1939) depicted life at Fort Grant on the southwestern frontier; *Trail Town* (1941) centered on marshal Tom Smith's hard-fisted control of

Abilene; and *Alder Gulch* (1942) narrated the frenzied activities in Alder
Gulch, Montana, and the deadly battles between the Plummer gang and
the Vigilantes. These novels were combinations of research and imagination; they joined historical figures like Grenville Dodge, General George
Crook, and Henry Plummer with Haycox's fictional characters. Hence, by
the appearance of *Bugles in the Afternoon* in 1943-44, Haycox had dis-
tilled a new blend that combined history and fiction, a brand that was
winning him increasing appreciation among connoisseurs of the Western.

Bugles in the Afternoon is Haycox's most widely read novel and one of
his best works. Published in book form one year after its serial appearance
in 1943 in *Saturday Evening Post*, *Bugles* centers on the defeat of General
George Armstrong Custer at the Battle of the Little Big Horn. These
events are told from the perspective of Kern Shafter, a former officer in the
Civil War, who has rejoined the army in 1875. When western scholars and
buffs are polled, they usually praise Haycox's novel for its drama, its narrative power, and its fidelity to fact. From their perspectives the book is a
well-crafted historical Western.[10]

No volumes in Haycox's large personal library (now in the Haycox
room at the University of Oregon library) are more heavily annotated than
his books about Custer and the events surrounding the summer of 1876.
Haycox was at home among Custer interpreters. Like the historian bent
on producing a first-rate monograph, he had read and thought about the
major book-length studies of General Custer. Notice for example, his perceptive comments to his publisher about the conflicting views of authorities
on Custer:

> I know of no other item in our history so completely unsullied by
> calm and detached judgment. . . . If I were to send the story to
> either Brininstool or Dustin[11]—both men who have given great
> amounts of time to the subject—they would instantly challenge
> my emphasis on Custer's leadership qualities, since neither man
> will admit any good at all in Custer. . . . By contrast, Captain
> Luce,[12] now superintendent of the Custer Battlefield and an ex-
> Seventh man, would blast everything I said, since Custer was
> God to him. The one man who comes nearer impartiality than any
> other is Colonel Graham[13] who wrote an excellent and tempered
> analysis of the battle and, as any army man, tried to keep out of
> trouble by not digging too deeply into Custer. Even so Brininstool
> pecked at him for years for his temperateness. It seems to be a
> fixed idea with these people. You cannot please them; and, dis-
> pleased, they will spend hours and days niggling over the most
> obscure items to controvert you. . . . This whole Custer thing is not
> in the hands of scholars. It is in the hands of partisans who started
> with a conviction and thereafter spent years hunting for facts to
> justify their view.[14]

Despite Haycox's reservations about the controversies that raged among
the Custer buffs, most of them were convinced that he had done his home-

work. Two noted Custer authorities pointed out that his novel was a well-researched account of the Seventh Cavalry and its leader.[15]

But *Bugles in the Afternoon* was more than a scissors-and-paste product of Haycox's reading in secondary sources. Not only had he weighed the various interpretations, but he had also read firsthand accounts of his subject and had interviewed persons closely associated with Custer.[16] The result of his research was an historical novel based on solid documentation in primary and secondary sources and a work that advanced a notable interpretation of a complex man and his involvement in a series of controversial events. Even a cursory reading of the novel reveals that Haycox knew where he was in the Custer embroilment and that he was willing to take a stand on his subject.

What was Haycox's view of Custer? He was convinced that the General was a bundle of contradictions. On one hand Custer was a gentle and loving husband, but he was also too impatient and too confident of himself. Near the end of the novel Custer is described as a man with a "fighter's heart" and "a fighter's tremendous energy." Haycox then adds,

> He scorned the cautions which held other commanders back, he had a blind faith in the naked power of a cavalry charge. On dash and surprise and swiftness he had made himself a general out of a boy lieutenant in four years and he could not change now. Nor wanted to change. Impatience and restlessness and a self-faith that never wavered were the stars that shone brightest before him, and moved him and made him.[17]

Most of all, Custer was driven to disaster by his enormous ambitions.

> He was a simple man so hungry for greatness that he could ride roughshod over the personal feelings of other men and not be aware of it; he was so naive in his judgments that even as he knew his enemies, he treated them in the manner of one who knows them to be entirely wrong and therefore to be treated charitably, indulged. He could be harsh and brutal for the sake of a soldierly ideal, but there was no gentle insight in him, no compassion, no deep sympathy. . . . All these things he was—an elemental complex of emotions and hungers and dreams never cooled, nor disciplined, never refined by maturity; for he had never grown up.[18]

General Terry's reflections, after he surveys the massacre of Custer and his battalion, sum up the views that Haycox seems to hold about the disaster at Little Big Horn.

> He knew, as he stood so gravely here upon this scene of defeat, how that defeat had come about. His trap, designed to snap shut, had been prematurely set off by the impetuous disregard of General Custer of his orders; wanting glory and blindly believing in himself and his regiment, Custer had not waited; the power of waiting was not in him.[19]

Although Haycox's treatment of Custer may be of primary interest to historians, most of the work deals with other characters and ideas. The major portion of the novel treats Kern Shafter and his attempts to reorder his jumbled private life, to realign himself with the Seventh Cavalry, and to understand his commander. In most sections of the plot, Shafter's story is combined with the Custer matters, and the result is a narrative whose meaning is augmented through this interlacing of personal and group concerns.

Had Haycox limited his work to these subjects—the Custer story and the narrative of Kern Shafter—he might have produced a memorable novel. But he was still tied to his serial markets and to the formula of the Western. These restrictions demanded that he drag in a heroine and a villain to complete the plot. Their appearance in the novel weakens its structure, for Shafter spends too much of his energy in winning the attentions of Josephine Russell and gaining revenge over his old enemy Edward Garnett. Although these actions are nearly always connected to Shafter's role in the affairs of the Seventh Cavalry, they often seem contrived and thus detract from the remainder of the novel.

The book's ending is also boxed in by the conventions of the Western. Once spring blossoms and the Seventh Cavalry embarks on its long-awaited march after the Sioux, Shafter carries along his hatred of Garnett, his love for Josephine, and his fear of Custer. Because Shafter is the hero of the Western and cannot lose his life, he is assigned to troop A under the command of Major Reno. Although severely wounded, Shafter survives, but Garnett falls before the Sioux charge. After General Gibbon arrives and rescues Reno's forces, Shafter and the other wounded are loaded on the steamer *Far West* and returned to Fort Lincoln. In the final scenes of the novel, Shafter and Josephine are reunited. She looks after Kern, who is saddened and still dazed from his experiences in the Custer tragedy.

Bugles in the Afternoon, then, is a hybrid. While it contains an accurate account of Custer and the Little Big Horn, the novel is strongly tied to the Western format. Too much of the novel is driven down the chute of the predetermined. In Shafter's story, history is not allowed free rein; it is prescribed by the conventions of a popular type. Although Haycox was moving toward a broader view of history and its use in his fiction, he was still limited by the restrictions of his market and bound by his inability or unwillingness to break loose from those demands.

From the serial publication of *Bugles in the Afternoon* until Haycox's death in 1950 was a short space of seven years, but in this brief span he showed more development as a writer than in any similar period in his life. During these final years he wrote less and spent more time on each project. After 1943 he published but one serial and one novel; two other novels appeared posthumously. In the previous seven years he had turned out nine serials. And the same proportion was evident in his production of shorter pieces. From 1937 to 1943, forty-one stories appeared, all in *Collier's*; but before his death, he added just twenty-eight more.[20]

In addition to slowing his production, Haycox was tinkering with the design of his novels. In this experimentation he received unexpected aid. During the Second World War, *Collier's* bought fewer serials, and thus Haycox, one of the magazine's steadiest serial writers, found himself squeezed out of his most lucrative market. The tightening purse strings at *Collier's* prompted Haycox to think once again of abandoning entirely the serial market, which he had threatened to do for nearly a decade. But once he arrived at this juncture in his thinking, he was not certain how to proceed. Convinced that he could not write a stream-of-consciousness novel or one that relied primarily on one character's reflections, he turned to a second kind of novel that he had pondered for some time.[21]

In his nearly ten years of experimentation with the historical Western, Haycox had found it difficult to keep his materials within the bounds of the serial. His abundant historical resources, his tendency to use several major characters, and his growing sense of the complexity of the past—all these threatened to burst the restrictive format of his serial Westerns. Slowly and tentatively he concluded that if he were to break out of the serial trap he would have to construct a "panoramic novel," one built on a large framework and one that allowed for numerous characters and several subplots. For Haycox, movement toward this goal was difficult because his literary agent, his editors, and many of his friends encouraged him to write better Westerns, but no one pushed him toward a complete break from his previous literary efforts.

And, as one might expect, Haycox did not make a sharp change. He repeated his earlier experiments with small innovations. In *Canyon Passage* (1945), a novel focusing on Jacksonville, Oregon, during its formative years, Haycox attempted his panoramic novel. But despite all the action and abundant character types, the novel is not effective. Too much reliance on stock figures and external motivation for the characters' actions weaken the work. Some of the same problems beset *Long Storm* (1946), which deals with Portland during the Civil War. In this book, Haycox's first novel after twenty-one serials, he tried to marry a series of reflective characters with an action plot; the marriage did not work, but Haycox was convinced that with more practice he could keep the union intact. His second attempt at a non-serial, *The Adventurers* (1955), proved that Haycox was still wide of his mark. He was dissatisfied with this story of life in Oregon in the 1860s and set it aside for further work. But he died before he was able to complete his revisions and to smooth out the abrupt transitions and faulty narrative perspective that marred the novel.[22]

Sometime during the last two or three years before he died Haycox came to the project he worked on for the remainder of his literary career. Since the early part of 1944 nearly all of his fiction had dealt with Oregon. Now he formulated a plan to cover the history of his state from 1840 until the turn of the century in several volumes of fiction. At first he planned four or five novels, but as he began writing the first of the series he decided on a trilogy. He had great hopes for the project because it would not only delineate important occurrences in the region's history but also embody his best writing. If he were to leave something for posterity it would be in his trilogy of historical novels about the Oregon country.[23]

The Earthbreakers, Haycox's final novel, is a summary of the last fifteen years of his writing career. It is, first of all, the closest he came to the "panoramic" novel he had promised as early as 1937. It is, again, historical fiction on the broad scale with emphasis on character conflict and some recounting of historical fact. More than this, it deals with man and his world, an emphasis that had become increasingly important to Haycox after the publication of *Bugles in the Afternoon*. He hoped, as he mentioned in 1948, that the novel would be an escape from his earlier novels and an "explanation of this little figure crawling on the earth whom we call man— so little and so potentially great."[24]

The novel treats a group of pioneers completing their long trek overland and entering the Oregon Territory in 1845. The plot carries them through one year of existence, the choosing of land, the building of cabins, the establishing of a frontier settlement, and the clash of manifold interests that arise in the revelation of the human situation. The novel contains several story lines, but Haycox weaves together the many relationships and is able to dissect the characters as he tells their story.

Yet in essence *The Earthbreakers* is a tale about Rice Burnett. Rice is at the center of the novel, and most of the relationships established among other characters implicate him. Having spent a portion of his life as a trapper, he has decided to divorce himself from his anarchic past and to build a grist mill in a new settlement. His background is similar to that of Cal Lockyear, another ex-mountain man, who has come along to Oregon. But the reactions of Lockyear to the new circumstances reflect an attitude toward civilization far different from Burnett's. Bob Hawn is the third mountain man. He preceded the other two men to the Oregon Country and is living with an Indian woman. His confrontation with the immigrants illustrates still another reaction to society.

Along the trail westward Burnett becomes interested in Edna Lattimore, as restless and ardent a woman as Haycox had portrayed. She wants a man and makes little attempt to disguise her desire for Rice. A more difficult woman for Rice to comprehend is Katherine Gay, the quiet and composed daughter of John Gay, the nominal leader of the group of settlers. A large part of the plot deals with the choice that Rice has to make between these two women.

Alongside and overlapping the problems of Rice Burnett are threads of several subplots. Doctor Ralph Witcomb is attracted to Lucy, the wife of George Collingwood, a man driven, above all else, to gathering the esteem of others. The rest of the community countenances the extramarital relationship because of their dislike for Collingwood, but when Lockyear is explicit in his inclinations toward Edna Lattimore, no similar sympathy is exhibited. Both are adjudged guilty of an immoral relationship, and no one condones the actions of either. In another subplot, Bob Hawn looks forward to the coming of the settlers. Not long after their arrival, however, he senses a difference in his Indian wife, Louisa. She suspects that he wants to return to his people and to leave her. He tries to quiet her doubts and so does Rice. But she leaves Hawn, largely because she thinks her suspicions are confirmed in the haughty attitude that the white women exhibit toward her.

The reflections of Rice Burnett provide the clearest glimpse of what Haycox has to say about the game of life and the part that participants ought to play. A man, Rice thinks, must understand Nature and play the cards she has dealt him; if he does not, life will seem meaningless.

> Nature, [he continues] hating the solitary thing—for the solitary thing has no function—had placed in man a sense of incompleteness which made him drift toward others; denied this closeness, he shrank and died. Not that she cared; for man was a vessel she created by the millions, and it didn't matter how many of these claypots were cracked along the way so long as a few survived to transmit the liquid she had poured into them; it was the liquid that mattered to her, not the pot. Man's dream of dignity was his own creation, not hers, and his suffering came of trying to make the dream real against the indifference of earth and sky to his individual fate.[25]

The final scene in the novel dramatizes this idea. The death of Katherine's father, John Gay, occurs at the moment that Rice and Katherine agree on marriage. The tragedy of the father's death must be seen in light of the younger couple's carrying on the content and force of his life. One vessel is destroyed, but the important life fluid is transferred to new ones.

Moreover, if the individual declares war against the odds and expects total victory, he is more likely than not to bring on his own defeat. Cal Lockyear is this self-defeating type. He viciously attacks the laws of the settlement and only gains thereby the hatred of all. His continued recalcitrance leads eventually to his being hunted like an animal and killed. Bob Hawn, on the other hand, tries to withdraw from society, but his desires reveal the inadequacy of his role. The answer is the one Rice finds. A man has to have, most of all, the will to exist, individually and as a part of a group. He must not expect victory, but at best a draw. Only perseverance of this type will bring satisfaction of any sort.

Rice Burnett is the most fully drawn of all of Haycox's characters. Prior to Rice, all heroes are confined within a rigid code of sexual morality. The author's previous reluctance to allow more than a flickering doubt or two in the hero's mind concerning his sexual drives was probably a hangover from his ties to the Western. But even in *Long Storm* and *The Adventurers*, Adam Musick and Mark Sheridan are kept from any indiscretions, although such possibilities are available. This is not the case with Rice. He succumbs to his passions as well as to the elemental desires of Edna. That he should do so seems consistent with his other actions, particularly in view of his search for the total meaning of life. Rice's character, when compared to Haycox's earlier heroes, is not, therefore, the result of dividing all men into the white and black hats and making explicit distinctions among them.[26] Rice is more complex, more ambiguous, and not merely a stock Western hero. Revealing in this connection are his musings about his relations with Edna. He thinks of her needs and desire for fulfillment and feels her presence.

> She came to him now as she had so many nights before; she settled warm-flanked beside him, laughing a little, whispering. This was the imperative reverie of a lone man, flesh's need tangled through the soul's need so that as he used her he endowed her with grace. Without grace it was brutal; without flesh it was bloodless. Lot White [the preacher] would have said that one was evil and the other perfection, but Lot was wrong, they were not two separate things, they were parts of one thing and so long as he was alive these alternate thrusts would have their way; the conflict had been built into him and he could no more change it than he could chop himself in halves and live.[27]

Human beings, Rice thinks, are combinations of good and evil. This duality of human nature was not easy for Haycox to deal with, but once he began to work with the subject he was excited about its possibilities in his subsequent fiction.[28]

In addition to drawing fuller and more persuasive characters, Haycox makes use of literary devices to augment the impact of his novel. The sequence of events begins in the fall and ends in the late spring. The moods of the settlers parallel the changing seasons. The disappointments of the early days in Oregon deepen into despair during the winter months of continual rain. But with the coming of spring the spirits of the settlers are revitalized. Here is Haycox's first use of the montage device. And though the mood of the novel is predominantly somber, periodic flashes of humor increase the scope of the novel in providing welcome relief from the dominant tone. The comic scenes in *The Earthbreakers*, principally in the conversations between the preacher, Lot White, and the married women, are

Haycox's first use of humor since he abandoned the sidekick figure in his Westerns of the early thirties.

The Earthbreakers is Haycox's best novel. It portrays universal themes—love, hate, and jealousy—in a convincing fashion. It combines smoothly the active and contemplative moods of its characters. It avoids the largest fault of the Western: adventure for adventure's sake. In short, it combines the impact of general and particular, of good and evil, and of active and reflective. It is not a Western but a novel of the West.[29]

What should be the final estimate of Haycox's writings? Interpreters of the western literary scene have had difficulty in answering this question. Shortly after Haycox died, Bernard DeVoto summed up Haycox's literary contribution when he remarked, "Ernest Haycox, who was the old pro of horse opera and came closer than anyone else to making good novels of it, left his mark—I should say his brand—on the style as well as the content." Recent writers of Westerns, he added, were "all trying to be Haycox and to go beyond him, though no one as good at the job as he [had] yet arrived."[30] Bill Gulick, a western writer, added an important footnote to DeVoto's appraisal: "Ernest Haycox's final and most exasperating problem . . . was breaking the bounds of the very form he had created —the Adult Western—and moving into the field of the Historical Novel, as he obviously was doing in his last few books, such as *The Earthbreakers* and *The Adventurers*."[31] Was Haycox, as DeVoto argues, an author of superior Westerns, or is Gulick correct in suggesting that Haycox moved beyond the Western in his final work? I am convinced that Gulick is closer to the truth in his evaluation of Haycox's accomplishments.

Throughout most of his career, Haycox never comprehended the fertile literary possibilities of the American West. He came to subjects not through a search for a region redolent with materials for serious fiction but mainly through his realization that the use of the West in his writings offered, at the time, the best possibility for sales. This being the case, it was several years before he came to respect the West in any terms other than economic ones. Even toward the end of his career he refrained from stressing the distinctive qualities of the region. He never, for example, made use of dialect, regional character types, or the sense of place in the fashion of two other writers of the Northwest, H. L. Davis and James Stevens. As one of his infrequent essays, published in *Northwest Harvest*,[32] indicates, he viewed the Pacific Northwest as another portion of the West, with few if any unique regional qualities. It was this attitude that made Haycox so different from Davis, who sensed the distinctive traits of his region and set out to put them pungently and realistically into his fiction. Davis maintained, along with Stevens, that Haycox, Robert Ormond Case, and their teacher, W. F. G. Thacher, were guilty of commercializing the West, of playing up the sensational in order to promote sales. Davis and Stevens added that Haycox and his literary friends were ignoring the abundant materials of regionalism that were so close to the surface in the Pacific Northwest and could be easily explored.[33]

It was only in his final novel that Haycox came close to writing a first-rate northwestern regional novel. Earlier, like Owen Wister, he had been guilty of writing about cowboys without the cows; but in *The Earth-breakers* he captured some of the rich essence of the pioneer experience. He asked the essential and meaningful questions: What was it like to come to an entirely new environment and to face hardships hitherto unknown? What happened to the optimistic pioneers, who were ill-prepared to grapple with the cruel and often brutal frontier circumstances? Did they most often work together or against one another? How were law and order to be maintained in a new community? How important were institutions and their representatives; what roles did preachers and schoolmasters play? How did the settlers feel about the government so far away in Washington? In picturing the working out of these problems Haycox attempted to treat the essence of a complex human experience, the goal of any work of literary art.

So evolved the literary career of Ernest Haycox. Commencing his treatment of the West within the prescriptions of a popular literary mode, he slowly refined the methods of his craft, along the way adding techniques that gave his Westerns a distinctive quality. Emphasizing history and character conflict, he began to write historical Westerns. Finally, in the most important break of his career, he tried to produce a significant northwestern novel. Unfortunately, he died before he could achieve the large goal of his last years. Haycox's growth was gradual, but his development illustrates an author determined enough to defy popular demands and honest enough to write fiction consistent with his changing literary beliefs.

---

1. Except for brief visits elsewhere, Haycox lived outside the Northwest only during his stint on the Mexican Border in the summer of 1916, his nearly two years in the First World War (1917-1919), and the months he spent in New York City in 1925-1926. He lived continuously in Portland after the late 1920s.
2. Among the other writers of the Northwest who contributed largely to pulp and slick magazines were Frank Richardson Pierce of Seattle, Robert Ormond Case of Portland, and Russell Bankson of Spokane. All wrote Westerns, and all were friends of Haycox. Recent commentary on the Western is much indebted to the work of John G. Cawelti, especially his essays on formula fiction and *Six-Gun Mystique* (Bowling Green, Ohio: Bowling Green Univ. Popular Press, 1971). His most recent work is *Adventure, Mystery, and Romance: Formula Stories as Art and Popular Culture* (Chicago: Univ. of Chicago Press, 1976), which includes a section on the Western, pp. 192-259. I have not relied heavily on Cawelti's discussions of the Western as formula fiction because I wish to put major stress on Haycox's career and his use of history.

3. Much of what follows is drawn from my "The Literary Career of a Western Writer, Ernest Haycox, 1899-1950," Diss. Univ. of Oregon, 1966.

4. I have traced some of the origins and lines of historical development of the Western in "Origins of the Western," *Journal of Popular Culture*, 6 (Spring 1972), 799-805, and "The Historical Development of the Western," *Journal of Popular Culture*, 7 (Winter, 1973), 717-26.

5. Ernest Haycox to W. F. G. Thacher, Feb. 1, 1929, School of Journalism Records, Univ. of Oregon, Eugene. All manuscript collections cited, unless indicated otherwise, are housed in the Oregon Collection at the University of Oregon.

6. Charles Alexander, "Haycox on Cows," Albany *Democrat*, Feb. 9, 1929, p. 4; Ernest Haycox to Charles Alexander, Feb. 15, 1929, Charles Alexander Papers. Another reviewer, commenting on the plot of *Free Grass*, said: "The plot follows a dusty trail into the Dakotas, sometimes at stampede rate, but always with interest. . . . Haycox puts no affected swagger into the story. He simply tells it and tells it so well, so vividly, that it becomes history as well as romance." Portland, *Oregon Journal*, Feb. 17, 1929, mag. sec., p. 4.

7. *Free Grass* (New York: Doubleday, Doran and Company, 1929), p. 8.

8. Haycox has Lorena dressed as a man, and in doing so he was following a dime novel tradition that Henry Nash Smith discusses at length in a chapter on the dime novel heroine in *Virgin Land: The American West as Symbol and Myth* (Cambridge, Mass.: Harvard Univ. Press, 1950). Emerson Hough was severely castigated by several reviewers for placing a woman among the cattle drovers in *North of 36*, a novel which was also published in the 1920s.

9. W. H. Hutchinson gives Haycox credit for being the first writer of Westerns to use the formula of two heroines. See his "Virgins, Villains, Varmints," *The Rhodes Reader* (Norman, Okla.: Univ. of Oklahoma Press, 1957), pp. xiv-xv.

10. *Bugles in the Afternoon* (Boston: Little, Brown & Company, 1944; New York: Bantam Books, 1962). Some of these ideas and phrases are drawn from my "Ernest Haycox: The Historical Western, 1937-1943," *South Dakota Review*, 5 (Spring 1967), 35-54.

11. E. A. Brininstool, *A Trooper with Custer* (Columbus, Ohio: The Hunter-Trader-Trapper Co., 1925); and Fred Dustin, *The Custer Fight* (Hollywood: privately printed, 1936), and Dustin, *The Custer Tragedy* (Ann Arbor: Edwards Brothers, Inc., 1939). All three books are in the Haycox Memorial Library at the University of Oregon and contain annotations in Haycox's hand.

12. Edward S. Luce, *Keogh, Comanche and Custer* (St. Louis: John Swift Company, 1939).

13. W. A. Graham, *The Story of the Little Big Horn* (New York: The Century Company, 1926).

14. Haycox to Ray Everitt [Haycox's editor at Little, Brown], July 14, 1943, Haycox Files, Little, Brown and Company, Boston.

15. Fred Dustin praises Haycox's historical research in Dustin to Little, Brown and Company, Feb. 1, 1944, Little, Brown files, Boston. A copy of E. A. Brininstool's *Crazy Horse* is in the Haycox Memorial Library and carries the following by the author on the frontispiece concerning *Bugles in the Afternoon*: the novel, Brininstool writes, "contains the most thrilling and most plausible account of the Custer fight of any other book."

16. While yet an undergraduate, Haycox began reading about Custer. His library contains copies of Mrs. Custer's *Boots and Saddles* (New York: Harper

and Brothers, 1913), and her *Tenting on the Plains* (New York: C. L. Web-
ster and Co., 1889). He also had read Brininstool's edition of F. W. Benteen,
The Custer Fight (Hollywood, privately published, 1933) and several other
firsthand sources. In addition, Haycox tried, whenever possible, to interview
anyone who had served with Custer or who was closely related to someone who
had been in the Seventh Cavalry. See Haycox to Arthur B. Epperson, April
26, [undated, 1930 or 1931], Haycox Papers.

17. *Bugles*, p. 203.
18. *Bugles*, p. 204.
19. *Bugles*, p. 239.
20. For bibliographical material I am indebted to a Haycox bibliography compiled
by Jill M. Haycox and Jack Chord, "Ernest Haycox Fiction—A Checklist,"
The Call Number, 25 (Fall 1963-Spring 1964), 5-27.
21. Haycox's uncertainties at this point in his career are documented in his correspondence on file at the University of Oregon and in the authors' files of Little,
Brown.
22. I have discussed this problem in "The Literary Career," pp. 175-77. Additional information is available in the Little, Brown files.
23. Robert O. Case to R. W. Etulain, Feb. 1, 1964. Ernest Haycox, Jr., "How My
Father Came to Write *The Adventurers*," *Wings* (January 1955), p. 5.
24. Quoted in V. L. O. Chittick, ed. *Northwest Harvest* (New York: Macmillan
Company, 1948), p. 39.
25. *The Earthbreakers* (New York: Bantam Books, 1959), p. 10.
26. Saul David, "The West of Haycox Westerns," *The Call Number*, 25 (Fall
1963-Winter 1964), 28-29; *Saturday Review*, 25 (March 1, 1962), p. 17.
27. *Earthbreakers*, p. 92.
28. Interview with Angus Cameron, Aug. 5, 1965, New York City. Cameron, who
was Haycox's last editor with Little, Brown, did much to help Haycox see the
complexities of human nature and encouraged him to avoid the stereotyped
characters of the Western. Cameron's letters to Haycox in the Little, Brown
files are filled with suggestions on how Haycox could leave the field of the
Western and become an historical novelist.
29. The reactions of Thacher to *The Earthbreakers* changed after its publication.
He read a draft "with growing delight, then with amazement, and finally with
the jubilant sense of vicarious triumph." Thacher, "Oregon Authors I Have
Known," Univ. of Oregon Browsing Room Lecture, April 8, 1953. Later, he
felt that the novel was too much a hybrid: the superimposing of "frank descriptions of sexual behavior on the substructure of *action*." Thacher to James
R. Nation, Sept. 6, 1956, Haycox Collection.
30. DeVoto, "Phaëthon on Gunsmoke Trail," *Harper's*, 209 (December 1954),
14, 16.
31. Gulick to R. W. Etulain, Sept. 27, 1965.
32. Haycox, "Is There a Northwest?" *Northwest Harvest*, pp. 39-51.
33. The criticisms of Davis and Stevens are contained in their pamphlet *Status
Rerum* (The Dalles: privately printed, [1927]). This attack on writers like
Haycox and Case is necessary reading for those wishing to understand the
Northwest literary scene in the twenties and thirties.

Idaho novelist Vardis Fisher portrays another subregion of the Pacific Northwest in the dry and lonely sagebrush country of the Snake River Valley. The cultural ties of this area link it, in some respects, more closely to the vast, arid-hearted West than to the populous, green Pacific coastal strip. In the following essay, Barbara Meldrum describes Fisher's Idaho and his fictional characters in terms of the classic "West" of Crèvecoeur and Frederick Jackson Turner and invites us by implication to test our conceptions of "Northwest" against these larger definitions. Barbara Meldrum is professor of English at the University of Idaho. She has written numerous articles on American literature and is currently working on a study of the image of women in the literature of the American West.

Vardis Fisher's Antelope People: Pursuing an Elusive Dream

Barbara Meldrum

From the earliest days of our country we have had an ambivalent attitude toward the West and what the West means. In 1782 Crèvecoeur expressed this ambivalence in his *Letters from an American Farmer*; the new American was a westward pilgrim best embodied in the class of freeholders, people "respectable for their industry, their happy independence, the great share of freedom they possess, the good regulation of their families, and for extending the trade and the dominion of our mother country." Crèvecoeur's happy farmers promoted material progress while achieving individual fulfillment through worthwhile labor, family affection, and a sense of independence and freedom. But Crèvecoeur also acknowledged the essential role played by the pioneers who were directly influenced by the rugged environment they sought to tame in the name of advancing agriculture—the "back settlers" who "appear to be no better than carnivorous animals. . . . They are a kind of forlorn hope" who precede the more civilized farmers. They become hunters and, "once hunters, farewell to the plough. The chase renders them ferocious, gloomy, and unsociable." They live off the land and become lazy and careless; "eating of wild meat . . . tends to alter their temper," and rather than manifesting a noble independence and freedom, they demonstrate "a strange sort of lawless profligacy."[1] But the freedom of the untamed, uncultivated frontier also had its appeal for Crèvecoeur; near the end of his *Letters* he wrote of the attractions of the thinly inhabited western regions where one might cheerfully go in quest of peace.[2] Although fundamentally Crèvecoeur was committed to an agrarian ideal, which he thought could coexist with the ideals of independence and freedom (or what might be termed "individualism"), he saw the lawless, degenerate frontiersman as an essential link in his chain of progress and he finally admitted to the attractions of the frontier life.

Henry Nash Smith has pointed out a similar tension in the Daniel Boone tales, where Boone was heralded both as freedom-loving frontiersman, a "child of nature who fled into the wilderness before the advance of settlement," and as "standard-bearer of civilization and refinement," one who rejoiced to see the inevitable influx of American freemen into the rich western lands.[3]

Frederick Jackson Turner is, however, the most articulate and important spokesman for our twentieth-century view of the meaning of the western frontier experience. In his delineation of the so-called frontier thesis he describes the social stages of typical frontier development. The western pioneer returns to "primitive conditions" as the "wilderness masters the colonist. . . . He must accept the conditions which [the frontier] furnishes, or perish." But this experience is described by Turner as a "development" through which a "perennial rebirth" takes place. On the frontier, defined as "the meeting point between savagery and civilization," the pioneer "little by little . . . transforms the wilderness." The result is not only the taming of the wilderness but the development of a new American character. In describing the "intellectual traits" of the new American, Turner states that

> to the frontier the American intellect owes its striking characteristics. That coarseness and strength combined with acuteness and inquisitiveness; that practical, inventive turn of mind, quick to find expedients; that masterful grasp of material things, lacking in the artistic but powerful to effect great ends; that restless, nervous energy; that dominant individualism, working for good and for evil, and withal that buoyancy and exuberance which comes with freedom—these are traits of the frontier, or traits called out elsewhere because of the existence of the frontier.[4]

For Turner, then, the American character owes its individualism, resourcefulness, and sense of freedom to the frontier experience. The existence of free land was essential, in Turner's view, to this development, and he remained strongly committed to the idea that an agrarian economy would best foster American democracy. What in Crèvecoeur was a clear distinction between the frontiersman and the agrarian becomes in Turner a unified ideal wherein the best traits of frontiersman and agrarian are combined and are realizable in the cyclical experience that occurs when one is "reborn" on the frontier and passes through the primitive to the civilized stage of development. Although Turner acknowledged some negative traits and side effects of this Americanization process, he is essentially positive. The American West offers an opportunity for individual fulfillment that is both materialistic (the attainment of property) and idealistic (the pride of self-achievement, independence, and freedom).

It seems to me, however, that the seemingly unified ideal of Turner is misleading. One problem is that Turner seems to be speaking about Americans generally (thus including women), whereas the experience he describes applies more to men than to women. As David Potter has pointed out, the Turner thesis speaks of opportunities that in fact "were opportunities for men and not, in any direct sense, opportunities for women." Potter concludes that the "frontier for American women" was the city, where women could achieve independence.[5] Turner fails to see that the frontier meant different things to women, and he ignores the impact of the woman's differing experience on the man with whom she was associated. Also, by failing to distinguish clearly between the frontiersman and the agrarian, Turner oversimplifies the nature of the western frontier experience. He sees the western venture in masculine terms, whereas there was really a tension between the masculine and feminine, the frontiersman and agrarian.

Perhaps my point can be made clearer by reference to the views of several literary critics. Roy Male, in *Hawthorne's Tragic Vision*, wrote that America has been "from its beginning . . . a predominantly masculine venture . . . a gamble that movement westward might assure not only prosperity but also some kind of moral purification. . . . In this predominantly masculine enterprise, the role of woman has always been anomalous."[6] He then proceeds to show how Hawthorne used the masculine-feminine dichotomy in his fiction to focus on some of the fundamental problems of human existence; in Hawthorne's fiction, man is space-oriented and characterized by a tendency to speculate; woman is time-bound and characterized by a tendency to conserve. Other critics have noted the masculine emphasis in much western fiction, particularly in the Westerns of the cowboy and gunfighter. Wallace Stegner writes of two forces, "the freedom-loving, roving man and the civilizing woman" (terms which recall Male's discussion of Hawthorne). "Almost every writer who has dealt with family stresses on the frontier has . . . [written of] male freedom and aspiration versus female domesticity, wilderness versus civilization, violence and danger versus the safe and tamed."[7] The dichotomy Stegner describes seems most reminiscent of the frontiersman versus agrarian that we have seen in Crèvecoeur's *Letters*. A recent critic, Jay Gurian, extends the dichotomy to include the two dominant myths of the West, the myth of the Garden and the myth of the Western Hero: "Behind the Myth of the Garden there is the Romance of Democratic Settlement, which affirms that the 'good' end—civilization, commerce, culture and church—was the guiding goal of the American settler. . . . Similarly, behind the myth of the Western Hero, there is the Romance of Lawlessness. . . . While one romance glorifies violence, death, and 'evil,' in the various frontiers, the other glorifies peace, order, welfare and natural goodness."[8] These dualities, I propose, can be seen as the conflict between masculine and feminine traits and values. The linking of masculine with the frontiersman is easily seen; the linking of feminine with the agrarian is not so simple and needs further clarification.

The alignment of the feminine force with the agrarian is most apparent when we consider the commitment to home, civilization, family responsibility, and the productivity of "mother nature." Also, the word *materialism* derives etymologically from roots which suggest both *mother* and *matter* or substance.[9] Classical mythology associates materialism with Demeter, the Greek goddess of corn, who is both matriarchal and agricultural. The title character of Willa Cather's *My Ántonia* provides one concrete example of this linking of woman with the agrarian and the material abundance of nature. However, in much western fiction woman does not find fulfillment in an agrarian life: she is trapped rather than free, she ages prematurely, she may even lose her sanity. Her husband, the male agrarian, is seldom wholly committed to the feminine-agrarian, but is usually a blend of the masculine-frontiersman and the agrarian. Just as Turner fails to distinguish clearly between the complementary but essentially conflicting claims of the frontiersman and the agrarian, so the western farmer seldom understands the duality of his own inner nature and his ambivalence toward these conflicting values, for he is both freedom-loving, individualistic frontiersman and home-loving, productive agrarian. If he does not achieve the realization of his dreams, his wife may seem to be responsible for his failure since she limits the idealistic speculation of the man, limits his freedom, ties him to family responsibilities, and promotes an empty materialism. But the woman too faces unrealized dreams, for her own avenues of fulfillment are dominated by the man upon whom she depends and whose "vision" has thrust her into the hard life of the frontier. Although by all our cultural expectations she should achieve her fulfillment in home and family and the productivity of nature, she is all too often overwhelmed and defeated.

Many western writers have dealt with the ideas discussed above. The purpose of this essay is to explore ways in which Vardis Fisher has portrayed the western frontier experience in three novels of the Antelope country of southeastern Idaho: *Toilers of the Hills* (1928), *Dark Bridwell* (1931), and *April: A Fable of Love* (1937).[10] As Fisher worked on his first novel,[11] he wrote a number of sonnets about the people of the Antelope Hills; some he destroyed, but thirteen were published in periodicals and anthologies.[12] These surviving sonnets provide vignettes of Idaho pioneers, some of whom reappear in the novels. Although the country they live in is beautiful, their lives do not reflect that beauty, and in various ways they evade life, living in fear and distrust, avoiding emotional involvements that might add meaning to their existence, haunted by doubts and lacking faith in the God they profess, overwhelmed by events they are powerless to change. One character "might now be a poet" if he but lived "where poetry's not transmuted into prose" ("Dick Rowe"). Another hates the mountains because they dwarf his own dominion; so he goes eastward to the city where, "Beneath a torn earth, sewer-foul and dredge-gutted, / He heard life building tunnels underground" ("Perg Jasper"). Another, Lizzie North, is surrounded with the drudgery of housework and baby tending, takes out her frustrations and hatred on her baby, and drones "one crazy song: / *Love is a gift to man, the woman pays.*" One character, however, is portrayed positively, and that is Joe Hunter; in a sonnet which anticipates Dock Hunter of *Toilers of the Hills,* Fisher tells how this pioneer entered "the grayest waste of Idaho," "clubbed the desert and . . . made it grow" until "he left the aged and barren hills aglo / With color." This man "poured his great dream into golden wheat; / Until his gnarled and calloused hands had wrought / A deep and quiet holiness of work."

Toilers of the Hills is Fisher's most consistently agrarian novel, and Dock Hunter provides a convincing portrait of the hard-working pioneer of vision and ingenuity who struggles to transform a wilderness into a garden. The novel focuses on two central conflicts: one the conflict between man and nature as Dock seeks to conquer nature and make it productive; the other, the conflict between Dock and his wife Opal, between the pioneer who lives and works for the future and loves the soil, and the woman who lacks his vision and his love of the land, who is haunted by the isolation, the loneliness of their pioneer life, and who longs for community life and the relative comforts of the valley they have left behind.

Fisher's tale begins with the Hunters' move into the Antelope Hills in about 1906. Dock breaks new ground, trying to dry farm, believing that these barren hills can be made to produce grain. He maintains that anything of value comes through hard work and that continued work will bring positive results. Although he loves the land, his love is not for the natural beauties—the wild flowers and birds—but for the potential productivity as man conquers nature. It is a formidable task, for the dry soil is hard and unresponsive to Dock's meager tools, the brush resists his grubbing efforts, and the essential moisture comes seldom and must somehow be made to count and not be wasted. But Dock's determination is equal to the task—" 'I'll conquer them brush or I'll bust my worseless neck,' " he exclaims (p. 26) ; and he believes this country needs " 'men who would never say die, men who would turn this place into fields of gold. Worse spots than this had been conquered by men; worse trials than these had been endured by them.' " He takes heart in the example of his own father who "had been a pioneer on new frontiers" (pp. 199-200). Dock conceives of his own task in a broad perspective which lends both dignity and hope to his endeavor.

> Men had conquered worse than weeds; they had endured worse than drouth. They were conquering the world day by day, inch by inch, and when this job was done, they would conquer all else in sight: the sun and the moon, if need be, and even the stars, if their minds turned that way. They would conquer the mountains, too, if that was their mind, and it would not surprise him a little bit if some day the mountains were orchards and fields of grain. Some time, by a strange turn of will, they would conquer lightning

and thunder, and they would make rain come when they wanted
it, and when they did not want it they would somehow send it
away. Had they not conquered all the wild animals of earth and
shut them up in pens or hitched them to plows or made them give
milk and lay eggs? . . . Men would invent perpetual motion before
they were done with it; they would make water run uphill as fast
as it ran down; and they would discover ways whereby to make
wheat an overbearer, like fruit trees and innumerable other things,
and once seed was planted, then the job would be forever done.
And these were only a scant few of the things, he could now see,
which men would do. They would invent machines that would
harvest crops without the need of a man at all, and they would
make fruit trees grow as big as pines and strawberry plants as
large as sagebrush. (pp. 230-31)

But Dock's achievement is slow in coming; year grinds on to year after
weary year, and Dock and Opal still live in a cottonwood shanty with a
sod roof that drips mud when rain falls, they still rely on water carried
from the distant river or hoarded from melting snow, their debts grow, and
Dock's grain is still scanty and weed-infested. But three factors eventually
lead to a qualified success for Dock. One is World War I, which brings
inflated prices for grain. The other is Dock's experimentation, the application of mind to matter, whereby he has developed dry farming techniques which eventually make his farm the most productive one in the
region. The third is the forbearance of nature itself which does not destroy
his bumper crop with hail or frost. Success comes, then, through a combination of luck, fertility of nature, and inner traits of human character and
intelligence. Dock's dream is fulfilled, perhaps not in the grandiose terms
of his early vision, and not in time for him to avoid the wearing effects of
his toil, but his dream has proven to be realizable.

Not so, however, has been Opal's dream. Hers was of a home with running water and minimal comforts, of neighbors nearby, community and
fellowship, of beauty and life. Her dream has been swallowed up by
Dock's dream; her dream had to die. In the conflict between Dock and
Opal and the resolution of that conflict we can see the deeper dimensions
of the pioneer agrarian's experience.

Dock conceives of his role in strongly masculine terms. To things inside
the house he gives feminine names; to things outside, masculine names
(p. 101). At times he senses an awing power in nature that makes him
aware of his own relative insignificance; but at other times, as he seeks to
conquer nature, he feels as though he could embrace nature "and make it
yield to him, make it moving and supple and eager like a woman's body"
(p. 66). Opal senses that to Dock the hills are so alive that he will want
to "marry one of them hills" (p. 100). As Dock tills the soil Opal sees he
is "scarring the gray breast of the earth" (p. 252). His work is an act of
conquest whereby he imposes his masculine will upon the feminine earth.

A frontiersman at heart, he idolizes his father and recounts tales of his father's exploits over man and beast (pp. 108-09). Even his name, Hunter, he believes to be a sign of his fighting nature and commitment to a goal he will reach (pp. 255-56). Physical strength and swearing are signs of masculinity (p. 44); if a neighbor's stray cow gets into his wheat field, he executes primitive law and justice to protect his own property (pp. 124-25); male children are valued because they will be of use, whereas girls are of no account (p. 61). Dock's concept of his wife's role is that she should stand by him and support his hopes and dreams, be pretty and not work in the fields like a man, cook his meals and keep his house clean, produce male children and care for them, and achieve her own sense of fulfillment in the realization of his own dreams. In Dock's male-dominated world, Opal his little chance to realize her own dreams.

Several key scenes demonstrate the conflict between Dock and Opal. When they first arrive at the place which is to be their home, Opal is depressed by the greyness of land and sky all around her. She cannot see the colors Dock promises to bring to this barren land, and she longs for a home in the valley they have left behind. While Dock prepares their bed for the night, she wanders into the night and fails to respond to Dock's calls; when he finds her, she is "looking westward . . . over round hills that were like gray silences." With terror in her voice, she cries, " 'I can't stand these hills and them lonely mountains!' " But Dock reprimands her: " 'You promise to love a man and stick to him through hell and high water and then you go a-bawlun for your mother. You ain't no sight of a wife for a farmer' " (pp. 14-15). Later, when the much needed rain comes thundering down, dripping mud from the sod roof into the house and drenching all within that flimsy shelter, Opal reminds Dock of his failures and complains of the wet and cold; but Dock talks on and on of his dreams, works to keep household goods dry, and Opal wonders "at his dauntless way in the face of a pitiless nature that crushed completely her will to live" (p. 107). As the storm subsides, Dock builds a fire, cooks food, dries the bedding, all the while telling Opal about his father and then shifting to tales of his own future and what he will accomplish. His example brings to Opal new love and understanding for her husband, and she minds less the mud-stained cottage and Dock's sweat-soaked clothing. In the beauty of the new morning she goes outside and picks blossoms for her home. But when she enters, her pleasure is crushed when Dock reprimands her for picking blossoms that would have ripened into fruit that they could have eaten.

> She found herself again among the ugly things she hated . . . .
> She gathered the blossoms and threw them out into the mud of
> the dooryard. . . . Bitter rage and loneliness were choking her,
> pushing her heart down into the hard lump that it must become if

she remained here. The blue sky mocked her now and the showers of blossoms and all the wet sweet things of the hills. Going behind a bush she wept and moaned at the pain reaching through her being, at the sharp ache of something imprisoned in her breast, pushing out vainly to new life and dying there as it had been dying now for a long year. (pp. 113-14)

To Opal, these hills foster ugliness, loneliness, and death. So long as she maintains her own dream but remains with Dock in these hills, her life is as grey as the hills around her.

What is required of Opal is a total self-effacement. This comes in the final scene of the novel when her own dream dies and she takes Dock's dream for her own. She acknowledges that she has been " 'no account as a wife,' " but resolves to be better in the future: " 'We'll make our home as lovely as we can.' " Opal looks "at the long grey road leading valleyward. It was a road to forget, for she had closed the door to her dreams." As she looks around her, she sees the color of the hills, the golden rays of the setting sun, the purple valley, the lilac and orange of a cloud-castle, the deepening blue shadows and the golden haze. "And little by little the gray road blurred and vanished" (pp. 360-61). The greyness is now identified with the valley; hand in hand with Dock, she sees the color and beauty of the life surrounding her.

Significantly, this resolution comes only after Dock's dream has been realized. They already have a new and better house, made possible by Dock's successful harvest and wartime prices; but making that house a "lovely home" is possible only when Opal renounces her dream and reconciles herself to the only home she will ever know. When early in the story Dock had reprimanded Opal for wanting to return to the valley, he had confessed, " 'I sometimes wonder why a man ever gets hisself a missus anyhow' " (p. 15). Indeed, one wonders whether he really does need Opal, for her nagging and her anticipation of defeat (that would enable her to return to the valley) certainly provide no help or encouragement for Dock. But the masculine vision of Dock needs woman to give significance to his achievement. This frontiersman pioneer wants home and family. The novel becomes, then, a classic portrayal of the male agrarian, who is both frontiersman and farmer, and his wife, who is imprisoned by the dimensions of her husband's world and who can find freedom and fulfillment only through total self-effacement.

In *Toilers of the Hills* Fisher maintains a detached perspective. Although much of the story is told from Opal's point of view, the overall effect is praise for Dock's indomitable pioneer spirit. In his next novel, however, Fisher expresses a much more ambivalent attitude toward agrarian values. *Dark Bridwell* begins with a prologue which describes the rugged Antelope Hills country to which Charley Bridwell takes his wife Lela. The first owners of their home had been a pioneer couple who had cleared enough acres for hay and a garden and had built a humble home. The man had loved the isolation of his mountain home, but his wife hated the loneliness and wild animals, so urged him to move away. The contrast sets the scene for Charley and Lela's drama, for Charley wishes to avoid the evils of civilization and brings his family here, believing his children will "grow up, with powerful bodies and clean minds" nurtured by nature (p. 316); but he has failed to account for inherited traits, the sinister effects of nature, and the opposing values of his wife.

Charley is a far cry from Dock Hunter. A frontiersman at heart, he disdains overalls as a sign of slavery. A vagabond in his early life, he settles down, but not to build a newer and better house or to till increasing acres; rather, he farms sporadically, hunts and traps, refuses to work a full day at a time, and enjoys life. He detests work because he believes work is a senseless striving for an accumulation of things of little value; as long as he can manage to get along without work, he is happy and content. When farmers come to ask him to help with harvest, he usually refuses and, when he points out the futility of labor to these men, the farmers blame their wives for making them work so hard (pp. 14-15).

Indeed, work is identified with woman in this novel; when Fisher contrasts the frontiersman with the agrarian, the frontiersman is clearly masculine and the agrarian, feminine. And both are identified with varying aspects of nature. Charley identifies with the mountains, which are "great hulks of philosophy and peace. . . they sat on their heels and let time move over them with good things." He also likes lakes, which are deep and still, rather than the river which annoys him with its constant striving, "as if it had work to do between its source and its graveyard of the sea. But it had nothing to do that was worth doing" (pp. 43-45). Lela, however, embodies the duality of mountains and river. She responds to the quiet beauty that surrounds her in this amphitheatre of the hills, the tranquility linking her with Charley, who nearly convinces her that she prefers the quietness of his indolent life. But she also identifies with the river, and this identification becomes increasingly stronger when Charley's domination of her life allows her creativity no outlet. Indeed, the anonymous narrator of the novel asserts that Charley's "greatest mistake" lies in his efforts to make Lela into "a kind of idle princess" who is not allowed to work. The river haunts her, makes her aware of her "desire to create, to build her life into a thing of meaning"; although its restless seeking seems to be as unchanging as the "chloroformed seasons of her life" (pp. 270-71), it keeps alive her ambition which is spurred into action by the dark side of Charley's nature.

Charley is both tender and violent, loving and cruel. Although he seeks to live attuned with nature, we soon learn that nature includes much which promotes cruelty. This aspect is most apparent in his son Jed, who is "schooled by savagery" and who feels both kinship and ageless enmity for rattlesnakes (pp. 152, 167). The solitude and ruthlessness of life in this mountain wilderness prompt him to reckless deeds; his growing hate for his father leads him to strive to exceed his father in cruelty (p. 153). Unlike Turner's frontier prototypes, the Bridwells are not reborn as upstanding American democrats through their immersion into the primitive wilderness; to Fisher, genetic inheritance usually counts more than environment, and nature can foster the dark side of man's nature as well as man's more socially acceptable traits.

Charley's two sons grow to hate him and leave home to seek a new life outside of the paradise Charley has sought to provide his family. His daughter is seduced by a sheepherder who seeks to revenge a cruel joke Charley once played on him, and the broken father forces a shotgun marriage. With her older children thus lost to her, Lela seeks some way to endure her life and prevent a repetition of disappointment in her newborn daughter's life when her nearest neighbor, Prudence Hunter, points the way for her: Prudence inspires her to work so that she can educate her daughter and tells her how to raise turkeys and make money from cheese, fruit, and vegetables. So is born a "new vision" for Lela who resolves to push aside her husband "and follow her path to freedom. No longer a house-fixture to be adored, sitting with useless lovely hands, she would go boldly into life, even as the river went" (p. 329). Undaunted in her ambition, she insists on mowing the hay herself in spite of Charley's complaint that mowing is man's work. But she joys in her work and even seems to grow younger (p. 340). Thus is framed her dream: "to earn and save money, to flee with Hetty, to find her sons" (p. 345).

For seven years she labors, successful in her agrarian efforts; never is her agrarian life an end in itself, but simply a means to an end; for her, freedom and fulfillment lie beyond these mountains, vaguely in the city where her sons have gone. Significantly, the goal is expressed as lying westward, even though literally it is eastward—just as Jed had followed his westward vision that would lead him east, for so deeply ingrained is our American sense of westering that we believe that vision must somehow lie westward even though for some, opportunity exists somewhere east of that presumed paradise which never really existed in the first place, or was more a prison than a paradise.[13]

And so Lela leaves, spurred to depart through a final brutal scene in which she believes Charley has corrupted her young son, her ambivalent hatred and love for Charley is resolved into a lively hate, and Jed returns in time to confirm that hatred and rescue his mother. Charley, alone in the desolation of his ruined paradise, tries to drown his grief with wine, then wanders off alone, "eastward . . . into the empire of solitude" (Epilogue). But he has been east before, and no opportunity beckons him; cursed and abandoned, he is damned to a living death of fragmented dreams.

It would seem that Lela's way has been best and that Charley has been proved wrong. But though Charley is defeated, he is not despised, and Lela's freedom is not the promise of new life. The narrator forewarns that her victory will be a hollow one, for he writes: "And in that hour of midwinter, seven years later, when she went forth into freedom, she forgot that deeper than ambition, as deep almost as motherhood itself, was her love for Charley Bridwell; and she did not remember until it was too late" (p. 335). The narrator also tells of Lela's sketches which she makes during the idle winter months. One of these is a painting of "the river buried under ice, its waters lost in a black and cold and flowing graveyard. Charley did not like this one. It made him think, he said, of something that had slaved all its life and then got lost, that had entombed itself with labor. . . . 'Hang it in the corner by the stove. Mebbe it'll thaw out'" (pp. 347-48). Then, in the last haunting image of the book, the narrator describes the abandoned and desolate Bridwell place: "Lying behind and under the stove are six empty wine bottles, deep with silence and age. And above hangs one of Lela's paintings, netted in spiderwebs. It shows a mighty river, caught in the power of its own unresting greed, smothering itself with bitter white death" (Epilogue). The ceaseless striving of the river of ambition leads not to life, but to death. Moreover, without love, endeavor is vain.

Fisher followed this powerful novel with his autobiographical tetralogy, also rooted in the Antelope Hills country of Idaho. Commenting years later about this period of his career, Fisher said, "I loathed and hated the Antelope country and was merely trying to come to some kind of terms with it."[14] That he did achieve a resolution to his own ambivalent attitude toward the region of his childhood can be seen, I believe, in his final Antelope novel, *April: A Fable of Love*. Fisher struggled with this book while writing his tetralogy, working through five different versions to produce the novel he later claimed was his favorite.[15] This short work of poetic prose is satirically comic in its portrayal of a homely fat girl who desperately wants to love and be loved but rejects the homely man who has patiently courted her since childhood because her lover is not like the romantic heroes she has read about in novels. The scene is still the Antelope Hills, but the impression of life is radically different from that of the earlier novels. We are not concerned with the pioneering era, but with a time of settled agrarian life. Yet even though the people portrayed are farmers, they do not seem to be working very hard. Physical needs are minimized in this fable which focuses on the problems of love.

The agrarian context is, however, still present and important. June's lover, Sol Incham, has lived in New York, Georgia, and Hollywood; although we learn nothing more specific about his background, we know that he is now a farmer, that he perceives the inner beauty of the homely June Weeg, and that he wants to marry her, thus suggesting that his years of wandering have led him to seek fulfillment of his dreams in a western agrarian life with wife and family. Sol's empty house becomes for June "a symbol of his need: something empty and unused, a loneliness waiting for a woman, for gentle ways to smooth it into beauty and repose" (p. 67). But the house haunts June, for she resists falling in love with Sol because she dreads the kind of married life she sees around her: marriage without love, the wife becoming nothing but a brood sow, beaten down by sweat and toil (p. 194). She longs instead for a gallant lover (a blend of frontiersman and knight in shining armor) who will come in beauty and strength and waft her away to a new life. Realizing her homeliness will not attract such a lover, she invents a new identity, which she names April for the beautiful month she likes best. But it is difficult to sustain such a fantasy, and she is continually brought face to face with the realities of a life she cannot come to terms with. She entertains various alternatives, each one an escape from the fate of an Antelope farmer's wife: she will become a nun, or a whore, or an actress; finally, she decides to leave and seek her fortune elsewhere. But before leaving, she is drawn to visit Sol once more to bid him farewell; not finding him at home, she notices how dirty his house is and how unlike Sol's home it was, for he was usually neat and clean. But she begins to realize that Sol's incentive to work and to keep a tidy home has been undermined by her apparently final rejection of him several months before. Without realizing why, she decides to clean up Sol's house before writing a farewell note (this is the first time in the novel that June engages in any work) ; then she decides to cook him a meal; then she sets the table for two, resolved to eat with him before leaving; finally Sol returns and, seeing "more in his face, more in his eyes, than she had ever found in books," she goes to his waiting arms (p. 206). This final scene, which was entitled "The Death of April" when Fisher published it separately as a short story, suggests that true beauty is of inner character, that self-fulfillment is more a matter of love than of material achievement, and that love can ennoble and give meaning to work. Only by facing the realities of life—which includes both beauty and ugliness—can one learn to give and to accept love.

Thus, in these three novels of the Antelope People, Vardis Fisher explores the possibilities of self-fulfillment through the western experience. *Toilers of the Hills* portrays the victory of the male agrarian in his pioneering struggle with nature; but that victory is measured against the consciousness of a wife who must surrender her own dream and adopt her husband's if she is to live with love and beauty. *Dark Bridwell* pits frontiersman against agrarian in a drama of conflicting dreams; although the narrative victory goes to the agrarian, that victory is undercut by the symbolism of the closing scene, and we know that all has been lost with the loss of love. In *April*, the love which gives meaning to life and to labor is found by both man and woman; self-effacement is not required, and beauty is found amidst the ugly realities of life. For Fisher, the West became much more than the meeting point between savagery and civilization; it became a state of mind, a paradise that must be found within, and that blossoms only through the dynamics of love.

---

1. J. Hector St. John de Crèvecoeur, *Letters from an American Farmer,* ed. W. P. Trent and Ludwig Lewisohn (New York: Albert and Charles Boni, 1925), pp. 72, 59-60, 67-68 (Letter III).
2. Crèvecoeur, pp. 287, 302-04, 315-18 (Letter XII). Crèvecoeur's narrator, James, decides that life with the Indians on the frontier is preferable to an agrarian life amid the perils of the Revolutionary War. Although recognizing that some hunting will be inevitable, he will try to avert the "charm of Indian education" which might induce his children to go completely native by encouraging agrarian labors as much as possible.
3. Henry Nash Smith, *Virgin Land: The American West as Symbol and Myth* (Cambridge: Harvard Univ. Press, 1950), pp. 55-56.
4. Frederick Jackson Turner, "The Significance of the Frontier in American History" (1893), in *The Frontier in American History*, ed. Ray A. Billington (New York: Holt, Rinehart and Winston, 1962), pp. 2-4, 37.
5. David M. Potter, "American Women and the American Character" (1959), in *History and American Society: Essays of David M. Potter*, ed. Don E. Fehrenbacher (New York: Oxford Univ. Press, 1973), pp. 280-84.
6. Roy R. Male, *Hawthorne's Tragic Vision* (Austin: Univ. of Texas Press, 1957), pp. 3-4.
7. Wallace Stegner, "History, Myth, and the Western Writer," in *The Sound of Mountain Water* (Garden City: Doubleday and Co., 1969), p. 195.
8. Jay Gurian, *Western American Writing: Tradition and Promise* (Deland, Florida: Everett/Edwards, 1975), pp. 4-5.
9. "mater-," in *American Heritage Dictionary of the English Language* (New York: American Heritage Publishing Co., Inc., 1969), p. 1527.
10. Page references are indicated in the text and are to the following editions: *Toilers of the Hills* (New York: Houghton Mifflin Co., 1928); *Dark Bridwell* New York: Houghton Mifflin Co., 1931); *April: A Fable of Love* (Caldwell, Idaho: The Caxton Printers, 1937).
11. Fisher wrote five novels which he destroyed; *Toilers* was his sixth, but first published novel. He wrote it, he said, "after reading the romantic foolishness of Willa Cather. There never were any pioneers of the kind she wrote about." *Vardis Fisher: A Critical Summary with Notes on His Life and Personality* (Caldwell, Idaho: The Caxton Printers, 1939), p. 6.
12. The Antelope People sonnets were published as follows. See *Voices: An Open Forum for the Poets*, 7 (March 1938), 203-04, for "Slim Scott," "Susan Hemp," "Konrad Myrdton," and 49 (April 1929), 134-36, for The North Family—"Charles North," "Baby North," "Lizzie North," "Sally North," "Jess North"; see *Anthology of Magazine Verse for 1928 and Yearbook of*

American Poetry, ed. William Stanley Braithwaite (New York: Harold Vinal, 1928), pp. 113-17, for "Slim Scott," "Susan Hemp," "Konrad Myrdton"; *Northwest Verse: An Anthology*, ed. Harold G. Merriam (Caldwell, Idaho: The Caxton Printers, 1931), pp. 137-39, for "Slim Scott," "Susan Hemp," "Konrad Myrdton," "Perg Jasper," "Joe Hunter"; see *Sunlit Peaks: An Anthology of Idaho Verse*, ed. Bess Foster Smith (Caldwell, Idaho: The Caxton Printers, 1931), pp. 74-75, for "Tim Doole," "Dick Rowe," "Hank Radder"; all but the last three sonnets were reprinted in Dorys C. Grover, *A Solitary Voice: Vardis Fisher* (New York: The Revisionist Press, 1973), pp. 50-55.

13. Jed looks "west, feeling that his path of life lay through that blue valley and beyond" and is lured by "the glory of cities and far shores." Although he looks westward, he imagines his journey will take him "eastward into the sun" across Nebraska, Iowa, the Atlantic, to France and beyond. When he actually leaves, he goes "westward," but on a "pilgrimage that was to lead him into many strange lands of earth" (pp. 214-15, 263-64). Thiel follows his brother "into the west" (p. 290). Lela is a "prisoner" in the supposed paradise of Charley's place and determines to "follow her path to freedom" to find her sons and to place her daughter in "a great and noble school" that could probably exist only in a city (pp. 275, 329, 345). A similar east-west confusion occurs in Rolvaag's *Giants in the Earth* when Per Hansa, lost in a snowstorm, keeps himself going with a vision of the Rocky Mountains which he regards as his westward gateway to the Pacific even though he is actually headed eastward. O. E. Rolvaag, *Giants in the Earth* (1927; rpt. New York: Harper and Row, 1965), pp. 255, 265-66.

14. Vardis Fisher, "Hometown Revisited 13: The Antelope Hills, Idaho," *Tomorrow*, 9 (December 1949), 18.

15. *Vardis Fisher: A Critical Summary*, p. 12. Fisher's opinion was published in 1939, before many of his books were written. Whether he still regarded *April* as his favorite book later in his career is not known. When asked in 1964 which of his novels he liked best, he replied, "This question, asked endlessly of writers, has always seemed to me to be childish." "Western Novel: A Symposium," *South Dakota Review*, 2 (Autumn 1974), 21.

George M. Armstrong received his Ph.D. in English at the University of California, Berkeley. His dissertation was on H. L. Davis and the westering experience in modern literature. In this essay Armstrong analyzes Davis's last published work, *Kettle of Fire*, to demonstrate Davis's skill in shaping deeply understood Oregon materials into an interpretation of the western experience as being fundamentally repetitive of the universal and unending search for meaning in human existence. Davis, Armstrong insists, was such a tough, uncompromising albeit compassionate, observer of the complexity and contradictions in life that he was incapable of reaching the easy and romantic answers that characterize so much writing about the American West. Professor Armstrong has taught in the English Departments at the University of Idaho and Washington State University. He has published several articles on H. L. Davis and is at work on a book on Loren Eiseley.

An Unworn and Edged Tool: H. L. Davis's Last Word on the West, "The Kettle of Fire"

George M. Armstrong

Aside from *Honey in the Horn*, kept alive partly by its actual merits and partly by its reputation as a Pulitzer Prize winner, H. L. Davis's work is unknown to most readers, even those with a predilection for western American subjects and authors. Critical notice of Davis has been infrequent if regular since his death in 1960.[1] His work has maintained a small but enthusiastic readership, with some scholarly interest in him as a representative western author but with little sense of his relevance to the larger context of American literature. The award of a Pulitzer to Wallace Stegner in 1972 for *Angle of Repose* has refocused critical attention on the place of western American writers of the mid-twentieth century within the American literary tradition, and it is my intention in this study of his last published work, the long story "The Kettle of Fire," to provide a view of Davis's fiction which might illustrate his relevance to, and stature within, that tradition.

Davis's mixed reception in his own lifetime was due to the very effort that he undertook. Like many of the best American artists (one might as well say "best artists"), he was consciously ahead of his time and behind it. His books are also hard to categorize, and thus difficult to criticize and market. They are characteristic American hybrids—Davis would not have shrunk at calling them bastards—western and yet not "Westerns"; modern in treatment of their themes and yet set in the past; historical but clearly not "historical novels." Such problems of categorization plague the critic and bookseller and too often in American literary history have resulted in unique works and authors simply being "shelved," rather than marketed, bought, and read.

I suspect that Davis's work will survive to become an enduring part of American fiction precisely because of those qualities which make its present position so tenuous. Like many hybrids, Davis's books exhibit an extraordinary vigor—they are lively, full of facts, fictions, tales, people, places, things, sounds, smells, and the feel of his love of them all. Davis's reader never really knows where he is going until he gets there, and then, like the fictional characters he has traveled with, he finds that he has been self-deceived in his idea of the destination, but that the trip itself was worth it.

The primary proof of an artist's worth lies in his work's literal viability, its continuing relevance to the changing life of its culture. Davis's writing has maintained its relevance because he strove to embody life, not merely lives, and to capture the feel of reality, even at the expense of realism. The difficulty of categorizing his works merely emphasizes their lifelike quality; living things, they refuse the stasis of category. Their appeal is powerful; they force life's complexity on the reader who seeks easy resolution of the problems they pose. He finds himself absorbing historical lectures where he had expected romantic action, snickering in the midst of life's tragedy, and sympathizing with the lowest common denominators of human behavior.

Davis's writing takes the myths held sacred in the tradition of western American literature and at once purifies and profanes them, bringing them down to earth so that western experience is usefully and lovingly integrated into the experience of twentieth-century Americans rather than degraded, or displaced into some false Golden Age.

Davis's literary ideal was always to unify western experience with the rest of history, to show from the "significant particulars" of western life that the human story is of a piece. As Hendricks, his spokesman for the importance of the past in his novel *Winds of Morning* (1952) put it: "Times change, but people don't,"—the one constant is, for better and worse, human nature. Davis's fictional canon begins with what he called "astringent" (and thus presumably *healing*) criticism both of "people" and "times" in the period of his association with H. L. Mencken's *Mercury*, moves to a slightly more sympathetic view of both in his first novel, *Honey in the Horn* (1935), and then turns to the job of building bridges between the American West and the various other "Wests" out of which it came, in *Harp of a Thousand Strings* (1947) and *Beulah Land* (1949). By the time of *Winds* (1952) he was enough at home with his own past and present to embody them in a novel at once intensely western in its specific materials and universal in its implications about the human condition. Having gained mature artistic control over his main fictional subject —his youth in Oregon and the legacies of the past which had formed it— he returned to a "long view" of the West in *The Distant Music* (1957), achieving a western panorama in time as he had achieved it in space in *Honey*, but maintaining better control over its expanse by keeping a close focus on the ever "diminishing center" of the land of his subject-family the Mulocks. After *Music* he turned to an even tighter focus, a frankly "autobiographical novel," tentatively entitled *Exit, pursued by a bear*,[2] which was to embody his own early life in Oregon. He never finished the work, dying on October 18, 1960. *Exit* was left in several fragmentary versions now owned by the Davis Collection in the Humanities Research Center of the University of Texas at Austin.[3]

The other major work which Davis was doing in the fifties, following the publication of *Winds* and paralleling his work on *Music* and on *Exit* (which was apparently begun in 1956),[4] was a series of articles on "western" subjects published in *Holiday* magazine.[5] They are all vivid pieces, products of the intense interest in portraying western life which he exhibited even during his final illness. The most important, however, is the last item in the miscellany of late Davis short prose, published under the title *Kettle of Fire* (New York: Morrow, 1959). This is the long tale entitled "The Kettle of Fire," originally printed in the University of Oregon's literary magazine *Northwest Review*.[6] Its plot is simple enough: Davis's narrator's recounting of a tale told him in his youth in Antelope, Oregon, by "a rundown old relic named Sore-Foot Capron [who] held the post of city marshal except when there was somebody loose who needed to be arrested."[7] Capron, whose surname approximates the Spanish and Italian words for both "goat" and "bastard," begins an angry young outcast, like most Davis protagonists:

> As he told it, he had run away from a respectable home in Ohio in the early eighteen-sixties, out of disgust with his parents because, after he had beaten his brains half out winning some prize in school, they had merely glanced coldly at it and reminded him that he was almost a half-hour late with his milking.[8]

Fourteen and puny, he tries to enlist in the Army to take part in the Civil War but is turned down. As the narrator puts it, he "castigates" his way west to St. Louis, where he finds a benefactor, Cash Payton, who arranges for him to come to Nevada with an emigrant train to work in Payton's silver mines. The train—composed of

> emigrants from Illinois and Missouri who were organizing to sneak past the frontier outposts and head west for a new start in unspoiled country, and also, though none of them brought the point up, to get themselves somewhere out of reach before they got picked up in the draft.[9]

—succeeds in evading the garrisons which are trying to stop emigration since no protection from Indians can be given emigrants due to the demands of the War. The party gets as far as the Malheur Desert before it has Indian trouble, loses its guide, and "busts" at an alkali waterhole.

Bad weather is coming on and Indians are all around. All the powder in the train is wet except that actually loaded in guns, and they can't make fire with that because shots might cause an Indian attack. Their wood is wet as well. People begin to fall ill. Young Capron, expendable, is chosen to ride south toward the Nevada mines and get help, or at least fill an old iron kettle with hot coals. He goes, gets the coals, mistakenly killing Cash Payton in the process, and comes back in time to save the emigrants. Warmed by his fire, they scrape up enough nerve to move on, and finally blunder into the settled region of Oregon.

The "Kettle story," as Davis referred to it, is a version of the Promethean myth which he chose as the closing frame of his last published work, *Kettle of Fire*. It is clear that he wished to give his collection of Oregoniana some absolutely universal dimension, a story that would unify western experience with "all times and places." My best evidence, mainly remarks in Davis's *Journal*, indicates that the story was first begun in 1956 and was intended as the *front* frame of his "autobiographical novel," *Exit*. One of the existing manuscripts is clearly the Kettle story arranged as the first chapter of that novel, which was to be both an autobiography *and* a western version of Shakespeare's *The Winter's Tale*, where the significant particulars of his life were to be raised to universal significance partly by analogy with a work of Shakespeare and *his* sources from apparently different worlds. There is some indication that at one point he intended to call his autobiographical novel *The Kettle of Fire* rather than *Exit*. But the thirty-eight-page fragment at Austin which melds the Kettle story with the highly symbolic and Shandean account of Davis's own conception in a fence corner under an overhanging rose bush, and other "reminiscences" of his early childhood in Roan's Mills, should be catalogued with the many other fragmentary first chapters of *Exit*, since at that time it was clearly intended to head *Exit*.[10] He apparently later crossed out the parts of the story that unified it with the rest of the novel's chapter and sent it off to *Northwest Review* with an added didactic final paragraph. Probably Davis's original notion was to use the Kettle story to provide an even greater frame of reference for the novel *Exit*, displaying its Shakespearean, Aeschylean and archetypal analogues and projecting them into the future in *Exit* by showing how his own life was an analogue of Capron's deed and burden, and how all men live "to bring home the fire, through the same hardships and doubts and adversities of one's life that make up the triumph of having lived it." This didactic tag on the end of the Kettle story would presumably have been unnecessary had it ever functioned as the first chapter of his autobiographical novel. Published as it was, first alone in the *Northwest Review*, and then at the end of the volume *The Kettle of Fire* as the symbolic summary of what he had to say about his microcosmic "Oregon," he felt that the moral must be pointed out boldly, even intrusively. To his protagonist Sorefoot Capron's typically western insistence on the temporal uniqueness of his own exploit in "bringing home the fire"—

> It's the only thing I'd do over again, I believe, if I had to. Not that I'll ever get the chance. Things like that don't happen nowadays

—Davis, unifier of all times, rejoins to the reader,

> He was wrong about that, of course. Such things change in sub-
> stance and setting, but they go on working in the spirit, through
> different and less explicit symbols, as they did through the cen-
> turies before emigrations West were ever heard of, and as they will
> for men too young to know about them now and for others not yet
> born.[11]

Davis's own "kettle of fire," the gift he had brought home in his novels
after wandering from Oregon to Oaxaca, was Promethean like Capron's,
although *his* gift to man was one of the later arts symbolized by the Titan's
fire—literature, described in *Prometheus Bound* as

> Number, number, queen of all the arts
> I showed them, and the craft
> which stroke to stroke
> Added, till words came and the letters spoke;
> The all-remembering wonder, the unworn
> And edged tool, whence every Muse is born.[12]

There is no question that he felt the torments of having chosen to be a
writer, and thus an exile, as much as Capron felt the kettle burning his
hand, as much as Prometheus his "spike adamantine." But, as Hendricks,
his character in *Winds of Morning*, had put it, "A man's got to find out
what he's good for, and then do it." The Kettle story was the last public
work Davis was able to do, and it is intended to confer, through "explicit
symbols," universal meaning upon specifically western experience—to "remember all" and thus prophesy all, since "times change but people don't,"
as Hendricks's saying has it. It is also, like all Davis's work, an "edged
tool" that cuts through to the unity of human experience by rejecting the
illusions of conventional western literary stereotypes, or at least identifying
them as such and providing a "tradition" which springs as he did, "out of
the country itself," rather than out of the needs of an eastern audience as
he believed the conventional western romances had.[13]

"The Kettle of Fire" is set in the same historical period as the end of his
novel *Beulah Land*, and the beginning of *The Distant Music* (1957): the
opening of the Civil War, a time when, as he puts it in the preface to *The
Kettle of Fire* volume,

> the West became a sort of backwash, populated by hand-to-mouth
> mining promoters, seedy politicians, Chinese coolies, and Border
> State draft-dodgers. There was nothing in the West that any-
> body was interested in, and writing, except for the war poems of
> Bret Harte, leveled down to light travel sketches and newspaper
> whimsies.[14]

This period, left "shapeless" in fiction because no serious writing had
linked it with the present, fascinated Davis. Much of his best fiction is

concerned with bringing it alive, and "The Kettle of Fire" is an attempt to bring the West as a "backwash" in the flood of the Civil War alive in story and to prove that all historical periods are equally vital and relevant.

A letter to George R. Stewart in the Davis Collection provides some insight into Davis's apparent composition of the Kettle story. It is an old tale of his, long pondered and finally rewritten when the editor of the *Northwest Review* asked him to contribute a piece to the *Review*'s handsome Centennial Edition of "contemporary arts in Oregon." Davis claimed that he had "dug out an old one I had sketched out once for the Satevepost and shelved because it was too long, and rewrote it for them. It turned out pretty well and ran about 12,000 words."[15] The Kettle story shows no signs of having been written hastily, but the characteristically nonchalant pose is continued in another letter, (this one to Pare Laurentz, Jr.) but with a bit more specificity:

> The collection [*Kettle*] beside the *Holiday* pieces, is to contain a squib on Western writing that I did once for the *New York Times* ("Preface: A Look Around"), and a longish short story that I ripped off a couple of weeks ago for the centennial edition of the U. of Oregon literary quarterly: pretty good, too, I think, an action story with a basis of literary satire—Zane Grey with overtones of Sainte-Beuve or somebody.[16]

The flippancy of that "or somebody" can't conceal the importance of the remark, one which might almost stand for Davis's literary effort *in toto*. He uses the western materials of Zane Grey: the land, the active outdoor life, the violence, and the movement. But they are interpreted through the eye of the critic, with his "long view" resulting from a classical education (in Davis's case, largely self-taught), the realist's extreme attention to detail both "human" and "natural," and the moralist's more complex conception of the function of literature. Davis was a critic of the West via his writing, and his conception of that criticism was like Sainte-Beuve, moral, as the end of "The Kettle of Fire" shows. Often his works' moral power lies in their emotional effect as much as in their explicit statement, in their carrying out of Pound's dictum that "the function of literature . . . is that it does *incite* people to continue living."

The reconciliation of Zane Grey with "Sainte-Beuve or somebody" is a difficult synthesis, but it is precisely the kind of effort Davis was always making, using the developed conscious critical eye and the "all-remembering wonder" of literature to unify the most conventionally disparate experiences and times. Davis, in the literary act of recording his search for the missing link between his own times and the many Wests lost to literature, becomes that missing link.

The "basis of literary satire" which "The Kettle of Fire" rests upon is important, and set deep into literary history, both of the American West and of Western Civilization. It is at once a satire of the Promethean myth, *and* of the Zane Grey "action story."

In many ways this tale is literary satire only—its physical detail is close enough to the actual histories of a number of emigrant trains. What it satirizes is the literary stereotype of the wagon train as a band of stalwart heroes with more or less perfect unanimity of will and ability, challenged only by the environment and a gratuitous villain or two. In that sense the satire is only apparent in a literary tradition; Davis's version inverts the literary notion that pioneers were altruistic heroes; history shows that they weren't (from, for example, the blunders and squabbles that caused the Donner disaster). "The Kettle of Fire," in this sense, performs the same function as the last third or so of his novel *Beulah Land* by realistically complicating the literary image of the peopling of Oregon—Oregon was settled by *some* clear-eyed manifest-destinarian heroes, but also by some half-breed Indians as in *Beulah Land*, and by some draft dodgers who "were not worth much, on the average,"[17] as in the Kettle story.

As an "action story," "The Kettle of Fire," also satirizes western literature of the Zane Grey stripe by introducing a very intense web of ironies intended to challenge the conventional Western's identification of the hero with morally controlled acts of violence. All action in "Kettle" (as in most of Davis's canon) has ironic results and is morally equivocal.

The narrator's introduction of Capron as a city marshal, traditionally a figure of righteous action in conventional Westerns, begins this irony. Capron has gone from his triumph of saving the emigrant train to being a marshal whose most significant quality is not his enforcement of the law with a ready gun. What he can do is manage the town water system "because he was the only resident who had been there long enough to know where the mains were laid."[18]

Capron's origins as a westerner are also ironic—he'd tried so hard *not* to be one—winning his school prize, and then trying to enlist in the war which was at that time making the West "a sort of backwash." When he does get caught up in the westward movement, it is as a tagalong to a bunch of refugees whose main motive, Davis implies, is cowardice. Capron's motive is materialistic; he hopes that Cash Payton, whose name clearly relates what *he* "stands for," will set him up in something lucrative in the West.

His one main "western" action is his mistaken killing of Payton, the man who had become a "second father" to him and represented all his "western" hopes. Furthermore he kills Payton during his quest for fire because he mistakes him for an Indian and yet "it was not even certain that there was anything in it to regret . . . a man shacked up in a Snake Indian lodge in that remote part of the desert must have had some business in hand besides organizing classes in Bible study or quilt piecing." There is the strong possibility that Payton, the self-styled "silver mine operator" is actually in the business of catching Indian children to sell as slaves in San Francisco, and, if he was, he "deserved shooting for it."[19] As usual with Davis, Payton's situation which causes his death and his apparent occupation are *historically* realistic. Their ironies, unremarked by the narrator, are only apparent within the context of the conventions of western fiction, where the enslavement of children is an Indian monopoly, and a hero, unlike Capron, can always distinguish "red" from "white."

Capron, having mistakenly shot a man whom he loved yet who probably deserved it, is caught in a moral trap: in Davis's work, unlike traditional Westerns, bullets seldom hit the person they are aimed at. When they do, it turns out to be the wrong person. When they do hit the right person, it is usually for the wrong reasons, as here. Capron, having shot Payton, still knows that he can talk his way out of the shooting and escape south with Payton's companions, leaving the "train" fireless. Ironically his shooting Payton and taking coals from his fire ensures that he must return with his burden, even disliking the emigrants as he does. Otherwise, as he says, "It would mean Cash Payton had died for nothing, for mere foolishness, because a streak of light had hit him the wrong way. The only way to make his death count for something was to get fire back to the train."[20]

In this choice is Capron's only heroism—he is loyal not to an ethical value, but to a feeling, to love: a primitive admiration and gratitude for Payton's bread and salt that causes him to act heroically in spite of the rational facts that Payton "deserved killing" and the people of the train were "not worth much." Capron fulfills Davis's belief that true humanity requires "disillusioned knowledge" by acknowledging both facts, and nevertheless acting out of the pain of his love for dead Payton in spite of the "gloom of knowledge" that Payton was almost certainly involved in evil, and that the wagon train was barely worth saving.

A further irony is that ultimately even the sacrifices of Capron's quest are unnecessary: he returns to the train to discover that one of the "observation posts" of the Snakes who are harassing it has been abandoned, leaving the smouldering coals of its watch-fire within easy strolling distance of the train. Payton's death and Capron's pains would have been unnecessary had any of the emigrants stumbled upon that fire, and it is mere accident that they did not, accident morally and causally unrelated to the sacrifices entailed in his "bringing home the fire." Capron feels "relieved and uplifted in spirit" that none of the party had found the Indians' fire. But even though he puts it out and preserves his heroism undiluted by *that* irony, they, like his parents with the school prize, do not much value his deed.

"They made me pay for the pony I lost," he said. "And the

saddle and bridle, too. Took it out of my wages, what little there
was of 'em."

"It don't sound like you'd got much out of it," I said. At the
time, it didn't seem to me that any story with such a frazzled-out
ending was worth spending all that time on. "It sounds like everybody had come out ahead except you."

"That was what they all thought, I guess," he said. "They're
welcome to their notions. None of 'em come out as far ahead as
they thought they had, and it's the only thing I've ever done that
I got anything out of that was worth hellroom."[21]

Capron's sacrifice and his valuation of it reveal Davis's belief that a
man's self-evaluation is of primary importance. Hendricks was the mature
Davis's spokesman for this in *Winds of Morning*: "It isn't what you get
out of life that matters, it's what you put into it." Obviously this is a
question that can be most accurately judged by the one who "does the
putting." Hendricks's belief that a man must do what it is that "he has to
do," regardless of "whether other people want it or not" is repeated in Capron's knowledge, as he rides away from the train on his fire-quest, that he
will try to return—not because of the good or ill opinion of the emigrants,
but because of the proddings of his own conscience. For he dreads to carry
the sounds of the dying camp "through all the years that he could reasonably expect to live, and maybe even beyond them."[22]

What Capron "puts into" the quest in terms of anguish, remorse, dread
of death, and physical exhaustion is told by him and assessed by the narrator. What he "gets out" of the experience is less clear, but obviously most
important. None of his gains are material; actually he loses money by the
exploit. None of his gains are public—the settlers are even less impressed
than the hearer, eleven-year-old Davis, who at least *remembers* the "story
with the frazzled-out ending." Capron does discover a moral:

A man had to live up to what he was, weaknesses and all. Finding
out what they were was probably not worth shooting a man for,
but it was a gain. The kettle had returned him that much for his
trouble, at least.[23]

What Capron gains is self-knowledge, an increment of consciousness, and
thus the ability to live life truly by knowing it truly.

One of the most important points about that self-knowledge is that he
becomes aware of the nature of the human self—that to a great degree
nature *is* the self, and vice versa. The parallel structure of natural seasons
with the seasons of human emotion and experience in *Winds of Morning*
had been one way of illustrating man as an extension of nature; the
"naturalizing" of man's works in Davis's many descriptions of ghost
towns and abandoned farms another, as was the dehumanizing by the
natural environment of people such as the "denizens of Shoestring Valley"
in the opening chapters of *Honey*. A journal entry just before Davis's

death illustrates what his works sought to express about the relationship of man to nature:

> An understanding of nature doesn't mean the ability to track down wild animals and classify wild plants and bird's nests. Certainly nobody is any worse off for knowing how to do such things, but what is needed is not to clear up any mystery of nature; it is to deepen one's knowledge of it as a mystery, as a succession of mysteries underlying mysteries. And it is not to know more things about nature, but to know the essential things more and more deeply. This is in itself an enlargement of experience, of living face to face with a constantly self-renewing mystery of which you yourself are a part.
>
> This would be complained of as metaphysical, I suppose, especially by those who don't know what metaphysics are. There must be some clearer way of putting it, something commoner and more concrete.[24]

Davis's tone here is reminiscent of a number of modern writers who have attempted to express the power of nature in terms that are physical and material, and yet lyric—still true to the actual emotions of awe that nature inspires. As the scientist Loren Eiseley complains at one point, "I have had the vague word 'mystic' applied to me because I have not been able to shut out wonder occasionally when I have looked at the world."[25] Davis died seeking his "more concrete way of putting it," but one of the main effects of his last public work, like all his works, is its stress on man as "a part of nature." Young Capron's return with the fire takes him through a stretch of "wild country" clearly symbolic of deeper and deeper revelations about the nature of man. It is as though Capron were actually traveling deeper and deeper into himself as he moved into the wild country, meeting himself in animal versions which reveal his animal "human nature" by analogy, and at the same time his "humanity" by contrast.

The passage relating Capron's return to the emigrants somewhat resembles several others in Davis's works, notably the country through which Clay passes immediately after Luce leaves him in *Honey* and the symbolic landscape in *Beulah Land* where "the various forms of animal life had not worked out the space each was entitled to . . . or the rate of increase that it [the land] would support among all of them,"[26] and the passenger pigeon nesting grounds dominate, for a term before their extinction, all of life's processes. In the Kettle story, however, the process of analogy between man and nature is more overt; as its final paragraph asserts, it is a story of "explicit symbols."

Leaving his human pursuers—Payton's companions—behind, having rejected the physical salvation offered by either bushwhacking them and taking their horses or simply laying claim to their friendship and lying about Payton's death, Capron leaves humanity behind, only to find in nature a series of presences which simultaneously threaten and resemble his conception of humanity. He first comes upon a country of sage rat burrows, "as bare as if it had been plowed and harrowed." The rats ignore him— "when all was said and done, the proper study of ratkind was rats."[27] This wry parody continues the analogy between the rats and people which began with the image of the rat territory as "plowed and harrowed." The analogy is further developed into a vision of "man naturalized" by "country":

> They were not much company. The worst of it was not their strangeness and preoccupation with themselves, it was the loneliness of the country that made young Capron adapt himself, without being aware of it, to their values and scale of living. A few more miles of them, he felt, and he would find himself growing feeler-whiskers, squeaking, and rearing up on his hind-legs to watch himself ride past and try for a second or two to figure out what he was. . . .[28]

The doubleness and confusion of identity are of course characteristic of the psychological state of the seeker in a name or identity search, of which the "Kettle of Fire" story is a version.

He pulls down a gully to escape the rats and discovers it full of owls, blinded by the daylight so they can't even see him. At the end of it is a rye-grass flat covered so densely with jackrabbits that "it looked gray and moving like a spread of water." They are weakened by bot-flies as they usually were

> in the years when they had run themselves down by overbreeding . . .
> A curious thing about it was that though disease had undermined their instinct for self-preservation, it had left their appetites unimpaired, or only a little slackened. They were still able to crop all of the green sprouts out of the dead rye-grass clumps, and they had not lost their interest in copulation, whatever might have happened to their ability. They were not noticeably energetic about it, but they stayed with it faithfully, working as the pony picked its way among them at the absorbing task of perpetuating their kind, bot-flies and all, and regarding nothing else as deserving of notice.[29]

Capron, in leaving humanity behind, finds that nature commits all the acts of man which are faults only in man, the animal who is conscious of his acts when truly, however rarely in Davis's view, humane. Man's preoccupation with himself—his pride of dominion which leads to the same dustbowl in *Honey* as the rats are creating here, the blindness of the owls, and the overpopulation, "bot-flies and all," of the jackrabbits—*is* natural. It's just that it belongs to the animal part of our nature; it is not truly human. Pope's "The proper study of mankind is Man," is a human and humane truth only when it is realized that there is a corollary need for

Emerson's "Know thyself: study nature." Man *is* a part of nature's "self-renewing mystery." He too is a self-renewing mystery, but he realizes his uniqueness, his true nature as a species, only when he is able to realize consciously that his fixation on "things human" is the same unconscious drive to dominate the rest of the environment which many other species display. Humanity consists partly in realizing that pride of dominion is not the primary sign of humanity, not even when it manifests itself in great migrations and great civilizations and great populations. Humanity consists of the conscious ability to resist the blind trust in action that results from the promptings all species have to "inherit the earth," and yet the necessary humility to surrender to nature's promptings for love and the actions it prompts, and live to tell the tale.

The satiric parallels between the blindness of the various animal populations Capron passes and the blindness of humanity to the rest of nature are clear enough. They all, as men in *their* materialistic pride of dominion are apt to do, ignore him or, like the wild geese he meets last, indignantly try to drive him away, "outraged with him for being there, without having the ghost of an idea what he was doing or the slightest interest in finding out."[30] Like the majority of humans, they are blind to other forms of life, to nature as a whole, and thus merely are part of the "sea of unconscious forces and counterforces," the physical building blocks of the transcendent mystery of nature described in a lyric passage of the novel *Harp of a Thousand Strings*.[31] Only Capron's story, unifying the animals' behavior with that of man in a moral construct, rises above that "sea" to human stature.

In the end Capron is reduced by the forces of nature (in the form of a wild horse herd that stampedes his pony) to a position where he has no choice at all: "Without a horse and without food enough for another day, the emigrant camp was the only place he could go."[32] Ironically, the "natural" force that reduces him to a point where he has no moral choice is the wild horse, one by-product of man's pride of dominion (and of course, the main western symbol of that pride, as Davis's first volume of poetry, *Proud Riders*, shows) which, once loosed, became uncontrollable. "Caused" by a restless drive in man which to Davis is biological, (despite whatever manifest-destinarian rationalizations it might have had) the western wild horse becomes an "unconscious counter force" in its own right, "recruiting" the emigrant's stock into its wild bands and providing the western Indians' main weapon, mobility. Indeed the tribes that have caused the train's, and Capron's, dilemma apparently did not exist as such until the introduction of the horse;[33] it is the actual *and* the symbolic basis of their culture as it is of the western white culture with which they are conventionally contrasted in western literature.

Capron's overmastering selfishness is revealed by his ordeal—it finally breaks him down, but for one saving factor, to the amoral level of non-human nature itself, the level at which Davis, always skeptical of human nature in the aggregate, felt that most humans spent most of their time. In the end Capron's values are inverted by the ordeal.

> It was humiliating to realize that his values had all been turned upside down, when he could welcome seeing a dead horse with buzzards around it and be downcast to think that people he knew might be keeping warm and cooking food and drying out their gunpowder.[34]

He is relieved to find them on the verge of disaster, as he had left them, and carefully covers up the Indian watch-fire that could have saved them. Capron's deed and Payton's death are both unnecessary, had the people of the train only known. Capron makes sure that they do not, but when he tells the story as an old man, he transmits that knowledge to his auditor and Davis's narrator passes it on. *We* get the truth about his deed because the truth of the story that is important to Davis is the irony itself, and Capron's recognition of it. The salvation of the wagon train is relatively unimportant: Oregon, as he points out in the essay "Oregon" in the same volume, was already fairly well peopled by the beginning of the Civil War.[35] Capron's act is not important in any material way for the development or survival of Oregon; its value lies in what it says about Man, not just western American man, nor the Oregon pioneers.

Davis is very clear about this. Capron's last words, "things like that don't happen nowadays," are immediately and directly contradicted by the narrator's "he was wrong about that, of course," and his didactic final paragraph which goes on to generalize the story's application to the past and future. Presumably the unfinished novel *Exit*, had the Kettle story been included in it, would have projected its meaning into Capron's future by telling of Davis's past life, *his* "bringing the fire home"; the "hardships and doubts and adversities" of his life that had made up "the triumph of having lived it."

Davis was always adamant in his belief in the continuity of human story and in his belief that the basic human stories such as "bringing home the fire" repeated themselves endlessly throughout human history. The clearest way in which the Kettle story can be seen as a repetition of a universal human experience is in its ironic variations on Aeschylus's *Prometheus Bound*. Davis was a lover of that play, and, as an avid amateur ethnologist, well aware that the Promethean myth was a human cultural constant. Even the editors of the *Northwest Review* seem to have recognized the Kettle story's classical analogues, placing it as the lead article of their very handsome Centennial Edition, followed by a free translation from Strabo by John B. Freedman entitled "Apatropaios."[36] In the placement of "Kettle" within the volume, Davis is recognized as Oregon's leading writer; in the placement of Freedman's translation next to it, Davis's story's meaning is acknowledged to be more than merely western.

I have mentioned Davis's stress on the power of nature in shaping human character and human institutions. Man's limitations, the "powers that be" in Davis's work, are natural: either the power of "external nature" over man, or more often, man's inability to rise above his corresponding inner nature, the "sea of blind energies" within him that results in his seldom attaining true humanity, true self-consciousness.

Capron's gift of fire keeps the people of the train from reverting to a state "where they are likely to fall into a panic and do things too disgusting to bear telling or thinking of."[37] It keeps them from reverting to the "brutish" state of men before Prometheus's original gift.

The character Capron functions in several ways. He is of course an inversion of the paradigm of the lawman in the conventional "Western." Chained to the town of Antelope by his badge and, more important, by his knowledge of the water mains, Capron, his liver being devoured by rotgut, is the opposite of the strong, silent man of action—a weak, garrulous man who "held the post of city marshal except when there was somebody loose who needed to be arrested. . . ." Yet even in his garrulity he is a hero, the savior of the train, because without him as its "interpreter," the train would have died in man's memory as surely as it would have died physically if he had not brought the fire. Capron, whose life's only material meaning is in his knowledge of the water mains (a more-or-less adventitious knowledge), *lives* through his position as a "maker," a transmitter of story. Capron gives himself and the train the only life that can transcend the forces of nature that claim all men, through their lives and at their lives' ends: he embodies himself, Cash Payton, and the train of shiftless refugees *in language* so Davis may give it life *in writing*, Prometheus's "all-remembering wonder."

Davis's remark about the Kettle story being "Zane Grey with overtones of Sainte-Beuve" is not just a throwaway. It is symptomatic of his attitude toward all of his own writing. That the West was a subject of undying interest to most Americans was an accomplished fact of our culture by the time he was born, and he spent all of his life trying to write western fiction, poetry, and prose that moved the reader from entertainment through beauty to a knowledge of the West that would have more than merely western or twentieth-century American application. As he said in an unpublished essay on the form and function of contemporary popular fictional forms such as the "Western" and the detective novel: "any form of writing that people find entertaining can be changed by art into something more than entertainment, as the blown up rant of *Tamburlane* and *The Spanish Tragedy* was changed into *King Lear* and *The Tempest*."[38]

Davis saw "art" in western writing as the bringing of a larger frame of reference to the western materials that most Americans have found important, a point of view that could make the "significant particulars" of his own experience relevant not only to the immediate western past and future, but to all of human history. He sought to provide not only particular missing links in our view of the history of the West that would fill in the blind spots the first generation of western writers had been unable to manage, but also to set up the concept of western writing as a perpetual filling in of the missing links with our many pasts. His own canon was to be "Exhibit A," a body of writing that placed the stories of Oregon forever in the great stream of the human comedy.

His writing was characteristically "unwestern" or "un-American" in its cautionary tone—its stress on the dangers of the pride of dominion whose chief symptoms in the West are materialism and the complacency that a belief in Manifest Destiny allows. Davis's writing always emphasized a continuity in material creation that gives the lie to a belief in man's special position in the world, showing how tenuously and rarely man achieves the consciousness that raises him momentarily above the realm of material accident.

To a subject matter whose fictional treatment had traditionally been marked by simple plot structures emblematic of a simple and wholly rationalized morality, Davis brought all of the moral complexity, and some of the concomitant structural complexity of twentieth-century literature. He gave a shape to the "shapelessness" of the present which conventional western writers, following Owen Wister, spurned. That shape was achieved not by rejecting its complexities, but by embodying them in paradox and the acceptance of a paradoxical state for man and a realization that the "good life" is a tenuous acceptance of the demands of man's pradoxical nature. Man, trapped by the demands of consciousness, "conscience," and the "gloom" of the disillusioned knowledge that he is trapped by human nature's correspondence to a nature's material causes, can only wander striving, immortalized by his own failures embodied in art. Davis never doubted that his writing was a lifesaver, bringing to life as it did the stories of the forgotten dead. His own personal kettle of fire was his knowledge that writing about the West in an unconventional manner was "what he had to do, whether other people wanted it or not." Scarred by what he felt was critical and popular rejection, he nevertheless left a body of work that deals with the problem of the discontinuous identity of the West, what Wallace Stegner has called the problem of "many Wests,"[39] in the microcosm of "many Oregons." Rejecting one of the poles of the western self-image, the ideal of static perfection of society in the "Garden of the Lord," he turns to a new version of the other, the "Long March" idealized by Frank Norris. Lacking faith in the worth of the dynamic, manifest-destinarian view of the West which earlier writers such as Norris had, Davis rejects the notion that the importance of the western movement is social or racial at all; he claims that any meaning it may have is in its endless repetition of basic human patterns of learning, loving, striving, and triumphing in spite of material failure. The Long March, man's errand in the wilderness, becomes an endless series of marches and countermarches correspondent to the physical "blind energies and counter energies" of the world. Man's triumph is to realize his condition, and to strive in spite of it—Davis's fiction functions primarily in its cautionary messages, its "gloom of knowledge" of the human condition. Its second function is to "incite its reader to continue living" by providing him with a model of consciousness, the love of life which torments man into "restlessness," into quest, and ultimately into immortal story.

1. The best published bibliography of Davis's works and Davis criticism is still George Kellogg's "H. L. Davis, 1896-1960: A Bibliography," *Texas Studies in Language and Literature*, 5 (Summer 1963), 294-303.
2. Harold Lenoir Davis, *Exit, pursued by a bear*, Ms. Works section of the Harold Lenoir Davis Collection at the Humanities Research Center of the Univ. of Texas, Austin.
3. *Exit* exists as five separate fragments (plus the "Kettle Story"), several of which are more developed drafts clearly meant to supersede earlier ones. The longest connected version, consisting of ninety-four typewritten pages with extensive handwritten notes and emendations, contains the first three chapters and the so-called "Fulton episode," which may have been intended as chapter four. There is also a handwritten manuscript, referred to as "/Exit, pursued by a bear: Notes and story development/," which extends the plan of the novel through a further 210 pages of Davis's characteristic "dialogues with himself" which mark the first planning stage of all his extant novel manuscripts.
4. The tentative date of August, 1956 comes from the earliest dated notes for the Kettle story in the Davis collection: "Ms. File (Davis, H. L.) Works, Misc. notes *re* The Kettle of fire. Tms 1956, Augs? ."
5. Following, in alphabetical order, are articles by Davis on "western subjects" which appeared in *Holiday*: "The Best Time for Camping," Sept. 1958, pp. 78-81; "Fishing Fever," Aug. 1953, pp. 56-60; "Oregon," June 1953, pp. 34-37; "Oregon Autumn," Nov. 1961, pp. 155-56, 173-77; "Our Resourceful Forests," July 1958, pp. 72-79; "Palm Springs," Oct. 1957, pp. 84-85; "The Pleasures of the Brook," July 1957, pp. 74-75; "The Puget Sound Country," May 1954, pp. 98-105 ff.; "Sheepherders: the Quiet Westerners," May 1959, pp. 19-22; "A Walk in the Woods," May 1954, pp. 88-90; "The Wilds of Mexico," May 1957, pp. 26 ff.
6. Harold Lenoir Davis, "The Kettle of Fire," *Northwest Review*, 2 (Summer 1959), 5-22.
7. *Kettle,* p. 165.
8. *Kettle,* p. 166.
9. *Kettle,* p. 166.
10. The 38-page fragment which shows the Kettle story set up as the "front frame" of *Exit* is identified in the Davis Collection under the title of "Ms. Works Kettle of Fire I." The prose connecting the Kettle story with the

description of the conception of *Exit*'s narrator is neatly crossed out in red pencil, isolating the story as it was finally published in *Northwest Review*.

11. *Kettle,* p. 189.
12. Aeschylus, *Prometheus Bound,* trans. Gilbert Murray (London: Allen and Unwin, 1952), p. 42.
13. "Ms. (Davis, H. L.) Works, /Notes on the Novel/ Ams./ inc. 23 pp. n.d. (1960?)," p. 1.
14. *Kettle,* p. 14.
15. Ms. (Davis, H. L.) Letters file in the Davis Collection. This is the letter dated May 16, 1959, one of thirty-six letters from Davis to Stewart collected at Austin.
16. Ms. (Davis, H. L.) Letters file. This is dated March 14, 1949, and is one of seven letters to Pare MacTaggart Laurentz, Jr., author of an unpublished thesis on Davis.
17. *Kettle,* p. 188.
18. *Kettle,* p. 165.
19. *Kettle,* p. 174.
20. *Kettle,* p. 178.
21. *Kettle,* pp. 188-89.
22. *Kettle,* p. 169.
23. *Kettle,* p. 175.
24. Ms. (Davis, H. L.) Journal file; entry dated Feb. 13, 1960.
25. Loren Eiseley, "The Mind as Nature," in *The Night Country* (New York: Scribners, 1971), p. 151.
26. *Beulah Land,* p. 237.
27. *Kettle,* p. 182.
28. *Kettle,* p. 182.
29. *Kettle,* p. 183.
30. *Kettle,* p. 184.
31. *Harp of a Thousand Strings* (New York: Morrow, 1947), pp. 264-67.
32. *Kettle,* p. 186.
33. Clark Wissler, *Indians of the United States* (Garden City: Doubleday, 1940), pp. 221-22, 261-64.
34. *Kettle,* p. 187.
35. *Kettle,* p. 25.
36. John B. Freedman, "Apotropaios," *Northwest Review,* 2 (Summer, 1959), 23.
37. *Kettle,* p. 169.
38. "Ms. (Davis, H. L.) Works "About Novels," T/cc. ms., n.d.," p. 4.
39. Wallace Stegner, Introd., *Great Short Stories of the West,* ed. J. Golden Taylor (New York: Ballantine, 1971), pp. xiv-xv.

In this final paper, Kermit Vanderbilt offers a major reappraisal of the great modern American poet, Theodore Roethke, who taught at the University of Washington from his arrival in the Northwest in 1947 until his death in 1963. Professor Vanderbilt, who was a colleague of Roethke's at Washington from 1958 to 1962, examines thoroughly Roethke's personal and poetic relationship with the Pacific Northwest—touched on in George Venn's essay—in what must become a most significant addition to Roethke criticism. Professor Vanderbilt now teaches at San Diego State University, where he was recently named that institution's outstanding professor. He is the author of two books, *Charles Eliot Norton: Apostle of Culture in a Democracy* and *The Achievement of William Dean Howells*, as well as numerous articles on American literature.

Theodore Roethke as a Northwest Poet

Kermit Vanderbilt

> There are those to whom place is unimportant,
> But this place, where sea and fresh water meet,
> Is important—
>
> Roethke, "The Rose" (1963)

To explore the relationship between Theodore Roethke and the North-west is very satisfying for several personal reasons. I was Roethke's colleague in his late years at the University of Washington. He knew I admired his poetry, but I was somehow unable to accord him the repeated and fulsome praise I knew that he deserved and almost insatiably required. I now intend to give proper homage to Roethke and make amends for the perversity of my earlier restraint. I shall also atone for my failure in never having shared with Roethke the regional impulse in his later poetry. After his posthumous *The Far Field* appeared in 1964, I began to discover how important the Northwest was to Roethke. Since then, I have followed the steady flow of critical analyses, revaluations, and rising estimates of his lyrical virtuosity and dynamic vision. (How the insecure Roethke would have savored this belated recognition!) Still absent in this criticism is the importance for Roethke of what D. H. Lawrence termed "the spirit of place."

The neglect is understandable. Testimony abounds that Roethke was in no sense to be mistaken for a regional poet. The evidence is formidable enough that I want to assemble it rather fully at once. I shall then argue the positive case for Roethke as a man and poet whose total career can be understood as a growing possession of his American geography and self-hood. Finally, I want to offer a few comments about Roethke in the light of standard conclusions which so often appear in discussions of literary regionalism, at least since recognition of Faulkner. I mean the *pro forma* consideration of regionalism as *initial* response. The writer of major talent then dissolves, transforms, and transcends this regionalism and moves out-ward to the national, international, and cosmic reaches of his sensibility. That a literary region in American might claim a healthy autonomy through its own shaping myths and archetypes, a unique reason for being that is fully realized in its own necessary form—this possibility has seldom been entertained seriously by our literary historians and critics. Allen Tate observed in 1929, for example, that American regionalists like Lindsay, Sandburg, and Masters, let alone the would-be epic poet like Hart Crane, suffered from the absence of a truly national literature, a "homogeneous body of beliefs and feelings into which the poet may be educated." In particular, "the spiritual well-being of the West," said Tate, "depends upon its success in assimilating the cultural tradition of the older sections." But Tate then hoped that future writers in the "provinces" could help somehow to solve the problem of a national literature by releasing local wellsprings and creating ancillary pipelines into an eventual mainstream culture (my imagery, not Tate's). Only recently, one of our best poetry critics, Fred Moramarco, reviewed a collection of dubiously "Western" poetry and then went on to advance the companion, or universal, theory of regional offerings. The best author will select his local materials with an eye and ear responsive to significant universals. Unlike Tate, Moramarco does not foresee a vital literary regionalism in the future from which larger "verities" can emerge, for he doubts that the distinctive region itself any longer exists. Instead, we live in "post-McLuhan media saturated global village uniformity." The sad result is that "the idea of a regional literature in any meaningful sense died in this country with the passing of Frost, Faulkner, Jeffers and a few other major literary talents who were able to isolate regional qualities and discover the universal verities within them."[1] Compulsively echoed and rephrased by lesser critics over the past fifty years, these demands for significant national and universal expression have encouraged a fair amount of misdirected ambition in the careers of American authors who might otherwise have been content to embrace and vitalize the particular history, folklore, and landscape of their region. Among the victims of this confused purpose, I am afraid, was our poet Theodore Roethke.

I.

No interpreter of Roethke, biographer or critic, has discovered that in his life or poetry Roethke drew either a strong identity or consistent nourishment from his locale. He was above all, we are told, a private, meditative, hermetic sort of man and poet. He derived from his natural surroundings a stream of correspondences to express the agonized progress of the lonely self in its mysterious and sometimes wondrous drive toward transcendence and beatitude.

Biographer Allan Seager writes, for example, that for Roethke, "It was himself he had to sing, not the circumambient world. He only used that."[2] And Seager confirms his judgment with the testimony of Stanley Kunitz, whose friendship dated from Roethke's first teaching job at Lafayette College in the early thirties: "Stanley Kunitz says [Roethke] was not a really close observer, and, of course, he did not need to be since everything around him was useful to him only as signatures of himself" (GH, 123). When Roethke traveled, he was interested in meeting a few interesting people rather than touring the monuments or natural wonder of historic places. Many of his friends and colleagues—from Lafayette to Michigan State to Pennsylvania State to Bennington and (after 1947) the University of Washington—would probably concur with Denis Donoghue that Roethke was the autonomous poet who never attached himself to an ideology or a geographical region: "He never set up shop as a Left Wing poet or a Right Wing poet or a Catholic poet or a New England poet or a Southern poet or a California poet; he never claimed privilege in any region of feeling."[3]

Donoghue's regional list was casual. We may inquire into his two prominent omissions—the Michigan Saginaw Valley of Roethke's childhood and the Pacific Northwest of his final sixteen years. Ample data suggests that Roethke felt no spirit of place in the environs of Saginaw. Seager puts it this way:

> There is no memory of Roethke hanging around the old folks listening, like Faulkner, and his old folks were German, anyway. Their stories would have led him back to the Old Country which never interested him. He also ignores all the vivid racy tales of the lumber boom, tales that expressed courage, will, and cunning that might have engaged another man. Unlike Allen Tate or Robert Lowell, he ignores in his poetry the events of his region's history. He must have been aware of the Indians, for he collected a shoebox full of flint arrowheads in his rambles along the riverbanks. But, of course, many boys did that. (GH, 8)

Years after, during the first mental breakdown in late 1935 that terminated his brief teaching stint at Michigan State University, Roethke recorded the following insight about himself in a long medical questionnaire: "Afraid of being localized in space, i.e. a particular place like W. E. Leonard in Madison. Question: What is the *name* of this? Hate some rooms in that sense, a victim of claustrophobia (sp)? Wasn't Dillinger a victim of this? Aren't many of the criminal leader types of this sort [*sic*]" (GH, 95). The illuminating reference to Dillinger connects with Roethke's poetic self-image as the outsider and points to his regional alienation even earlier. In one of his college essays at the University of Michigan, Roethke had discussed "the poet as criminal," the instance being François Villon (GH, 59). Early on in Michigan, then, Roethke felt himself a lonely poet and species of outrageous free spirit. Or as Seager provocatively sees it, Roethke "may have begun to suspect that poetry, having no voice in the community where he lived, was antisocial. . . . Poetry was akin to crime. Strange and unwelcome in middle-class America, the poet was a criminal" (GH, 60). Though he admired Whitman, the young Roethke would not emulate the people's bard and camarado. He was, instead, the tough-guy poet. "I may look like a beer salesman, but I'm a poet," he announced defensively by way of introduction to the president of Bennington College at a job interview in New York early in the forties (GH, 56). Even through the fifties and into his final years, he continued to fashion and embroider the fiction of the gangster element in his life. He would relate how he had once been on close terms with the Detroit underworld and that the notorious Purple Gang had once "offered to bump my Aunt Margaret off for me. As a favor, you understand" (GH, 58). The cadences here might have been lifted directly out of one of the fabrications of Jay Gatsby.

Seager effectively discounts these "memories" of regional outlawry. "In the Thirties, Ted was not near Detroit long enough to ingratiate himself with the gang lords" (GH, 58). Excepting the one year in Michigan during the mid-thirties, he was successively at Harvard, Lafayette, and Penn State, safely out of touch with Michigan and its urban underworld.

His first two books of poetry firmly support the thesis that Roethke was never a midwestern regionalist, either by sympathetic identity or literary example. Before *Open House* appeared in 1941, ten of the poems were anthologized in a volume titled *New Michigan Verse* (1940). Hungry for a reputation, Roethke was delighted to be published but, says Seager, "he had a few misgivings also because he did not want to be known as a regional poet" (GH, 133). Roethke rather explicitly denies, also, any regional impulse in the Saginaw greenhouse poems which create the celebrated breakthrough in the mid-forties and dominate his second book, *The Lost Son* (1948). When he comments on this work in progress to Kenneth Burke, Roethke stresses not the significance of local place but rather the intention to "show the full erotic and even religious significance that I sense in a big greenhouse: a kind of man-made Avalon, Eden, or paradise."[4] The inspiration and metaphor of the organic greenhouse world appeared to be mythic and not regional. Outside the childhood greenhouse, to be sure, were a community and a region, but the growing youth came to feel this area as annihilating space, either a claustrophobic "particular place" or a pitiless waste land. In a vivid notebook jotting later in the fifties, Roethke remembered "the Siberian pitilessness, the essential ruthlessness of the Middle West as I knew it."[5]

Roethke came to the Northwest in 1947 to join the English faculty at the University of Washington, and it remained his academic address until his death in the summer of 1963. Yet some colleagues who were closest to him there have told me that he was never a chamber of commerce spokesman for the Northwest. Even before he took up residence in Seattle, Roethke in the East expressed "misgivings about going even further into the provinces" than ever before.[6] When he arrived in mid-September of 1947, he mentioned his initial fears to Kenneth Burke: "I'm afraid I'm going to be overwhelmed by nice people: it's a kind of vast Scarsdale, it would seem. Bright, active women, with blue hair, and well-barbered males. The arts and the 'East' seem to cow them." Neither pub life nor cafe society had much of a chance in this Northwest outpost. "I found, to my horror," Roethke continued, "that you have to go a mile from the campus even to get beer, and there are no bars for anything except beer and light wines in the whole of Seattle, except in private clubs. And there are no decent restaurants, either, as far as I can find out."[7]

Several months later, he wrote again to Burke. Living in the Northwest, it was now clear, amounted to a sort of physical and spiritual exile. "I tell you, Kenneth," he wrote, "this far in the provinces you get a little nutty and hysterical: there's the feeling that all life is going on but you're not there."[8] Within the year, he had reverted to the earlier self-image of the poet as at best an outlaw celebrity in his tame middle-class community. "As the only serious poet within 1,000 miles of Seattle," he wrote another friend in the East, "I find I have something of the status of a bank robber in Oklahoma or a congressman in the deep south."[9]

In 1951 he moved out of the University district to North Edmonds, where the house offered a splendid view of Puget Sound. "But oddly enough," he wrote to Babette Deutsch, "it's lonely and I resent the 30 minutes drive each way" (GH, 197). After his marriage in 1953 he lived in Bellevue on Lake Washington and finally bought a house across the lake nearer to the University in 1957. But one should not easily conclude that Roethke had slowly become a loyal Northwesterner. Throughout his tenure at the University of Washington, he was inquiring into jobs elsewhere or applying for Fulbrights and other grants that might bring him relief or delivery from the scene at Seattle and the University.

This alienation was caused, in part, by what to him was a depressing climate in the Northwest. In his first or second year, he entered the following verses in a notebook.

> What eats us here? Is this infinity too close,
> These mountains and these clouds? On clearing days
> We act like something else; a race arrived
> From caves. . . [sic]
> Bearlike, come stumbling into the sun, avoid that shade
> Still lingering in patches, spotting the green ground.
>
> (SF, 38)

Writing to Princess Marguerite Caetani (founder and editor of *Botteghe Oscure*), he ruefully exclaimed in 1954, "Such a stupid letter! —even worse than usual. But it's partly the weather, I think—the sun hardly ever gets out in these parts. (San Francisco and Berkeley were wonderfully warm & non-foggy the week I was there.)"[10] The climate affected not only his disposition. His physical health also deteriorated. Seager writes: "His arthritis grew worse and became more painful in Seattle's damp climate. (He kept trying to get a job in California for the winter terms where he could be in the sun. He liked the sun.) He seemed to have a permanent bursitis in his elbow, and what he called 'spurs' in his shoulder for which he often got cortisone injections" (GH, 251).

Small wonder, then, if Roethke in his later poetry appears not to celebrate the Northwest but, instead, meditates upon death and the Roethkean soul's "drive toward God." Frederick Hoffman recalled that in the summer of 1957, Roethke confided "that he was much concerned with the mysteries and paradoxes of death, and that his new poetry reflected these concerns. It did just that. . . ."[11] Even in the "North American Sequence," William Snodgrass eloquently dismisses the native and regional note and hears instead a predominant urge to regression and death. The "burden" of such poems as "Meditation at Oyster River" and "The Long Waters," says Snodgrass, is "a desire to escape *all* form and shape, to lose all awareness of otherness . . . through re-entrance into eternity conceived as womb, into water as woman, into earth as goddess-mother."[12]

Other critics have echoed this conclusion, and some have gone on to remark that Roethke in the Northwest years scarcely seems to have acknowledged the ordinary human life of his community and region, let alone the political and social crises of the nation and world. Perhaps the capacity to respond to a regional *ethos* in America is linked to the capacity to respond to a national *ethos*—to feel the pulsebeat of the nation in the whole and in its distinguishing parts. The people of Washington State after the War were affected not only by the Canwell Committee political witchhunts, or logging and aircraft prosperity, but more broadly by Little Rock, McCarthyism, Eisenhower and Nixon, and a standardized civilization exploding with machines, gas pumps, and supermarkets. Where does this life appear in the poetry of Roethke? Simply, it is not there. But in recent years we have glimpsed, in the published notebooks, a Roethke to some degree conscious of both the humdrum and "provincial" and also the national temper of Cold War life in the Eisenhower fifties. But he appears through it all a man tormented by his incapacity to absorb this life, either concretely or abstractly, into his imagination, to ventilate his airtight broodings of self with poems ranging from his Seattle A & P to the shoddy goings-on of Joseph McCarthy and Richard M. Nixon. Being aware of a regional America, he muses, is to be sensitive to the lonely limits of the "provincial" experience lived simultaneously within an American civilization of major shortcomings and meager returns. In short, he cannot go the poetic route of a Hart Crane, Williams, Lowell, or Ginsberg. The following prose excerpts from the published notebooks reveal something of the distinguishing tone of the postwar decade—from Seattle to the nation's capital—which a lonely Roethke heard and felt but was unable to convert into his poetry.

> Me, if I'm depressed, I go down to the A & P and admire the lemons and bananas, the meat and milk. (SF, 213)

> Crane's assumption: the machine is important; we must put it in our lives, make it part of our imaginative life. Answer: the hell it is. An ode to an icebox is possible, since it contains fruit and meat. (SF, 239)

> Perhaps our only important invention is the concept of the good-guy. (SF, 240)

> After Mr. Richard M. Nixon, I feel that sincerity is no longer possible as a public attitude. (SF, 240)[13]

> ... there are intense spiritual men in America as well as the trimmers, time-servers, cliché-masters, high-grade mediocrities. (SF, 240)

> Democracy: where the semi-literate make laws and the illiterate enforce them. (SF, 240)

> Was it my time for writing poems about McCarthy or my time for sending out fresh salmon or the time of playing happy telephone or my time for dictating memoranda about what's wrong with America? ... or my time for crying. (SF, 88)

> I think no one has ever spoken upon the peculiar, the absolute—can I say—cultural loneliness of the American provincial creative intellectual. I don't mention this as something to be sighed over, worried about, written about—simply say it is simple fact that the American is alone in space and time—history is not with him, he has no one to talk to—Well, the British do. (SF, 228)

> As a provincial, an American, no fool, I hope, but an ignoramus, I believe we need Europe—more than she needs us: the Europe of Char, of Perse, of Malraux, of Michaux, those living men with their sense of history, of what a freeman is. (SF, 242)

An argument can be fashioned, nevertheless, that despite his poetic escape from the ordinary or critical affairs of his fellow earthlings, Roethke in Seattle was, in the most expressive and traditional manner, the poet of his place and time. In his dark confessional pages he spoke powerfully of the poet's spiritual despairs and searchings. Were they not shared, however diffusely, by Northwest folk and in fact, by all addled Americans whose lives were without ties and ballasts in the new global chaos of the mid-twentieth century? Another vivid notebook entry, presumably self-descriptive, supports this view of Roethke's American career and might aptly serve as the poet's own modern epitaph:

The grandeurs of the crazy man alone,
Himself the middle of a roaring world.

(SF, 84)

II.

Other Roethkes insistently emerge from the biographical pages. They blur together to suggest the man and poet who related himself positively to a place of birth, a region of his formative youth, a native land, and finally, a second region of his mature years. Allan Seager underplays this opposite story. The temptation is familiar to all who have conceived or labored to write the coherent biography of a complicated human being. Roethke's shifting masks and identities were varied and complex. He was a man of fierce, self-rending ambivalences. In addition to the previous examples of disaffection from region and country, leading to final escape into the metaphysical, one discovers also Roethke's embracement variously of the communal, the regional, and the national.

Though I am in search of a Northwest Roethke, I should briefly touch the earlier years for the evidence that he felt a certain positive spirit of place and attachment in America before 1947. In the early forties when Roethke arrived at rich and presumably sophisticated Bennington, Seager was struck by his new colleague's "ambiguous fear and admiration of the rich, his ambiguous fear and admiration of the East" which seemed to stir "all sorts of atavistic and Middle Western antagonisms" in the man (GH, 135-36). Seager did not know then that this Midwest identity had recently become a central concern for Roethke. He had applied for a Guggenheim grant just before. The poetry would advance beyond the private rejection and anger he had earlier expressed in regard to provincial Michigan and the "hideous" life of his youth. "A series of poems about the America I knew in my middle-western childhood," he wrote, "has been on my mind for some time; no flag-waving or hoopla, but poems about people in a particular suburbia" (GH, 133). Though he failed to receive the grant, Roethke persisted, and in his successful Guggenheim application three years later he described two of his three projects to be the writing of a distinctly regional verse:

> (1) a dramatic-narrative piece in prose and verse about Michigan and Wisconsin, past and present, which would center around the return of Paul Bunyan as a kind of enlightened and worldly folk-hero.
> (2) a series of lyrics about the Michigan countryside which have symbolical values. I have already begun these. They are not mere description, but have at least two levels of reference. (GH, 148)

To William Carlos Williams, who would understand this regional programme, Roethke worried over "the Paul Bunyan idea. The more I think
about it, the less I like it. But I've got to get some device to organize some
of my ideas & feelings about Michigan, etc.—not too solemn or God bless
America or Steve Benétish. Maybe it's worth trying, anyway."[14] When
The Lost Son appeared in 1948, readers would find that Roethke had or-
ganized his "ideas & feelings about Michigan" not within the Bunyan
myth but rather in a primordial myth of the child's Edenic greenhouse
world. In the "Michigan" poetry, Roethke did not fulfill his intensely
regional undertaking after all. Nor did the outer vegetal life register on
the inner Roethke except largely as a human metaphor, to be equated,
shaped, verbalized. But the urge to regional description and symbolization,
as well as to natural immersion and union, had begun. It remained a part
of his creative impulse which he would continue to explore and ultimately
frame and express in the Northwest.

In a 1953 appearance on BBC's "The Third Programme," Roethke introduced himself as a poet of unmistakably regional origins. "Everyone
knows that America is a continent," he said, "but few Europeans realize
the various and diverse parts of this land." He then described his own
Saginaw Valley and termed it "a wonderful place for a child to grow up
in and around."[15]

Again in an interview shortly before his death, Roethke fondly reminisced about Michigan scenes of his childhood which "still remained in
his mind" to influence his poems (GH, 275). Other testimony is now at
hand to support this version of Roethke who clearly felt a decisive part of
his identity as a man and sensibility as a poet had received salutary strength
from the region of his earliest years. It remained as a residue of positive
and cherished memory to sustain the maturing poet and enrich the strong
poems in his last book which I shall turn to in a moment.

Sometime in his early development, as Roethke understood himself to
be an Upper-Midwesterner, he also sensed another part of his identity
which should be noted before we enter the Northwest phase. He came to
feel his roots as an American. The process is too subtle to trace with absolute certainty. After he became assured of a reputation, Roethke almost
emphatically portrayed himself as having been, early on, a national poet in
the American grain. Though he was an avid reader of the English poets
and dramatists, he recalled first of all his American masters whom, he said,
"*early*, when it really matters, I read, and really read, Emerson (prose
mostly), Thoreau, Whitman."[16] And to a degree his memory is corrobo-
rated by student documents. His notes from a college course in American
literature at Michigan in the late twenties include these releaving comments on Whitman:

What are we to say of Whitman as poet? Selection? Defied rules.
Can art be formless NO!

1) An undying energy of life—a tang—vitalizing something.
2) A certain largeness—deals with deep things in life on a large
scale.
3) Most great poetry is primal? (GH, 54)

In a composition for his rhetoric class, Roethke's theme was his strong
response to nature. Again are the hints of a developing American consciousness: "I know that Cooper is a fraud—that he doesn't give a true
sense of the sublimity of American scenery. I know that Muir and Thoreau
and Burroughs speak the truth" (GH, 55). One can scarcely detect these
"American" influences in the deeply private poetry that would soon come
from Roethke's pen in the early post-college years. No doubt he had to
discover other aspects of selfhood—his personal, sexual, and family identity—before he possessed any version of a representative Roethke, Midwesterner or American.

Soon after *Open House* appeared in 1941, Roethke seems to have felt a
new growth away from the tight limits of this early poetic form and experience as well as, so we may infer, a movement toward a larger, a more
inclusive identity. "My first book was much too wary," he wrote Kenneth
Burke a few years later, "much too gingerly in its approach to experience;
rather dry in tone and restricted in rhythm."[17] And in a pair of anecdotes
to Allan Seager in the mid-forties, Roethke illuminates the early making
of a self-consciously national poet. The first is a letter after he arrived at
Bennington: "It seems I was hired because, according to the president,
Lewis Jones, I'm 'a grass roots American with classic tastes.' So, simple
fellow that I am, I'm to teach a course in American literature (just people
that interest me) next year."[18] Though he is amused by this American
version of himself, the man and poet with an as yet plastic and uncertain
self-image regarded the comment revealing enough to remember and
repeat.

The other occurrence, however, made him belligerently nationalistic. In
July, 1946, a less amusing version of the American Roethke had arrived
from England. The London *Horizon* had returned his new greenhouse
poems. "It seemed to us that your poetry was in a way very American,"
the rejection letter announced, "in that it just lacked that inspiration, inevitability or quintessence of writing and feeling that distinguishes good
poetry from verse." Seager comments that "this letter made him wrathy
and he was still fulminating against the 'god-damned limeys' when I saw
him later in the summer" (GH, 151-52).

The sting of this criticism may still have festered when Roethke
presently wrote an introductory comment on *The Lost Son* poems to be
included in John Ciardi's *Mid-Century American Poets* (New York:

Twayne, 1950). He now insisted that this poetry was very American and possessed a strong inspiration, inevitability or quintessence of feeling.

> Some of these pieces, then, begin in the mire; as if man is no more than a shape writhing from the old rock. This may be due, in part, to the Michigan from which I come. Sometimes one gets the feeling that not even the animals have been there before; but the marsh, the mire, the Void, is always there, immediate and terrifying. It is a splendid place for schooling the spirit. It is America.[19]

So much for American beginnings. In his Northwest years, when Roethke was bidding for and finally winning the cherished poetry prizes against his native competition, we can recognize a highly attuned "American" poet. Indeed, the competitiveness in the old tennis coach (incredibly, one of his duties at Lafayette and Penn State) had fully surfaced in the poetry career the year before the Seattle period began, when the leading influence on American poets was England's top seed, T. S. Eliot. Roethke had sent a manuscript copy of his poem "The Lost Son" to Eliot's current archenemy, William Carlos Williams. Roethke included the following comment: "It's written . . . for the ear, not the eye. . . . And if you don't think it's got the accent of native American speech, your name ain't W. C. Williams, I say belligerently." But Roethke's adversary was not Williams; it was the influential exile in England who irritated both men. "In a sense ["The Lost Son" is] your poem, yours and K. Burke's," he continued to Williams, "with the mood or the action on the page, not talked about, not the meditative T. S. Eliot kind of thing. (By the way, if you have an extra copy of your last blast against T.S.E., do send it to me. I can't seem to get a hold of it anywhere.)"[20] Roethke clearly understood that the Eliot cult must be discredited in America before the judges could hear and consider Roethke's (and Williams') native accents. By 1949 he was encouraged. He wrote to Kenneth Burke of new signs that "the *zeit-geist*, ear-to-the-ground boys in England" were coming over to his side and now calling it Roethke over Eliot: "[They] think I'm the only bard at present operating in the U.S. of A., that everybody is tired of Tiresome Tom, the Cautious Cardinal."[21]

One of Roethke's gratifying intimations of a growing reputation in Eliot's country came in 1950 when John Malcolm Brinnin told him that Dylan Thomas, on his first American tour, wanted especially to meet America's Theodore Roethke. Roethke was very proud of that and enjoyed Thomas immensely. Here was an authentic "roaring boy," a British admirer, and no rival for the American prizes. Finally in 1954 Roethke won his first big award, the Pulitzer, for *The Waking*. (But he remained envious when Aiken, not Roethke, won the National Book Award that year.)[22] The following year, Roethke was Fulbright lecturer in Florence. Like many American writers before him, he now comprehended his native

land more keenly from the vantage point of Europe. His concern, predictably, centered not on the characteristic travails of political democracy
in an election year, but rather on the state of American letters. He sized
up once again the relative strengths of modern American poets:

> Sometimes I think the fates brought me here for my own develop-
> ment: to see my contemporaries, and elders, in their true perspec-
> tive. And some of the American biggies have dwindled a good
> deal in my sight. For instance, Hart Crane, whom I once thought
> had elements of greatness. Except for the early poems, he now
> seems hysterical, diffuse—a deficient language sense at work.
> Williams, for the most part, has become curiously thin, self-
> indulgent, unable to write a poem, most of the time, that is a
> coherent whole. (This last saddened me a good deal, since I'm
> really fond of Bill.) Etc. People who *have* held up are Bogan,
> Auden, and of course old Willie Yeats, whom I'm not lecturing
> on; and Tate, for instance, looks better all the time, as opposed to
> Winters, whose work is often dead, rhythmically, and so limited
> in range of subject-matter and feeling.[23]

After *Words for the Wind* (1958) won him most of the major prizes in
America he had not yet claimed, including the National Book Award,
Roethke was clearly preparing now to beat the world. He was ready to go,
finally, after the big one, "to bring the Nobel in poetry to America," as he
said with a veneer of patriotism. But the egotism was not far behind. He
wrote his editor at Doubleday, "Certainly I'm a vastly better poet than
Quasimodo, and this French man [Perse] is good but does the same thing
over and over. I think Wystan Auden should be next, then Pablo Neruda,
then me. . ." (GH, 273). He had arrived at this "cold, considered objective judgment" (GH, 273) of his native genius after a final repudiation
of "the Pound-Eliot cult and the Yeats cult." As he told critic Ralph Mills,
neither "Willie" Yeats nor "Tiresome Tom" Eliot was ever Roethke's
master:

> In both instances, I was animated in considerable part by arro-
> gance: I thought: I can take this god damned high style of
> W.B.Y. or this Whitmanesque meditative thing of T.S.E. and use
> it for other ends, use it as well or better. Sure, a tough assignment
> But while Yeats' historical lyrics seem beyond me at the mo-
> ment, I'm damned if I haven't outdone him in the more personal
> or love lyric. . . . Not only is Eliot tired, he's a [expletive deleted
> by editor] fraud as a mystic—all his moments in the rose-garden
> and the wind up his ass in the draughty-smoke-fall-church yard.[24]

The next year, in a London interview, Roethke named the American
poets he most admired: Auden, Elizabeth Bishop, and Stanley Kunitz.
The last two certainly were no threat to his ambitious climb to the top of
the heap. And Auden might be seen not only as a poet ambiguously Amer-

ican, but also a leader of the Roethke cheering section. The year before, as Roethke recalled, Auden had passed along to a mutual acquaintance the compliment that "at one point he was worried that I was getting too close to Yeats, but now he no longer did because I had out-done him, surpassed him, gone beyond him."[25]

One formidable American remained to challenge Roethke in the poetry sweepstakes. This was Robert Lowell, whom Roethke met in summer of 1947 at Yaddo Writers Colony. He had grimly vanquished Lowell in all the recreational contests. "I was croquet, tennis, ping-pong and eating champion," he reported at the end of the summer (GH, 157). Seager writes perceptively here of the distinctly American myth of success and ardor for combat that lay within Roethke's hunger for greatness: "He was like Hemingway. To view literature as a contest to be won is a Saginaw Valley, Middle-Western, American set of mind, and throughout Ted's career he saw Lowell loom larger and larger as his chief opponent" (GH, 192). In this contest with Lowell, Roethke received the most punishing defeat publicly in July of 1963 shortly before his death. An admirer of Lowell, the Irish poet Thomas Kinsella, was in Seattle at Roethke's invitation, staying as Roethke's houseguest until later in the week when he gave a poetry reading. Seager recreates the harrowing climax of that evening:

> Ted sat in the front row. The reading was well-received and afterward Kinsella permitted a question-and-answer period. Someone asked, "Mr. Kinsella, who do you consider the greatest living American poet?" With Ted in the front row at the high tide of his renown, this was not, in a way, a genuine question but a solicitation of a compliment.
>
> But Kinsella, helplessly candid, hypnotized into tactlessness by his honest opinion, said, "Robert Lowell."
>
> Ted did not explode, but at the party he and Beatrice were giving for Kinsella later that evening, he grumped to his other guests, "That bastard, damn him. Did you hear what he said?" until Beatrice told him it would look better if he just shut up, and, oddly enough, he did. Later, calmer, more sober, Ted realized that Kinsella had a right to his opinion, forgave him and they parted friends. (GH, 284-85)

Perhaps one can rightly infer that the competitive Roethke traced Lowell's national success to his impressive roots in his American region. If so, the challenge to the leading younger poet of the Northeast might come in one manner, then, if Roethke could square off as the leading poet of the Northwest. But aside from the national ambition, Roethke for a number of years had been discovering the natural—and poetic—resources of the Northwest with that "obsessive quality of emotional ownership" that Richard Hugo looks for in the authentic regional poet.[26]

I have recorded earlier Roethke's negative reactions to the environs of
Seattle. Once more, the response to place in the mercurial Roethke has a
dynamic, positive side as well. One of his first references to a possible academic residence in the Far West comes in a letter of late 1946 when he was
on his first Guggenheim Fellowship and afraid that Bennington would not
invite him to return (he was technically still on leave from Penn State).
He admitted that he had been "brooding about the West Coast" (GH,
154). Shortly after, he wrote to George Lundberg, sociology professor
at the University of Washington whom he had known at Bennington.
Lundberg recommended him to the English department chairman, Joseph
Harrison. After some of his characteristic haggling about salary, Roethke
arrived in Seattle in September 1947 to become associate professor of
English at $5,004 (GH, 170-71).

The Northwest had one salutary effect on him at once. Some eleven
years before, a bookless Roethke in Michigan had lamented to Louise
Bogan on his twenty-eighth birthday, "No volume out and I can't seem to
write anything. You can say what you want, but *place* does have a lot to do
with productivity."[27] An ounce of rationalization in the frustrated poet
may be present here. By contrast, however, he exploded with ideas and
poems after he arrived in Seattle. Seager speculates on the causes: "Whether it was the stimulation of a new setting, the West Coast with its opu-
lence of natural life in its almost English climate, or whether he felt that
he had been idle too long (and 'idle' meant not that he had not been
writing but that he had gone too long without publishing a book) . . . he
filled more notebooks and more loose sheets with poetry in these two years
than in any period of his life" (GH, 185). He moved out to Edmonds
after several years of residence in the University district, finding it "more
Northwestern."[28] And for all his restless applying for grants or other jobs
to take him away from the University of Washington, Roethke in spring
of 1957 did buy the Seattle house on Lake Washington, an act which most
money-conscious Americans make when they confirm a place as their
home. Roethke was assuredly money conscious.

He was also, by then, *the* reigning poet of Seattle. I met him not long
afterward, and can attest to the fertile results of his presence. He was no
longer the only serious practicing poet for one thousand miles around.
Poetry readings seemed to be happening almost nonstop—usually on the
second floor of Hartman's Bookstore in the District or on campus in the
Walker Ames Room of Parrington Hall. Roethke's local students were
appearing, while ex-students were returning to Seattle to read from their
work. I recall the reading appearances of such visitors as Marianne Moore,
Snodgrass, Merwin, Kunitz, Wright, Langland, Ginsberg, Bogan, and
Leonie Adams—all of them come to Seattle or detoured there en route
down or up the coast because Roethke had made the Northwest a vital

corner of American poetry. Roethke himself, not to be outdone, made his own flamboyant public performances, now legendary in Seattle, appearing as the Northwest bard and declaiming his verses to his fellow townspeople, from savants to bourgeoisie, with an effect that would have cheered and amazed the bardic Whitman himself.

A "Northwest Renaissance" in poetry was proclaimed by Seattle poet Nelson Bentley, one of the Roethke faithful. During 1963 in San Diego, where I had gone to teach in a somewhat sunnier climate, I asked John Ciardi when he came through, "Are you conscious in the East of a 'Northwest Renaissance'?" He replied, "I don't know about any Northwest movement, but we all know that one poet named Theodore Roethke is out there."

How intensely Roethke was engaged in his private Northwest movement, a love-hate affair with a locale in which the critical citizen helped to form the integrity of feeling in the poet, we can now begin to gauge in the published notebooks. I mentioned earlier the entries where he comments on the isolation of a "provincial creative intellectual" in America and records the sterile, prosy observations of a frustrated citizen in Seattle. The notebooks also reveal the exhilarating process of a poet exploring his adopted Northwest landscape and converting it into usable tropes and images. But I leave this examination of the notebooks, a fruitful subject, to future students of Roethke and regionalism and turn instead to the published poetry itself.

III.

Roethke's first book of poems in the Northwest appeared in 1951. *Praise to the End!*, his "tensed-up" version of Wordsworth's *Prelude*, carried nine new poems which can be read, in one sense, as Roethke's completing the "lean to beginnings" in the previous *Lost Son* collection.[29] Once more he tracked his voyage of the mind's return to the dream logic, Mother Goose rhythms, and purposeful gibberish of childhood, and then back again to the varieties of rebirth after these mythic descents. He will return to this early Michigan in the late Northwest poems, but the goblin fears of childhood are no longer present. To a degree, then, he was ready, after *Praise to the End!*, to experiment with a new stage of poetic expression that had lain in embryo within the first Northwest notebooks.

A promise of the regional poems to come begins to appear in the new verses of his next book, *The Waking: Poems: 1933-53* (1953). "A Light Breather," to select one, reveals a joyous dynamism of the spirit, "small" and "tethered" as before but now "unafraid" and "singing." Together with the unhurried grace of the title poem, these lines point to the dearly earned resolutions shaped in the Northwest settings of his final long poems.

Symptomatic of a new phase, too, are poems like "Elegy for Jane," which Seager calls "the first of his poems to have its whole origin on the West Coast" (though one will discover "a sidelong pickerel smile" in Roethke's 1938 notebook).[30] Finally are the more ambitious efforts of the 1953 volume which show a Roethke who is escaping from his prison of the self to engage the ambient world and the being of other living creatures. "Old Lady's Winter Words" is one instance, and Roethke will enlarge this empathy in the "Meditations of an Old Woman" sequence of his next book. Of equal significance in 1953 is the first great sequence of metaphysical love poems, "Four for Sir John Davies." Here Roethke at last is able to reach outside the dance of the solitary self, merge with a partner, and experience a quasi-Dantean transcendence into mature love, the "rise from flesh to spirit." Not surprisingly, these love poems forecast an imminent involvement for Seattle's forty-four-year-old bachelor-poet. Any colleague at the University who read these poems in earlier journal publication might have advised Roethke that he was beginning to sound increasingly vulnerable to the presence of any marriageable woman. On a December evening in 1952 on his way to a reading in New York City, he inadvertently met along the street a former Bennington student, Beatrice O'Connell. He courted her every day thereafter, and at the end of a month they were married. Allan Seager believes that Roethke's marriage presently led him to a heightened awareness of the Northwest world. As his capacity of feeling reached out to his young Beatrice, "hesitantly, even reluctantly perhaps, he admitted her into those labyrinths within himself where his father still lived, and he began to love her, not in the same way that he loved his father but with a true love nevertheless. And from this time forward, she participated in his growth, encouraged and supported it. Then he could see the mountains, the siskins, the madronas, and begin to use them" (GH, 238).

Viewed in this regard, the "Love Poems" segment of the next book, *Words for the Wind: Collected Verse* (1958), is considerably more than occasions for Roethke to range through his varieties of lecherous punning, metaphysical wit, and Dantean love of a modern Beatrice. The love poems, thoroughly studied for their passionate metaphors of wind and seafoam, light and stones and rippling water as "spirit and nature beat in one breastbone," will perhaps reveal the true beginnings of that distinctive Northwest sensibility which fully emerges in Roethke's last book. Useful also to that end, although for other reasons, are the final three sections of *Words for the Wind*, with their natural stream of correspondences tallying the movements of the soul, downward to the spiritual DTs and harrowing plunges and upward to the ascensions and harmonious resolutions with an "agency outside me. / Unprayed-for, / And final."

And so we arrive at *The Far Field* (1964), the final volume which

Roethke, almost providentially it now seems, had lived to write. At this zenith came his death. There would be no descent, no failing of creative energy. *The Far Field* becomes the logical culmination of Roethke's poetic and American sojourn out of the Midwest and through his native land to maturity and reconciliation in the Northwest.

The year before his death, Roethke wrote to Ralph Mills, Jr.: "I am still fiddling with the order and composition of certain final poems."[31] Only weeks before his death, he settled on a structure of *The Far Field* in four parts: "North American Sequence," "Love Poems," "Mixed Sequence," and "Sequence, Sometimes Metaphysical." The first, or "North American," sequence of six poems includes the title poem, "The Far Field." (An original title for the book, "Dance On, Dance On, Dance On," had come from the final poem.) Perhaps I am swayed unduly to believe that in changing the book's title, Roethke was signalling the reader that the opening section with "The Far Field" would carry the crucial burden of the entire volume. In any event, the "North American Sequence" has become the great achievement in Roethke's last book. It might properly be called the "Northwest Sequence" for reasons I hope will be apparent in fairly short order.

The genesis of this sequence may be traced, in one fashion, to the summer of 1950. Roethke had bought his first car and had driven it back to Seattle. The trip created the stirrings of a "symbolical journey," his own spiritual version of a Northwest passage. It suggested "for next or possibly later book . . . a happy journey westward"; but there would be a uniquely Roethkean variation of this traditional passage—"in a word, a symbolical journey in my cheap Buick Special toward Alaska and, at least in a spiritual sense toward the east of Russia and the Mongolian Plains whence came my own people, the Prussians, those poop-arse aristocrats, my father called them, who fed their families into the army or managed the hunt for Bismarck and Bismarck's sister—all this in Stettin in East Prussia, now held by the Poles" (GH, 194).

By the end of the decade, Roethke had modified this journey. It was now an exclusively North American and ultimately regional experience. He told Zulfikar Ghose in an interview in London in 1960, during his Ford Foundation fellowship, about his shifting conception and emphasis: "My imagery is coming more out of the Northwest rather than the whole of America." The nature of the journey had changed. In Ghose's words, it was "not like driving a car across America, but an exploration of the North-West" (GH, 269).

He had, in fact, developed a triple motif of outer-inner journeys. First is the Northwest passage to the dark oceanic "stretch in the face of death," and the periodic resolution experienced at the Pacific Coast shoreline, a journey out to the physical "edge" and metaphysical "beyond" and then back to reconciliation "where sea and fresh water meet" in the Northwest corner. The second passage or journey is a return to his origins, a movement eastward to the Michigan of his father's greenhouse and Roethke's childhood. Gone in this experience, as I hinted earlier, are "the muck and welter, the dark, the *dreck*" which burden the poems in *The Lost Son* and *Praise to the End!*[32] Third is a "journey to the interior," imaged in an inland American geography perhaps equivalent, temporally, to the middle period of Roethke's initial breakdown in that "Siberian pitilessness, the essential ruthlessness of the Middle West." Here he moves beyond the child's insulation from time and death and forward to the mature man's encounter with the voids and abysses and multiplicity of challenges to his spiritual growth. But he does not attain to the outer thresholds of vision, the achieved moments of outer-and-inner union and transcendence that belong to the Northwest passage. Ranging forward and back across the American landscape in the "North American Sequence," then, Roethke's speaker can understandably admit in "The Far Field": "I dream of journeys repeatedly."

Of the three journeys, the Northwest passage is by far the richest and most dominant in the six poems of the sequence. Roethke gathers within it the shifting motifs of selfhood within the Northwest's natural plenitude, identifications with birds, fish, trees, and flowers (and occasionally as relief, with the stillness of rocks, clam shells, driftwood, and nature's minimals); the imagery of edges, abysses, and thresholds; the desire for convergence, resolution and union with the natural scene of salt water, fresh water, air, and earth; and on occasion, when blessedly aided by the soft regional light and wind, the speaker feels the shimmerings of immanence which create a felt convergence, a moment of transcendence and beatitude. By entering upon the other two journeys inland from time to time, he enriches and paces the sequence in alternating rhythms of charged meditation and dynamic movement across American space. The speaker, classically a migratory American, travels inward and outward across the North American terrain in pursuit of his total selfhood. But he returns always to the Northwest shoreline for an ultimate synthesis.

These interlacing journeys and themes and alternating rhythms are sounded in the first poem, "The Longing," and then are centered on a longed-for passage, finally with an American Indian vigor of exploration, to the threshold of full spiritual awareness. Just as this initial poem becomes, musically, a prelude, almost an overture, to the entire sequence, the final poem, "The Rose," will climax and recapitulate the sequence.

"The Longing" opens "In a bleak time, when a week of rain is a year." (We can assume the speaker is in Seattle.) But this is not life-giving rain. The speaker's spirit is in a slump amid the reigning "stinks and sighs, / Fetor of cockroaches, dead fish, petroleum" and the pointless angst of nightclub crooners and their self-pitying, lust-fatigued audience, an un-savory scene of

> Saliva dripping from warm microphones,
> Agony of crucifixion on barstools.

In a regressive aside, he associates pure joy only with children, dogs, and saints. The Roethkean interrupting question focuses the list and impels the poem onward: "How to transcend this sensual emptiness?" The North-west scene, natural and manmade, fumes in its putrefaction. In bleak contrast to the free-soaring gull we remember at the onset of Hart Crane's *The Bridge*, Roethke's Northwest seagulls "wheel over their singular gar-bage." Images which later will foreshadow immanence—the regional light and wind—are invoked in this spiritual torpor to deepen our sense of their absence.

> The great trees no longer shimmer;
> Not even the soot dances.

The spirit, slug-like, recoils. But it retains the hunger for a new start, like "a loose worm / Ready for any crevice, / An eyeless starer."

So the sequence begins in one of the bleak rainy spells with which Roethke in Seattle was all too familiar. In the two remaining sections of "The Longing," we follow the Roethkean voyage of the modern soul in its tormented quest for light and wholeness. He conducts this soul-search initially by going back to the beginnings of elemental life. The clues of the way toward transcendence are sensed in the spareness of the natural world.

> The rose exceeds, the rose exceeds us all.
> Who'd think the moon could pare itself so thin?

A sign is also received in the unnatural light that cries out of the "sunless sea" in the same measures of longing.

> I'd be beyond; I'd be beyond the moon,
> Bare as a bud, and naked as a worm.

Roethke captions this retrogression and desire in the final lines of the sec-tion: "Out of these nothings / —All beginnings come."

The conclusion is introduced with a Whitman catalog of the speaker's longing for identification and convergence with the plenitude and benefi-cence he now feels he may possess in the world, by contrast with the open-ing section and the ascetic vacuity that followed upon it. In the poems to follow, the desire to pace his spiritual growth in harmony with his natural surroundings will be, at the same time, an esthetic search for a shaping, concrete language that will also express the inexpressible: "I long for the

imperishable quiet at the heart of form." But as of now, the speaker has
received only the intimation of future thresholds. He anticipates, meanwhile, a rite of passage through the North American interior.

> . . . the mouth of the night is still wide;
> On the Bullhead, in the Dakotas, where the eagles eat well,
> In the country of few lakes, in the tall buffalo grass at
> the base of the clay buttes. . .

Does the aging spirit dare to go primitive? No, if subjected to the ruthless
plains of the interior. Yes, if sustained amid the inland waters.

> Old men should be explorers?
> I'll be an Indian.
> Ogalala?
> Iroquois.

"Meditation at Oyster River," the second poem of the "North American Sequence," begins at twilight on the east coast of Vancouver Island.
Roethke's explorer looks eastward to the "first tide-ripples," briefly im-
merses his feet in the water, and then partakes of earth and air as well by
ascending to a perch on the cliffside. In the Northwest "twilight wind,
light as a child's breath," the spirit quivers with alertness. A soundless
pause has readied the time for meditation after urgent longing in the
previous poem.

Section two finds the speaker half in love with easeful death, persisting
"like a dying star, / In sleep afraid." He yearns for escape from the lonely
self, for oneness with the deer, the young snake, the hummingbird—the
shy and alert creatures of land and air. "With these I would be. / And with
water." At this threshold of poised awareness, "In this first heaven of
knowing," Roethke takes us, in section three, on a backward motion
toward the source, to "the first trembling of a Michigan brook in April."
He feels the old quickenings of a younger spirit which, like the melting
Tittebawasee in early spring, could awaken, expand, and burst forward
into a new season of becoming.

The meditation finally returns to Oyster River and closes with the harmonious resolution of youth and age as he is "lulled into half-sleep" in a
Whitman-like sea-cradle. After his journey back to Michigan and forward
once more to the waters of the Northwest, he merges now in quiet joy with
the waves and the intrepid shorebirds. The poem closes in a radiant, although not fully composed, vision:

> In the first of the moon,
> All's a scattering,
> A shining.

Arrivals on the threshold of naturalistic grace are momentary and precarious. In the third poem, "Journey to the Interior," the speaker returns to the yawning mouth of the night which awaited him at the close of "The Longing." He now embarks on that second American journey into the past, between Michigan beginnings and Northwest consummations.

As in "The Longing," he begins in dislocation, though not, this time, in spiritual dullness. Roethke initially presents "the long journey out of the self" in a vague, geographical metaphor: to pass through the perplexed inner workings and torments of the emerging self is like steering a lurching automobile through detours, mud slides, dangerous turns, flash floods, and swamps "alive with quicksand." Finally, the way narrows to a standstill, "blocked at last by a fallen fir-tree, / The thickets darkening, / The ravines ugly."

From this introductory standstill, he sets forth on a new soul's journey. In section two, this exploration takes the form of an actual trip westward through the North American interior. The explorer, appropriately, is neither child nor man now but a reckless youth careering over gravel at full throttle, scorning to "hug close" like the fear-ridden older motorist he would become in the previous stanza. With the arrogant confidence of youth, he courts danger and death on the American roadway head-on: "A chance? Perhaps. But the road was part of me, and its ditches, / And the dust lay thick on eyelids,—Who ever wore goggles?" (Roethke is here falling back on his own self-made legend that he had been once the extroverted American roaring boy. In fact, the hyper-sensitive youth from Saginaw had grown beyond forty before he owned a car and made this western journey through the interior. For an emerging identity, however, Roethke knew well that fantasy is as powerful and "true" as fact.) The second section concludes as the trip advances through the western prairies and beyond the Tetons. The past merges with the present, the random fluidity of the land journey is abated, and "time folds / Into a long moment" for the youth become, in the remembrance, confident father of the troubled man.

In the final section, the speaker can still feel his "soul at a still-stand," but this time with a difference. Thanks to the remembered journey through the American interior which has intervened, he again moves to the edge of water in the Northwest. Reconciled to change and death, united with the soft elements of his region, he can "breathe with the birds" while he stands "unperplexed" looking out on the Pacific scene. All extremes dissolve on that "other side of light," and

> The spirit of wrath becomes the spirit of blessing,
> And the dead begin from their dark to sing in my sleep.

"The Long Waters" was apparently written after but appears before

"The Far Field." Presumably, Roethke felt the need for a tranquil, sustained meditation piece to separate "Journey to the Interior" from "The Far Field" (which was originally titled "Journeys"). "The Long Waters" occurs in a setting closely resembling Oyster River. The poem moves quietly among three Roethkean stages—retrogression (closing at times to infantile regression), thresholds, and convergence. These movements are experienced largely in Northwest images without the backward journey motifs of the previous poems. Roethke creates, instead, an alternating rhythm of gentle ebbing and flowing, action and reaction. In a transparent outline modeled and elaborated after Roethke's own example (GH, 187), we may see the internal structure of the five sections to develop this way:

1. *Initial retrogression (ll. 1-12).* The speaker celebrates the joyous minimals of earth, water, and air—the worms, minnows, and butterflies. He confesses his childlike "foolishness"—his "desire for the peaks, the black ravines, the rolling mists," but also the opposite need for security amid "unsinging fields where no lungs breathe, / Where light is stone."

Threshold to convergence approached (ll. 13-19). He returns to a fire-charred "edge of the sea . . . Where the fresh and salt waters meet, / And the sea-winds move through the pine trees" in near-concert with the burnt-yellow grass and peeling logs.

2. *Retrogression again (ll. 20-32).* He invokes protection of a Blakean mythic mother against the quietly distressing motions of the worm and butterfly and the "dubious sea-change" but he knows that change and death are also the mothers of pleasure and beauty.

3. *Convergence approaches unawares (ll. 33-48).* The abundant varieties of Northwest coastal images—the leaping fish, the ivy rooting in sawdust alongside the uprooted trees, the casual osprey and dawdling fisherman, and a sea surface full of imagined flowers both alive and dead—bring the casual speaker almost to a reconcilement of extremes, to feelings of beatitude and immanence.

> I have come here without courting silence,
> Blessed by the lips of a low wind,
> To a rich desolation of wind and water,
> To a landlocked bay, where the salt water is freshened
> By small streams running down under fallen fir trees.

4. *Threshold reappears (ll. 49-53).* "In the vaporous grey of early morning / . . . . A single wave comes in."

Retrogression once more (ll. 54-59). But when the wave reaches "a tree lying flat, its crown half broken," the speaker, vaguely troubled, recalls "a stone breaking the eddying current / . . . in the dead middle way, / . . . A vulnerable place."

5. *Convergence followed by a light transcendence is briefly achieved*

(ll. 60-78). His receptive "body shimmers with a light flame" in the sea wind as the "advancing and retreating" sea, which images the risings and fallings of the poem, now yields up a visionary "shape" of "the eternal one." The undulant long waters attenuate in the long poetic line, shaping for the speaker a transformed moment of union and renewal.

> My eyes extend beyond the farthest bloom of the waves;
> I lose and find myself in the long water;
> I am gathered together once more;
> I embrace the world.

With "The Far Field" the sequence now returns to the opening of "Journey to the Interior"—the metaphorically "narrowing" trip by automobile to a final stalling "in a hopeless sand-rut." (One glimpses in the images the American affliction of Poe and the late Mark Twain.) From this still-stand of the spirit, Roethke again searches the way out by going back. The journey in this case will not be to the interior but an extended return to a timeless childhood, to moments of immanence in that "far field, the windy cliffs of forever, / The dying of time in the white light of tomorrow." In that field, "one learned of the eternal" in the child's world of dead rats and cats, of life-nestings in the field's far corner. For nature's casualties, his young "grief was not excessive." The warblers always heralded Maytime renewal and nature's plenitude. With similar ease, the child could ponder the evolution of mindless shells or indulge his innocent fancies of reincarnation.

Returning to the adult's present, the speaker, no longer constricted, can sense "a weightless change, a moving forward." The earlier narrowing of section one is repeated, but in an image of release, "As of water quickening before a narrowing channel / When banks converge." He emerges to face outward to sea. Like the philosopher's man of Wallace Stevens, he is able to confront an ultimate Protean reality, with more insouciance, even, than the wondering child he once was.

> The murmur of the absolute, the why
> Of being born fails on his naked ears.
> His spirit moves like monumental wind
> That gentles on a sunny blue plateau.

The poem rises into gentle transcendence. The "finite things" which in previous lines of the sequence recalled "a vulnerable place" or a disturbing juxtaposition of death and life, now compose in a constellation of Northwest images that the tranquil mind discovers to be the shape of "infinitude":

> The mountain with its singular bright shade
> . . . .

The after-light upon ice-burdened pines;

. . . .

Silence of water above a sunken tree:
The pure serene of memory in one man,—
A ripple widening from a single stone
Winding around the waters of the world.

The final poem, "The Rose," sums up and completes the "North American Sequence." All three of the American journey-motifs are here, together with all of the inner stages of the soul and their supporting images. More fully than any of the preceding single poems, "The Rose" is Roethke's Northwest poetic creation par excellence. It appeared in *The New Yorker* the month before his death. The thorough critic of Roethke's poetry would want more than a score of pages to explicate this beautiful poem and account for it within the entire sequence. I shall try to manage a fraction of the assignment in a few pages.

Appropriately with these verses that close the sequence, Roethke can begin with near-feelings of convergence that by now have been earned. We understand his opening assertion about the Northwest seacoast:

There are those to whom place is unimportant,
But this place, where sea and fresh water meet,
Is important—

He then draws the bountiful natural life into this ultimate song of himself. In the next fifteen lines, he describes some dozen Northwest birds and at the same time, predictably, he unites them to air, earth, and water. He no longer requires the agonizing interior journey through and out of the perplexed self. He can "sway outside myself / Into the darkening currents" with the quiet grace of the intrepid hawks he has just described (lines 4-5).

Section two advances the easy motions of grace onto a pacific ocean "As when a ship sails with a light wind— / . . . dipping like a child's boat in a pond." Still, in its apparently buoyant ease of passage, his spirit feels obscurely troubled, somehow adrift and incomplete. The realization he is seeking now approaches on the Northwest shoreline before his feet. His guide to this knowledge, both fact and symbol, is the single "rose in the sea-wind," the transcendent rose he had briefly invoked in "The Longing." Its own excuse for being, the wild rose silently instructs by a dynamic staying "in its true place," by "flowering out of the dark," widening in noonday light, and stubbornly resisting encroachment upon its solitary life. The meditation upon the individualized wild rose leads the speaker associatively to one final journey to the greenhouse world of his childhood. In the reminiscence, the aged man repossesses the glories he had known when "those flowerheads seemed to flow toward me, to beckon me, only a child, out of myself." The child had merged with the roses and both had flourished in the bountiful Eden created by his sufficient, protective father:

> What need for heaven, then,
> With that man, and those roses?

The childhood memory then triggers the other, or later, journey into the past. Section three first echoes the early morning "sound and silence" of the Northwest scene in the opening lines of the poem. We are then taken on a last journey into the "interior," to gather up and catalog the inland "American sounds in this silence"—a Whitman excursion among industrial noises, the bravuras of birds, "the ticking of snow around oil drums in the Dakotas, / The thin whine of telephone wires in the wind of a Michigan winter," and more. His second journey eastward into the past completed, the old explorer has reached the final definition of himself. His longing for "the imperishable quiet at the heart of form" had first occurred within the fluid Whitman catalog of the first poem. He now hears the imperishable quiet in the "single sound" that issues in the Northwest setting of "The Rose" at the heart of this Whitman free form. Phrased another way, his question in "The Longing" had been "How to transcend this sensual emptiness?" He has discovered the answer: the sensual emptiness has been transcended in the sensual fullness of the Whitman-Roethke gatherings of American plenitude, as in these fluid interior "American sounds in this silence." And this possession, be it noted, has occurred within a primary context of the regional. After extended longing, he has found the place of his desire. It is glimpsed, significantly enough, not as an ultimate paradiso or a child's insular garden of flowers, but as a transcendent landscape of earth composed both of languid shimmerings and Roethkean edges. The moment then dissolves in the precarious balance of a rapt instant of earthly beauty. The closing lines of the penultimate section of "The Rose" suspend an image of life wakening into, or indistinguishable from, death.

> And a drop of rain water hangs at the tip of a leaf
> Shifting in the wakening sunlight
> Like the eye of a new-caught fish.

The speaker emerges from the vision to explain himself in the final section. Thanks to the final journeys of private and native—and esthetic— self-realization that were stimulated by the rose's expansive self-containment, he has again embraced his present world, his Northwest, and can accept even

> the rocks, their weeds,
> Their filmy fringes of green, their harsh

> Edges, their holes
> Cut by the sea-slime. . .

Like the space-time curvature of this journey poem, the poet's spirit match-
ing the condition of the rose in the sea-wind, he has "swayed out. . . /
And yet was still." He can also rejoice equally with the bird, the lilac, and
the dolphin in the calm and change which they accept in air, land, and
water. In the lovely closing lines, he absorbs in his controlling solitary
symbol the diversity of experience and imagery in this climactic poem.

> [I rejoiced] in this rose, this rose in the sea-wind,
> Rooted in stone, keeping the whole of light,
> Gathering to itself sound and silence—
> Mine and the sea-wind's.

So ends an intensive drive toward definition of the many Roethkean
selves, of the perplexed American in his country and his region. The
"North American Sequence" can be read as Roethke's final portrait, not
unlike those late photographs of the poet in a Northwest landscape, his
face variously lined with what Robert Heilman read as "suffering endured,
dreaded, inescapable, and yet survived and, in an ever maturing art, sur-
mounted."[33] Even Roethke's "drive toward God" was climaxed in the ultimate landscape of the Sequence. The northern coast and oceanic far field
of his adopted region served him perfectly to frame and extend his religious
journeys in and out of time and space and even to resolve them in fleeting
moments of joyous, tranquil union.

Finally, this sequence enabled Roethke the poet to assimilate those
American peers who meant the most to him without permitting the national echoes to disturb or overpower the regional tonalities. The mastery
of this casual plagiarism offers one of the surest signs of the major poet
coming into possession of his own definable voice. Merely the final lines
of "The Rose," which echo the close of "When Lilacs Last in the Dooryard
Bloom'd," show how well Roethke had learned his poetic orchestration
from Whitman. The larger motifs of the sequence—the passages through
nature and America and beyond to a total selfhood—are indebted similarly
to Whitman, especially the "Song of Myself," "Out of the Cradle," and
"Passage to India." Echoes of the symbolical American journeys of Hart
Crane, likewise a transplanted Midwesterner, and William Carlos Williams's immersion in a local America also abound, as do the parallels and
instructive differences with the experimental Eliot of *The Waste Land* and
the Tiresome Tom of the *Four Quartets*. Clearly important to Roethke,
too, are the sensual Stevens of "Sea Surface Full of Clouds" and the more
philosophical Stevens of "Sunday Morning," "Asides on the Oboe," and
"Notes Toward a Supreme Fiction." And we hear the Emily Dickinson of

seasonal thresholds, nuances of light, and the edges of death. Sounding clearly, also, are the American nature notes of Emerson's "Rhodora" and Frost's "West-Running Brook," as well as the correspondences of New England coast and self in Robert Lowell—less transcendental but historically richer than Roethke's. But enough. An annotated "North American Sequence," obviously, would extend the references almost endlessly. Astonishing, then, for all Roethke's allusive and emotional range and intensity in this late sequence is the account from his biographer that these culminating long poems "came easily with an unwonted confidence—he knew what he wanted to say and he was sure of his means" (GH, 252).

Roethke's American debts for this regional achievement lead naturally, in turn, to the question of his own possible influence on the younger practicing poets of the region. Richard Hugo, William Stafford, Carolyn Kizer, and David Wagoner have carefully evaded the idea of any Roethke "school" in the Northwest while they praise his brilliant example of the verbal pressures and cutting edges possible in a highly disciplined poetry. Surely this is a healthy and necessary spirit of poetic autonomy. The "school" with its intimidating master voice has more often curbed than liberated vital literary expression, regional and otherwise. I suspect, however, that Roethke's regional experience at the end had been fashioned too powerfully not to have become a part of the consciousness of poets writing today in the Northwest. If so, this need not be totally bad. The Roethke idiom has generated intimations, if you will, of a receivable and emerging heritage. But the nature of Roethke's contribution to a Northwest poetry will obviously not be known for some time to come, just as anything nearing a definitive notion of a Northwest ethos awaits the regional intuitions of individual poets, novelists, scholars, and memorializers to come.

IV.

Had he lived, would Roethke have continued to mine the Northwest vein of his "North American Sequence"? Elsewhere, the final volume only clouds a possible answer. He had gone on to include more of the torments, the voids, and the self-disintegrations of the past. The best of these metaphysical lyrics include "The Abyss," "In a Dark Time," and "In Evening Air." He did extend himself, however, in the rare sequence of final love poems. With the same daring that led him earlier to create the feminine voice of his "Meditations of an Old Woman" (feminists today might call the effort ill-advised) he aimed in his final love poems to express the perhaps more difficult voice of a sensitive young woman in love. But in previous years he seemed always too restless, too experimental and ambitious to repeat many of his successful innovations. He would throw most of them out the window, as James Dickey once said, and then start anew. In his continuing art as in his religious meditations, Roethke would probably have strained again to "go beyond," "to be more," to outdo himself. The new love lyrics or the "North American Sequence," then, had been tried and completed. Perhaps it would be time, once again, to move on.

One exciting possibility remains on record to point a way that Roethke might have taken had he lived. His wife reported that when Roethke once visited the grave of Chief Seattle, "he knelt in the grass and [crossed himself] seriously" (GH, 199). The gesture may tell how soberly he had assumed his late ambition to write an epic of the North American Indian. His structural device would be, once more, a passage across the nation's heartland. The speaker would stop to commemorate the scenes of tragic undoing which various tribes suffered at the hands of the white marauders and military. In this epic drama, which Roethke hoped to create, he said, "through suggestive and highly charged symbolical language," the heroic figures, indicated in his notes, were to include the Nez Perce's Chief Joseph, the Oglala's Black Elk and Crazy Horse, as well as white adversaries like Generals Custer and Crook. The theme would be "the guilts we as Americans feel as a people for our mistakes and misdeeds in history and in time. I believe, in other words, that it behooves us to be humble before the eye of history."[34]

Such a culminating work, as I suggested at the beginning, would have been utterly *de rigueur* in the eyes of literary critics and Nobel committees—the regional writer impressively widening his range to become the national epic poet and, even more, an American conscience in the world's history. The Nobel-haunted Roethke was all too aware of the required pattern. A passage he entered in the late notebooks almost completely mirrors his anguish. He defiantly justifies his major work as faithfully "American" despite, or even because of, its being "provincial" (he continues to use, somewhat wryly, this pejorative term for the regional). Implicitly and belligerently he is advising the Nobel people to stuff their award.

> There's another typical stance: only *I* hear it. Then just listen: hump, schlump, bump—half the time: a real—did I say real?—I mean *unreal*, unnatural—thumping away in stupid staves, an arbitrary lopping of lines, rhythms, areas of experience, a turning away from much of life, an exalting of a few limited areas of human consciousness. All right, I say, make like that, and die in your own way: in other words limited, provincial, classical in a distorted and—I use the word carefully—degraded sense; "American" in the sense American means eccentric, warped, and confined. (SF, 243-44)

But we can set aside this too-obvious concern over obligatory soarings upward and outward to national epic, universal archetype, and the larger "areas of human consciousness" and indulge our pride in the native poet whose versatile powers and range of vision expanded *within* the Northwest landscape and seascape. Immersion in the local and the "confining," the "exalting" of the solitary self in our own "true place," the poet Roethke is saying at last, brings us intermittently to experience in the only way that knowing is finally possible—that is, privately in the desire of the heart—those deep responses and truths that others may wish to elevate with the abstract labels "American" or "Universal." This distinctive regional expression, which he bled for and slowly earned over the years, is what we have overlooked or undervalued in Roethke. By *The Far Field*, he was virtually creating the Northwest as a regional source of poetic truth. Inevitably with Roethke, expressing the spirit of place also had to mean a revealing of his mature identity as a man and poet. In the transcendental vision of the important last poems, Roethke and his Northwest had finally come to One.

---

1. See Allen Tate, "American Poetry Since 1920," *Bookman*, 68 (1929), 507-08; and Fred Moramarco, "A Gathering of Poets," *Western Humanities Review*, 30 (Winter 1976), 89. For a similar statement of these views, this time that Southwest literary regionalism is "strikingly thin" because the writers' approaches to the legendary culture of the area "have failed to produce a body of literature that transcends the romantic or regional," see Larry Goodwin, "The Frontier Myth and Southwestern Literature," in *Regional Perspectives*, ed. John G. Burke (Chicago: American Library Association, 1973), p. 176.
2. *The Glass House: The Life of Theodore Roethke* (New York: McGraw-Hill, 1968), p. 123; hereafter indicated in the text as GH.
3. "Roethke's Broken Music," in *Theodore Roethke: Essays on the Poetry*, ed. Arnold Stein (Seattle: Univ. of Washington Press, 1965), p. 158; referred to hereafter as Stein.
4. To Burke, Feb. 27, 1945, in *Selected Letters of Theodore Roethke*, ed. Ralph J. Mills, Jr. (Seattle: Univ. of Washington Press, 1968), p. 113; hereafter indicated in the notes as SL.
5. *Straw for the Fire: From the Notebooks of Theodore Roethke, 1943-63*, sel. and arr. by David Wagoner (New York: Anchor-Doubleday, 1974), p. 98; unless indicated otherwise, all excerpts from Roethke's notebooks are taken from this edition, hereafter indicated in the text as SF.
6. To Seager, July 29, 1947, SL, p. 132.
7. Sept. 18, 1947, SL, p. 134.
8. Jan. 19, 1948, SL, p. 138.
9. To Edward Nichols, March 13, 1948, SL, p. 144. See also SF, p. 205, for Roethke's amused notebook variation on this public self-image.
10. March 10, 1954, SL, p. 200.
11. "Theodore Roethke: The Poetic Shape of Death," in Stein, p. 95.
12. "'That Anguish of Concreteness'—Theodore Roethke's Career," in Stein, p. 87.
13. Roethke did write, but never published, a mildly obscene ballad on Vice President Nixon. The rough drafts are in the Roethke collection, University of Washington Library, Box #42, Notebook #187 (dated March 26, 1960).
14. *Circa* 1944, SL, p. 112.

15. "An American Poet Introduces Himself and His Poems," in *On the Poet and His Craft: Selected Prose of Theodore Roethke*, ed. Ralph J. Mills, Jr. (Seattle: Univ. of Washington Press, 1965), pp. 7-8.
16. To Ralph J. Mills, Jr., June 12, 1959, SL, p. 230.
17. Feb. 27, 1945, SL, p. 114.
18. May 8, 1943, SL, p. 109.
19. "Open Letter," repr. in *On the Poet and His Craft*, p. 40.
20. May 8, 1946, SL, p. 122.
21. Sept. 6, 1949, SL, p. 154.
22. To Marguerite Caetani, March 10, 1954, SL, p. 200.
23. To Robert B. Heilman, March 20, 1956, SL, p. 209.
24. June 12, 1959, SL, p. 231.
25. To Mills, June 12, 1959, SL, p. 231.
26. "Problems of Landscape in Early Stafford Poems," *Kansas Quarterly*, 2 (Spring 1970), 37.
27. May 25, 1936, SL, p. 37.
28. To Richard Eberhart, July 14, 1952, SL, p. 177.
29. My text for the poetry is *The Collected Poems of Theodore Roethke* (New York: Doubleday, 1968).
30. GH, 193, 162. "Elegy for Jane" is a persuasive instance of the way Roethke's work falls into place when we see him *of* rather than merely writing *in* the Northwest. His student at the University of Washington, Jane Bannick, had been fatally thrown by a horse. Another student, Lois Lamb, also fell from a horse and described it to Roethke. Further, because she had been raised on a farm in central Washington, she was able to communicate to Roethke, no lover of the animal world in the past, something of her "intuitive understanding" of animals (GH, 187). Seager believes she also may have helped Roethke to get the animals right in some of his children's poems. One can argue genetic regional links, then, where none had seemed likely, among "Elegy for Jane," the animal nonsense poems, and even the mastered nursery-rhyme cadences of *Praise to the End!*
31. March 23, 1962, SL, p. 252.
32. The phrase here is from Roethke's "Open Letter" introduction to the *Lost Son* poems in Ciardi's *Mid-Century American Poets*, cited earlier (cf. *On the Poet and His Craft*, p. 40).
33. "Theodore Roethke: Personal Notes," *Shenandoah*, 16 (Autumn 1964), 57.
34. To Ford Foundation, Jan. 22, 1959, SL, pp. 224-25. See also GH, 279. Like his discarded Paul Bunyan idea in the earlier Guggenheim proposal, Roethke's projected Indian epic may appear little more than calculated grantsmanship. But after writing these comments, I sampled the Roethke collection at the University of Washington Library. In Box #43, Notebook #200 (dated April 3, 1961), I discovered six large notebook pages in which Roethke sketched rather extensively the mood, landscape, and portions of the action of his Indian saga. He wrote one sustained poetic passage on the death, apparently, of General Custer, whom he planned to demythicize as "the liar" and "a slip-faced schemer."

Ward Tonsfeldt has a doctorate in comparative literature from the University of California, San Diego. Although trained in the medieval aspect of comparative literature, Professor Tonsfeldt is currently working seriously on the fiction of the twentieth-century Pacific Northwest. He has been a lecturer in English at San Diego State University and at UCLA. He is currently an assistant professor in English at Central Oregon Community College in Bend, Oregon.

The Pacific Northwest: A Selected and Annotated Bibliography

Ward Tonsfeldt

I. General Bibliographies

Belknap, George N. *Oregon Imprints: 1845-1870*. Eugene: Univ. of Oregon Press, 1968. An annotated bibliography that updates McMurtrie, Douglas C. *Oregon Imprints: 1847-1870*. Eugene: Univ. of Oregon Press, 1950.

Bromberg, Eric. "Bibliography of Theses and Dissertations Concerning the Pacific Northwest and Alaska." *Pacific Northwest Quarterly*, 40 (1949), 203-52, and 42 (1951), 147-66.

———. "Bibliography of Theses and Dissertations Concerning the Pacific Northwest and Alaska." *Oregon Historical Quarterly*, 59 (1958), 27-85, and 65 (1964), 362-91.

"Checklist of Northwest Books" in *Pacific Northwest Library Association Quarterly*. Annual bibliography of books about the region or by Northwest authors published in each fall issue.

Coleman, Rufus A. *Northwest Books*. Portland: Binfords and Mort, 1942.

———. *Northwest Books: First Supplement, 1942-1947*. Lincoln: Univ. of Nebraska Press, 1949. Annotated listings of regional writing with some information about the writers.

Inland Empire Council of Teachers of English. *Northwest Books*. Missoula, Mont.: H. G. Merriam, 1933. The first of the bibliographies in the *Northwest Books* series.

Smith, Charles W. *Pacific Northwest Americana*. Ed. Isabel Mayhew. Portland: Binfords and Mort, 1950. Books and pamphlets relating to the history of the Pacific Northwest.

II. Special Bibliographies

Albion, R. G. *Naval and Maritime History: An Annotated Bibliography*. 4th ed. Mystic, Conn.: Munson Inst. of American Maritime History, 1972. Books, theses, and published documents on maritime history with a section on the Pacific Northwest.

Appleton, John B. *The Pacific Northwest: A Selected Bibliography*. Portland: Northwest Regional Council, 1939. A list of materials relating to the natural and human resources of the region.

Davis, Lenwood G. *Blacks in the State of Oregon: 1788-1974*. Monticello, Ill.: Council of Planning Librarians, 1974. Published works and unpublished source materials on the lives and achievements of Blacks in Oregon.

Hewlett, Leroy. *Indians of Oregon: Bibliography of Materials in the Oregon State Library*. Salem: Oregon State Library, 1969.

Lowther, Barbara J. *A Bibliography of British Columbia: Laying the Foundations, 1849-1899*. Victoria: Univ. of Victoria Press, 1968.

III. Reference Works

Corning, Howard M. *Dictionary of Oregon History*. Portland: Binfords and Mort, 1956.

Farmer, Judith A., and Kenneth Holmes. *An Historical Atlas of Oregon*. Tualatin, Ore.: Geographical Area Study, 1973.

Highsmith, R. M., and Robert Bard. *Atlas of the Pacific Northwest*. Corvallis: Oregon State Univ. Press, 1973.

Loy, William G. *Atlas of Oregon*. Eugene: Univ. of Oregon Press, 1976.

McArthur, Lewis A. *Oregon Geographic Names*. 2nd ed. Portland: Oregon Historical Soc., 1974. Packed with information and a superb example of books of this kind.

Phillips, James W. *Washington State Place Names*. Seattle: Univ. of Washington Press, 1971.

Schmitt, Martin. *Catalogue of Manuscripts in the University of Oregon Library*. Eugene: Univ. of Oregon Press, 1971. Over 1,000 manuscript collections described in judicious and helpful detail.

Washington, State University Libraries. *Dictionary Catalogue of the Pacific Northwest Collection*. 6 vols. Boston: G. K. Hall, 1972. Published and unpublished sources from perhaps the largest collection of Pacific Northwest materials—indexed by author, subject, and title.

Who's Who Among Pacific Northwest Authors. Pacific Northwest Library Assn. checklist, published occasionally over the past twenty years.

IV. General Treatments of the Region

Bancroft, Hubert Howe. *History of Oregon*. 2 vols. San Francisco: The History Co., 1888.

————. *History of Washington, Idaho and Montana.* San Francisco: The History Co., 1890.

————. *History of British Columbia, 1792-1887.* San Francisco: The History Co., 1887. Bancroft's works remain the point of departure for serious study of the Pacific Northwest.

Cantwell, Robert. *The Hidden Northwest.* Philadelphia: Lippincott, 1972. A Northwest man of letters conceptualizes his region.

Dodds, Gordon B. *Oregon: A Bicentennial History.* New York: W. W. Norton and Nashville: American Assn. for State and Local History, 1977.

Griffith, Thomas. "The Pacific Northwest." *The Atlantic,* Apr. 1976, pp. 46-93. Contemporary overview.

Holbrook, Stewart. *Far Corner.* New York: Macmillan, 1952. Essays on Northwest life.

Johansen, Dorothy O., and Charles M. Gates. *Empire of the Columbia.* New York: Harper and Row, 1967. Best general textbook on the region.

Lavender, David. *Land of Giants: The Drive to the Pacific Northwest.* Garden City, N.Y.: Doubleday, 1958. Readable and reliable treatment of the Pacific Northwest.

Ormsby, Margaret A. *British Columbia: A History.* Toronto: Macmillan of Canada, 1958. Traditional treatment; especially solid to 1900.

Pomeroy, Earl. *The Pacific Slope.* New York: Alfred A. Knopf, 1965. Sophisticated treatment of the twentieth-century American West.

Vaughan, Thomas, ed. *The Western Shore: Oregon Country Essays Honoring the American Revolution.* Portland, Oregon: Oregon Historical Soc. and American Revolution Bicentennial Commission of Oregon.

Warren, Sidney. *Farthest Frontier.* New York: Macmillan, 1949. Social and cultural history of the Pacific Northwest up to about 1911.

V. Regionalism and the Pacific Northwest

Binns, John H. "Northwest Region—Fact or Fiction?" *Pacific Northwest Quarterly,* 48 (1957), 65-75. Lively consideration of the question.

Davis, H. L. *Kettle of Fire.* New York: Morrow, 1959. Stories and sketches on the meaning of the Oregon experience.

Frykman, George A. "Regionalism, Nationalism, Localism: The Pacific Northwest in History." *Pacific Northwest Quarterly,* 43 (1952), 251-61. Survey of Pacific Northwest historiography.

Gastil, Raymond D., Norman Clark, Richard W. Etulain, and Otis A. Pease. "A Symposium: The Pacific Northwest as a Cultural Region." *Pacific Northwest Quarterly*, 64 (1973), 147-62. Provocative approach to a definition.

Gastil, Raymond D. *Cultural Regions of the United States*. Seattle: Univ. of Washington Press, 1975. Useful in making comparisons.

Howard, Joseph Kinsey. *Montana: High, Wide, and Handsome*. New Haven: Yale Univ. Press, 1943. Unflinching account of Montana history and life.

Jensen, Merrill, ed. *Regionalism in America*. Madison: Univ. of Wisconsin, 1965. Papers from a 1949 University of Wisconsin conference on regionalism, approaching the topic from a variety of disciplines, including history and literature.

VI. History

Ashby, LeRoy. *The Spearless Leader: Senator Borah and the Progressive Movement in the 1920's*. Urbana: Univ. of Illinois, 1972.

Bakeless, John. *Lewis and Clark: Partners in Discovery*. New York: Morrow, 1947.

Burton, Robert. *Democrats of Oregon: Patterns of Minority Politics 1900-1956*. Eugene: Univ. of Oregon Press, 1970.

Berton, Pierre. *The National Dream*, and *The Last Spike*. Toronto: McClelland and Stuart, 1970, 1971. A two-volume popular history of the Canadian Pacific Railway.

Campbell, Marjorie W. *The North West Company*. Toronto: Macmillan of Canada, 1957.

Clark, Norman. *Mill Town*. Seattle: Univ. of Washington Press, 1970. Everett, Washington from its founding to the Everett Massacre in 1916.

Cohn, Edwin J. *Industry in the Pacific Northwest and the Location Theory*. New York: King's Crown Publishing Co., 1954. Application of an economic theory to the Pacific Northwest.

Coman, E. T. and Helen Gibbs. *Time, Tide and Timber: A Century of Pope and Talbot*. Stanford: Stanford Univ. Press, 1949. Case study of lumber, water transport, and marketing.

Cox, Thomas R. *Mills and Markets: History of the Pacific Coast Lumber Industry to 1900*. Seattle: Univ. of Washington Press, 1974.

Cook, W. L. *Flood Tide of Empire*. New Haven: Yale Univ. Press, 1973. Spanish exploration and ambition on the Northwest coast.

Dubofsky, Melvyn. *We Shall be All*. Chicago: Quadrangle, 1969. Best history of the Industrial Workers of the World.

Friedheim, Robert L. *The Seattle General Strike*. Seattle: Univ. of Washington Press, 1964.

Friedman, Ralph. *Tales Out of Oregon*. 1967; rpt. Sausalito, Calif.: Comstock Eds., 1972. Offbeat stories from Oregon's past.

Galbraith, John. *The Hudson's Bay Company as an Imperial Factor, 1821-1869*. Berkeley: Univ. of California Press, 1957.

Ghent, W. J. *The Road to Oregon*. New York: Longman, Green, and Co., 1929. Analysis of motives and experiences on the Oregon trail.

Gough, Barry M. *The Royal Navy and the Northwest Coast of British Columbia, 1810-1914*. Vancouver: Univ. of British Columbia Press, 1971.

Greever, William S. *Bonanza West: Story of the Western Mining Rushes, 1848-1900*. Norman: Univ. of Oklahoma Press, 1963.

Hidy, Ralph, Frank Hill, and Allan Nevins. *Timber and Men: The Weyerhaeuser Story*. New York: Macmillan, 1963.

Hitchman, James H. *The Waterborne Commerce of British Columbia and Washington, 1850-1870*. Bellingham: Western Washington State College, Center for Pacific Northwest Studies, 1976. Compares and contrasts local and international trade.

Howay, F. W., W. N. Sage, and H. F. Angus. *British Columbia and the United States*. New Haven: Yale Univ. Press, 1942. Standard account; still useful.

Hutchinson, Bruce. *The Fraser*. New York: Rinehart, 1950. Readable pocket history of the river.

Innis, H. A. *The Fur Trade in Canada*. Toronto: Univ. of Toronto Press, 1927. A landmark in the literature of the fur trade.

Jensen, Vernon. *Lumber and Labor*. New York: Farrar and Rinehart, 1945. The labor movement in the forest products industries.

Johansen, Robert W. *Frontier Politics and the Sectional Conflict*. Seattle: Univ. of Washington Press, 1955. Joe Lane and political factions in Oregon in the 1850s.

Jones, Nard. *The Great Command*. Boston: Little, Brown and Co., 1959. Popular treatment of the Whitmans in the Oregon country.

Kerfoot, Denis. *The Port of British Columbia*. Vancouver: Tantalus Research, 1966. A study of British Columbia ports and trade with useful historical statistics.

LeWarne, Charles Pierce. *Utopias on Puget Sound, 1885-1915.* Seattle: Univ. of Washington Press, 1975.

MacColl, E. Kimbark. *The Shaping of a City: Business and Politics in Portland, Oregon, 1885-1915.* Portland: Georgian Press, 1976.

Malone, Michael. *C. Ben Ross and the New Deal in Idaho.* Seattle: Univ. of Washington Press, 1970.

Meinig, Donald. *The Great Columbia Plain.* Seattle: Univ. of Washington Press, 1970. Historical geography by a leader in the field.

Merk, Frederick. *Fur Trade and Empire: George Simpson's Journal.* Cambridge: Harvard Univ. Press, 1931. Scholarly editing of the Hudson's Bay Company governor's journal.

———. *The Oregon Question.* Cambridge: Harvard Univ. Press, 1967. Thirteen essays covering the period 1818-1848.

Mills, Randall V. *Stern-Wheelers up the Columbia.* Palo Alto, Calif.: Pacific Books, 1947. Economic and social history of steamboating on the Columbia and Willamette.

———. *Railroads Down the Valley.* Palo Alto, Calif.: Pacific Books, 1950. Informal history of Oregon short line railroads.

Morgan, Murray. *Skid Road: An Informal Portrait of Seattle.* New York: Viking Press, 1951.

Newell, Gordon, ed. *The McCurdy Marine History of the Pacific Northwest.* Seattle: Superior, 1966.

Oliphant, J. Orin. *On the Cattle Ranges of the Oregon Country.* Seattle: Univ. of Washington Press, 1969. Definitive study of the range cattle industry in the Pacific Northwest.

Paul, Rodman. *Mining Frontiers of the Far West, 1848-1880.* New York: Holt, Rinehart, and Winston, 1963. Treats technical as well as historical aspects of western mining.

Phillips, Paul. *No Power Greater: A Century of Labour in British Columbia.* Vancouver: British Columbia Federation of Labour, 1967. Scholarly work on the role of labor in provincial development.

Richardson, Elmo. *The Politics of Conservation.* Berkeley: Univ. of California, 1962. Emphasizes the Ballinger-Pinchot controversy.

Robin, Martin. *Rush for the Spoils: The Company Province, 1871-1933.* Toronto: McClelland and Stuart, 1972. Stresses impact of big business on British Columbia.

Swan, James Gilchrist. *The Northwest Coast, or, Three Years' Residence in Washington Territory.* New York: Harper, 1857. Firsthand account by a perceptive observer.

Throckmorton, Arthur. *Oregon Argonauts: Merchant Adventurers on the Western Frontier.* Portland: Oregon Historical Soc., 1961. Business and social history of early western Oregon.

Tyler, Robert L. *Rebels of the Woods.* Eugene: Univ. of Oregon, 1967. Focuses on social and cultural as well as economic aspects of the I.W.W.

Turnbull, George. *History of Oregon Journalism.* Portland: Binfords and Mort, 1939. Still the definitive work.

Wright, E. W., ed. *Lewis and Dryden's Marine History.* Seattle: Superior, 1967. Maritime history of the Pacific Northwest from its origins to about 1895.

VII. Autobiography, Biography, and Journals

Anderson, Bern. *Survey of the Sea: Life and Voyages of Captain George Vancouver.* Seattle: Univ. of Washington Press, 1960.

Applegate, Jesse. "A Day with the Cow Column." *Oregon Historical Quarterly* 1 (1900), 371-83. Classic reminiscence of the "Great Migration" of 1843.

Beaglehole, J. C. *Life of Captain James Cook.* Stanford: Stanford Univ. Press, 1974. Monumental biography of Cook.

Blankenship, Russell. *And There Were Men.* New York: Knopf, 1942. Essays on some colorful personalities of the late frontier.

Burnett, Peter. *Recollections and Opinions of an Old Pioneer.* New York: D. Appleton, 1880. Important Willamette Valley settler who became first governor of California.

Clark, Malcolm Jr., ed. *Pharisee Among the Philistines: The Diary of Matthew P. Deady, 1871-1892.* 2 vols. Portland: Oregon Historical Soc., 1975. Informed account of Portland society in the vein of Samuel Pepys.

Coe, Urling C., M.D. *Frontier Doctor.* New York: Macmillan, 1939. Recollections of a Bend, Oregon general practitioner.

DeVoto, Bernard, ed. *Journals of Lewis and Clark.* New York: Houghton Mifflin Co., 1953. Judicious abridgement of original journals.

Douglas, William O. *Autobiography: Go East, Young Man.* New York: Random House, 1974; rpt. New York: Delta, 1975. The shaping influence of environment on young Douglas.

Drury, Clifford M., ed. *First White Women Over the Rockies.* 2 vols. Glendale, Calif.: Arthur H. Clark, Co., 1963-1966. Diaries of Narcissa Whitman, Eliza Spalding, Mrs. William H. Gray, Mrs. Asa B. Smith, Mary Richardson Walker, and Mrs. Cushing Eells.

————. *Marcus and Narcissa Whitman and the Opening of Old Oregon.* 2 vols. Glendale, Calif.: A. H. Clark Co., 1973. Life of the Whitmans by the leading authority.

French, Giles. *Cattle Country of Peter French.* Portland: Binfords and Mort, 1964. Best biography of the eastern Oregon cattle baron. Author is no relation to the subject.

Garcia, Andrew. *Tough Trip Through Paradise.* 1967; rpt. Sausalito: Comstock Editions, 1976. Picaresque recollections of an early Montana figure.

Geer, Theodore T. *Fifty Years in Oregon.* New York: Neale Publishing Co., 1912. Autobiography of influential political figure.

Hedges, James B. *Henry Villard and the Railways of the Northwest.* New York: Russell and Russell, 1930. Assessment of a leading figure in Pacific Northwest transportation.

Hendrickson, James E. *Joe Lane of Oregon: Machine Politics and the Sectional Crisis, 1849-1861.* New Haven: Yale Univ. Press, 1967. Life of Lane with emphasis on his career in the Pacific Northwest.

Holmes, Kenneth. *Ewing Young, Enterprising Trapper.* Portland: Binfords and Mort, 1967. Treats a key person in transition from fur trade to settlement.

Hyde, Dayton O. *Yamsi.* New York: Dial Press, 1971. Journal of a year's activities on a southern Oregon wilderness ranch.

Lamb, W. Kaye, ed. *Letters and Journals of Simon Fraser, 1806-1808.* Toronto: Macmillan of Canada, 1960. Concise, authoritative biography introduces the firsthand materials.

Loewenberg, Robert J. *Equality on the Oregon Frontier: Jason Lee and the Methodist Mission, 1834-1843.* Seattle and London: Univ. of Washington Press, 1976. Revisionist treatment of Lee and the Methodists in Oregon.

McCarthy, Mary. *Memories of a Catholic Girlhood.* New York: Harcourt, Brace, 1957.

MacDonald, Betty. *The Egg and I.* Philadelphia: J. B. Lippincott, 1946. A young couple scratches out a living raising chickens.

————. *Onions in the Stew.* Philadelphia: J. B. Lippincott, 1955. Author's family life on Vashon Island.

McNaughton, Margaret. *Overland to the Cariboo.* Toronto: W. Briggs, 1896. Firsthand account of life in the British Columbia wilderness.

Martin, Albro. *James Hill and the Opening of the Northwest.* New York: Oxford Univ. Press, 1977. Most recent biography of the founder of the Great Northern.

Morgan, Dale L. *Jedediah Smith and the Opening of the West*. Indianapolis: Bobbs-Merrill, 1953. Best biography of the American explorer and fur trader.

Morgan, George T. *William B. Greeley—A Practicing Forester*. St. Paul: Forest History Soc., 1961. Concise assessment of the famous forester.

Nesbit, Robert C. *"He Built Seattle:" A Biography of Judge Thomas Burke*. Seattle: Univ. of Washington Press, 1961.

Ross, Nancy Wilson. *Westward the Women*. New York: Knopf, 1944. Biographical sketches of striving Northwest pioneer women.

Sage, Walter. *Sir James Douglas and British Columbia*. Toronto: Univ. of Toronto Press, 1930. Competent treatment of the Hudson's Bay Company Chief Factor.

Sheppe, Walter, ed. *First Man West: Alexander MacKenzie's Journal of his Voyage to the Pacific Coast of Canada in 1793*. Berkeley: Univ. of California, 1962. Perceptive biographical sketch introduces the journal.

Sampson, William R., ed. *John McLoughlin's Business Correspondence, 1847-1848*. Seattle: Univ. of Washington Press, 1973. Helpful biographical sketch by the editor.

Smith, A. Robert. *Tiger in the Senate*. Garden City, N.Y.: Doubleday, 1962. A well-known journalist takes the measure of Wayne Morse.

Smith, Helen K. *With Her Own Wings*. Portland: Beattie and Co., 1948. Essays on women in the Oregon Country.

Whiteley, Opal. *The Story of Opal: The Journal of an Understanding Heart*. Boston: Atlantic Monthly Press, 1920. The author's fanciful childhood experiences mark the beginning of a bizarre life.

Winthrop, Theodore. *Canoe and Saddle*. 1863; rpt. Portland: Binfords and Mort, 1955. An observant Yale man's encounters with the Northwest landscape, settlers, and Indians in the 1850s.

VIII. Pacific Northwest Indians

Barnett, Homer. *Indian Shakers: A Messianic Cult of the Pacific Northwest*. Carbondale, Ill.: Southern Illinois Univ. Press, 1957.

Beal, Merrill D. *"I Will Fight No More Forever:" Chief Joseph and the Nez Perce War*. Seattle: Univ. of Washington Press, 1963.

Beckham, Stephen Dow. *Requiem For A People: The Rogue Indians and the Frontiersmen*. Norman, Okla.: Univ. of Oklahoma Press, 1971. Scholarly treatment of a neglected Indian group.

Clark, Ella. *Indian Legends of the Pacific Northwest.* Berkeley: Univ. of California Press, 1953. Convenient collection of myths most of which explain the origin of physical features in Oregon and Washington.

Cressman, Luther S. *The Sandal and the Cave.* Portland: Champoeg Press, 1964. An anthropologist analyzes evidence of early native peoples in Oregon.

Drucker, Philip. *Indians of the Northwest Coast.* New York: McGraw-Hill, 1955.

————. *Cultures of the North Pacific Coast.* San Francisco: Chandler Publishing Co., 1965. Both Drucker's works are authoritative and clearly written.

Duff, Wilson. *The Indians of British Columbia.* Victoria: Provincial Museum of Northwest History and Anthropology, 1965. Stresses impact of white society on Indian culture.

Haines, Francis. *The Nez Perces: Tribesmen of the Columbia Plateau.* Norman: Univ. of Oklahoma Press, 1955. Readable introduction to the Nez Perce with emphasis on their skill as horse breeders.

Hawthorn, Harry B., C. S. Belshaw, and S. M. Jamison. *The Indians of British Columbia: A Study of Contemporary Social Adjustment.* Toronto: Univ. of Toronto, 1958.

Jacobs, Melville. *The People Are Coming Soon: Analyses of Clackamas Chinook Myths and Tales.* Seattle: Univ. of Washington Press, 1960. Seeks to discover whether supplementation of literally translated words and phrases furthers comprehension and allows more aesthetic appreciation than the reading of the translations alone.

Josephy, Alvin M. *The Nez Perce Indians and the Opening of the Northwest.* New Haven: Yale Univ. Press, 1965. Thoroughgoing and sympathetic treatment.

Judson, Katherine B. *Myths and Legends of the Pacific Northwest.* Chicago: A. C. McClurg, 1910. Early collection of Indian tales.

McFeat, Tom, ed. *Indians of the North Pacific Coast.* Seattle: Univ. of Washington Press, 1967. Essays by various authorities on Indians such as the Nootka, the Kwakiutl, the Haida, and the Tlingit with special focus on class stratification and ceremonials.

McWhorter, Lucullus V. *Hear Me, My Chiefs.* Caldwell, Idaho: Caxton Printers, 1952. Best study by a white writer who knew the Nez Perce and wrote from their point of view.

Murray, Keith. *The Modocs and Their War.* Norman: Univ. of Oklahoma Press, 1959. Rather objective treatment of a topic much distorted by many writers.

Ramsey, Jarold. *Coyote Was Going There*. Seattle: Univ. of Washington Press, 1977. Indian legends of the Oregon Country.

Ruby, Robert H., and John A. Brown. *Half-Sun on the Columbia: A Biography of Chief Moses*. Norman: Univ. of Oklahoma Press, 1965. The authors resurrect a little-known chief of the middle Columbia region.

————. *The Chinook Indians: Traders of the Lower Columbia River*. Norman: Univ. of Oklahoma Press, 1977. Impact of white traders on red.

Splawn, A. J. *Ka-Mi-A-Kin: Last Hero of the Yakimas*. 1917; rpt. Portland: Binfords and Mort, 1944. Dramatic and sympathetic in tone.

Stern, Theodore. *The Klamath Tribe*. Seattle: Univ. of Washington Press, 1965. Scholarly study of the Klamaths and their reservation.

Swanton, John R. *Indian Tribes of North America*. Washington, D.C.: U.S. Govt. Printing Office, 1952. A still reliable handbook of tribal locations and affiliations.

Thompson, Stith. *Tales of the North American Indian*. 1929; rpt. Bloomington: Indiana Univ. Press, 1966. Points out persistence of recurrent patterns in American Indian tales.

Underhill, Ruth M. *Indians of the Pacific Northwest*. Riverside, Calif.: Sherman Inst. Press, 1945. Still useful and very readable.

IX. Literature: General Anthologies

Geddes, Gary, ed. *Skookum Wawa: Writings of the Canadian Northwest*. Toronto: Oxford Univ. Press, 1975. Selections from both historical and contemporary writing.

Holbrook, Stewart, ed. *Promised Land*. New York: McGraw-Hill, 1945. A collection of Northwest literature.

Jordan, Grace, ed. *Idaho Reader*. Boise: Syms-Youk, 1963. An anthology of Idaho writers.

Lee, W. Storrs, ed. *Washington State: A Literary Chronicle*. New York: Funk and Wagnalls, 1969. Selections from Washington writers and writers about Washington.

Lucia, Ellis, ed. *This Land Around Us*. Garden City, N.Y.: Doubleday, 1969. A survey of writing by Northwest authors. Updates Holbrook.

X. Literature: Nonfiction Nature-Writing

Haig-Brown, Roderick. *A River Never Sleeps*. New York: William Morrow, 1946. A noted British Columbia author and angler reviews a fisherman's year.

Higman, Harry W., and Earl J. Larrison. *Union Bay*. Seattle: Univ. of Washington Press, 1951. Description of the natural activities of a city marsh.

Heckman, Hazel. *Island in the South*. Seattle: Univ. of Washington Press, 1962. Sensitive treatment of life on Puget Sound.

Hoagland, Edward. *Notes From the Century Before*. 1969; rpt. New York: Ballantine, 1972. An urban novelist writes of the upper British Columbia backcountry.

Jackman, E. R., and Reub Long. *The Oregon Desert*. Caldwell, Idaho: Caxton Printers, 1969.

Lampman, Ben Hur. *The Coming of the Pond Fishes*. Portland: Binfords and Mort, 1946. How the warm-water fish species came to the Northwest.

Peattie, Roderick, ed. *The Cascades: Mountains of the Pacific Northwest*. New York: Vanguard, 1949. Essays by various hands on aspects of the Cascades.

Sharp, Dallas Lore. *Where Rolls the Oregon*. Boston: Houghton Mifflin, 1914. Early account of Oregon's natural wonders.

Stanwell-Fletcher, Theodora. *Driftwood Valley*, 1946; rpt. New York: Ballantine, 1971. A naturalist and her trapper husband build a cabin and live in the British Columbia wilderness.

XI. Literature: Pre-World War II Fiction

Balch, Frederick Homer. *The Bridge of the Gods*. 1890; rpt. Portland: Binfords and Mort, 1965. Classic romantic and sentimental historical novel of Indian life on the Columbia.

Binns, Archie. *Lightship*. New York: Reynal and Hitchcock, 1934. Adventure set aboard lightship off the Washington coast.

——. *The Laurels Are Cut Down*. New York: Reynal and Hitchcock, 1937. Brothers on the Olympic Peninsula and in the Siberian intervention.

——. *Timber Beast*. New York: C. S. Scribner, 1944. A logging family and their experiences, including those with the I.W.W.

Cantwell, Robert. *Laugh and Lie Down*. New York: Farrar and Rinehart, 1931. Faulknerian first novel of young people in a Northwest mill town.

——. *Land of Plenty*. New York: Farrar and Rinehart, 1934. Proletarian novel concerning a strike in a coastal veneer mill.

Case, Robert O. *The Yukon Drive*. Garden City, N.Y.: Doubleday, Doran, 1930. Concerns an actual cattle drive from Oregon to Alaska.

Davis, Harold Lenoir. *Honey in the Horn*. New York: Harper, 1935. Pulitzer Prize-winning novel about the homesteading period in Oregon. Essential to a study of Northwest literature.

————. *Team Bells Woke Me and Other Stories*. New York: William Morrow, 1953. A collection of some of Davis's best stories.

Fisher, Vardis. *Dark Bridwell*. Boston: Houghton Mifflin, 1931. Charley Bridwell's tragic attempt to impose an isolated Idaho life upon his family.

————. *In Tragic Life*. Garden City, N.Y.: Doubleday, Doran, 1933. First of Fisher's partly autobiographical novels set in Idaho's desolate valleys. See also his *Toilers of the Hills*. Caldwell, Idaho: Caxton Printers, 1933.

Foote, Mary Hallock. *The Cup of Trembling and Other Stories*. Boston: Houghton Mifflin, 1896. Four long stories dealing with Idaho.

Jones, Nard. *Swift Flows the River*. New York: Dodd, Mead, 1940. Novel set in the steamboating era on the Columbia.

McKay, Allis. *They Came to a River*. 1941; rpt. Portland: Binfords and Mort, 1961. A young girl grows up with the country along the Columbia near Wenatchee.

Miller, Joaquin. *Selected Writings of Joaquin Millre*. Ed. Alan Rosenus. Eugene, Ore.: Urion, 1977. Notes, stories, diaries, drawings, and photographs are included. See also Rosenus's recent edition of Miller's *Unwritten History*.

Niven, Frederick J. *The Flying Years*. 1935; rpt. Toronto: McClelland and Stuart, 1974. Although available, this work on the Canadian West may be of less interest to Northwesterners than Niven's earlier, out-of-print books.

Sinclair, Bertrand W. *Poor Man's Rock*. Boston: Little, Brown, 1920. Social concerns and human values in British Columbia's salmon fishery.

Stevens, James. *Big Jim Turner*. 1945; rpt. Albuquerque: Univ. of New Mexico Press, 1965. Semi-autobiographical novel of Northwest logger-poet.

XII. Literature: Post-World War II Fiction

Berry, Don. *Trask*. 1960; rpt. Sausalito, Calif.: Comstock, 1976. Ex-mountainman searching for new land on the Oregon coast turns to self-discovery. The locale appears again in Berry's third novel, *To Build A Ship*.

————. *Moontrap*. 1962; rpt. Sausalito, Calif.: Comstock, 1976. Mountainmen cannot assimilate with early Willamette Valley settlers.

Brautigan, Richard. *The Hawkline Monster*. New York: Simon and Schuster, 1975. A gothic western set in eastern Oregon.

Craven, Margaret. *I Heard the Owl Call My Name*. 1973; rpt. New York: Dell, 1974. A young white man discovers his life and death among the coastal Indians of British Columbia.

Cushman, Dan. *Stay Away, Joe*. New York: Viking Press, 1953. Comic novel treating contemporary Indian life in western Montana.

Guthrie, A. B. *The Big Sky*. 1947; rpt. New York: Bantam, 1972. Classic mountainman novel set in Montana in the 1820s and 1830s.

————. *The Way West*. New York: W. Sloane Associates, 1949. Dick Summers of *The Big Sky* guides a wagon train to Oregon. The series on western settlement is concluded by *These Thousand Hills* and *Arfive*.

Halcox, Ernest. *Canyon Passage*. 1945; rpt. New York: Signet, 1974. Adventure novel set in Rogue River country at the time of the Indian War.

————. *The Earthbreakers*. New York: Little, Brown, 1952. Haycox's most successful attempt to break out of the formula-western in this novel of early Willamette settlement.

Kesey, Ken. *One Flew Over the Cuckoo's Nest*. 1962; rpt. New York: Viking, 1973. Mental asylum inmates against "the Combine" in this widely popular first novel.

————. *Sometimes a Great Notion*. 1964; rpt. New York: Bantam, 1965. A logging family on the Oregon Coast defies the elements, the town, and the union.

Leahy, Jack. *Shadow on the Waters*. New York: Knopf, 1960. A white boy grows up on the Olympic Peninsula in the shadow of a dying Indian culture.

LeGuin, Ursula. *The Lathe of Heaven*. New York: Scribners, 1971. Science fiction set in the future Portland.

Lowry, Malcolm. *October Ferry to Gabriola*. Ed. Margerie Lowry. New York: World, 1970. Posthumously published novel by the noted author of *Under the Volcano*.

Malamud, Bernard. *A New Life*. 1961; rpt. New York: Pocket Books, 1973. An "outsider," although he taught at Oregon State University for 12 years, Malamud offers a comic look at the "insiders."

Marion, Elizabeth. *The Keys to the House*. New York: Crowell, 1944. Coming to maturity in the eastern Washington dry farming country.

Okada, John. *No-No Boy*. Tokyo and Rutland, Vermont: Charles E. Tuttle, 1957; rpt. Seattle: Univ. of Washington Press, 1978. A Japanese-American boy in Seattle struggles with his identity after interment in World War II.

Stegner, Wallace. *Angle of Repose*. 1971; rpt. Greenwich, Conn.: Fawcett, 1972. Conflict of Eastern and Western values in this story based upon the life of Mary Hallock Foote.

Watson, Sheila. *The Double Hook*. Toronto: McClelland and Stuart, 1966. Difficult, rewarding work by a novelist of the Cariboo country.

XIII. Literature: Pre-World War II Poetry

Davis, H. L. *Proud Riders and Other Poems*. New York: Harper and Row, 1930. Oregon's premier novelist was also her finest early modern poet.

Harrison, Henry, ed. *Oregon Poets*. New York: Henry Harrison, 1935. Includes poems by the "Portland Group," of whom Howard M. Corning is the most important.

Merriam, Harold G. *Northwest Verse: An Anthology*. Caldwell: Caxton Printers, 1931. Ambitious anthology of the best Northwest poetry of the twenties, with perceptive introduction.

Miller, Joaquin. *The Poetical Works of Joaquin Miller*. Ed. Stuart P. Sherman. New York: Putnam's, 1923. Illustrates the range of Miller's verse.

XIV. Literature: Post-World War II Poetry

Bertolino, James. *Northwest Poets*. Madison: Quixote, 1968. Introduction emphasizes the theme of self-sufficiency in Northwest poetry, including some earlier poets.

Birney, Earle. *Selected Poems, 1940-1966*. Toronto: McClelland and Stuart, 1966. Representative poems from an important Canadian poet.

Hugo, Richard. *The Lady in Kicking Horse Reservoir*. New York: Norton, 1973. Montana setting as opposed to the coastal Northwest of his earlier *Death of the Kapowsin Tavern* and *A Run of Jacks*.

Roethke, Theodore. *The Collected Poems of Theodore Roethke*. Garden City, N.Y.: Anchor-Doubleday, 1975. Roethke's *North American Sequence* has special significance for the Northwest.

Skelton, Robin, ed. *Five Poets of the Pacific Northwest*. 1964; rpt. Seattle: Univ. of Washington Press, 1968. The five are Kenneth O. Hanson, Richard Hugo, Carolyn Kizer, William Stafford, and David Wagoner.

Snyder, Gary. *The Back Country*. New York: New Directions, 1968. This volume of Snyder's poetry reflects his background in the rural Northwest.

Stafford, William. *Traveling Through the Dark*. New York: Harper, 1962. Oregon images meet with those of the poet's midwestern past in this early collection by the region's foremost living poet.

Strelow Michael, ed. *Northwest Review*, 14 (1975). A special issue featuring Northwest poetry.

Yates, Michael, ed. *Contemporary Poets of British Columbia*. Vancouver: Sono Nis Press, 1970. Representative anthology of British Columbia poets.

XV. Literature: Critical and Bibliographical Works

Chittick, V. L. O., ed. *Northwest Harvest: A Regional Stocktaking*. New York: Macmillan, 1948. Northwest writers and critics survey the region's literature.

Etulain, Richard. "Novelists of the Northwest: Opportunities for Research." *Idaho Yesterdays,* 17 (1973), 24-32. Survey of the critical reputation of Northwest novelists. Includes bibliography.

————. *Western American Literature: A Bibliography of Interpretive Books and Articles*. Vermillion, S.D.: Dakota Press, 1972. Includes material on Northwest writers.

Fiedler, Leslie. *The Return of the Vanishing American*. New York: Stein and Day, 1969. Former Montana professor Fiedler treats Kesey in his study of the rebirth of the Indian in American literature.

Flora, Joseph M. *Vardis Fisher*. New York: Twayne, 1965. Book-length study of the Idaho novelist.

Gohdes, Clarence. *Literature and Theatre of the States and Regions of the U. S. A.: An Historical Bibliography*. Dunham: Duke Univ. Press, 1967. Includes good coverage of the Northwest.

McCourt, Edward A. *The Canadian West in Fiction*. Toronto: Ryerson Press, 1949, rev. ed. 1970. Supplements Stevenson's 1926 *Appraisals of Canadian Literature*.

Powers, Alfred H. *History of Oregon Literature*. Portland: Metropolitan Press, 1935. Optimistic survey of the state's writing.

Rhodenizer, Vernon B. *Canadian Literature in English*. Montreal: Quality Press, 1965. A helpful section is entitled "The Northwest."

Stegner, Wallace. *The Sound of Mountain Water: The Changing American West*. Garden City, N.Y.: Doubleday, 1969. A collection of Stegner's critical essays on western literature, much of which is relevant to the Northwest.

Stevens, James, and H. L. Davis. *Status Rerum*. The Dalles, Ore., 1927. Two of the Northwest's best writers reject the region's local-color fantasy, and formula writing.

Western American Literature. Published by the Western Literature Assn. and Utah State Univ. Quarterly issues and annual bibliography include critical studies of Northwest writers.

Western Writers Series. Eds. Wayne Chatterton and James H. Maguire. Boise: Boise State Univ. Press. Recent pamphlets on western writers, including Fisher, Davis, Kesey, and Berry.

Index